FORTUNE'S
SPEAR

POLICE DE LA CITÉ DE LONDRES

Portrait, signalement et fac-similé de la signature de **GERARD LEE BEVAN**, demeurant ci-devant au Carlton Hotel, Londres, S.W., et à Littlecote, près Hungerford, dans le comté de Wiltshire en Angleterre, contre lequel un mandat d'arrêt a été délivré dans cette ville pour fraude comme administrateur de la City Equitable Fire Insurance Company, Limited, 3-4, Lothbury, Londres, E.C.

Age, 52 ans; taille, 1 m. 77; corpulence moyenne; yeux noisettes ou bleus; cheveux blonds, tendant à boucler sur les côtés, clairsemés au sommet de la tête; front haut; d'habitude complètement rasé. Parle français couramment.

Disparu d'Angleterre le 8 février 1922.

On est prié de communiquer tous renseignements utiles relatifs à ses mouvements au Commissaire de Police de la Cité de Londres, 26, Old Jewry, Londres, E.C. 2.

S'il est trouvé à l'étranger, une demande d'arrestation et d'extradition sera faite par voie diplomatique.

Le Commissaire de Police
de la Cité de Londres :

J. W. NOTT-BOWER.

Commissariat de Police de la Cité,
26, Old Jewry, Londres, E.C. 2.
Le 7 Mars 1922.

FORTUNE'S SPEAR

*A Forgotten Story of Genius,
Fraud, and Finance in
the Roaring Twenties*

MARTIN VANDER WEYER

Skyhorse Publishing

Picture credits: Newspaper articles 23 June 1922, 18 August 1922, 19 August 1922, 20 February 1923 © Mirrorpix. Wanted poster 7 March 1922 © The Times.

Extract on page 34 © R.A Church, Kenricks in Hardware: A Family Business, 1791-1966
(David & Charles, 1969). Extract on page 45 © Margaret Ackrill and Leslie Hannah,
Barclays: The Business of Banking, 1690-1996 (CUP, 2008). Extracts on pages 51 and 246
from Very Private Enterprise by Aylmer Vallance © 1955. Reproduced by kind permission, Thames & Hudson Ltd, London. Extracts on pages 57 and 149 © Harley Granville
Barker, The Voysey Inheritance (1905). Reproduced by kind permission, The Society of
Authors, Literary Representative of the Estate of Harley Granville Barker. Extracts on
pages 98-99 © Evelyn Waugh, Vile Bodies (Chapman and Hall, 1930; Penguin Books,
1938, 1996). Notes and introduction © copyright Richard Jacobs, 1996. Reproduced by
kind permission of Penguin Books Ltd, and Back Bay Books, 1991. Extract on page 279 ©
Death at the Bar by Ngaio Marsh (1939). Reproduced by kind permission
of HarperCollins Publishers Ltd. Extract on page 293 © George Orwell, George Orwell:
Essays, with an introduction by Bernard Crick. First published as The Collected Essays,
Journalism and Letters of George Orwell vols 1-4 (Martin Seeker & Warburg, 1968; this
edition Penguin Books 2000). Copyright © the Estate of Sonia Brownell Orwell, 1984.
Introduction copyright © Bernard Crick, 1994. Reproduced by kind permission of Penguin
Books Ltd. Extract on page 299 © Anthony Powell, To Keep the Ball Rolling (1983) and
on page 304 © Anthony Powell, The Kindly Ones (1962). Reproduced by kind permission
of Random House and University of Chicago Press. Extract on page 316 © Alejo Carpentier, Explosion in a Cathedral (University of Minnesota Press, 2001).

10 9 8 7 6 5 4 3 2 1

Library of Congress Cataloging-in-Publication Data is available on file.

ISBN: 978-1-63450-278-8

Printed in the United States of America

Contents

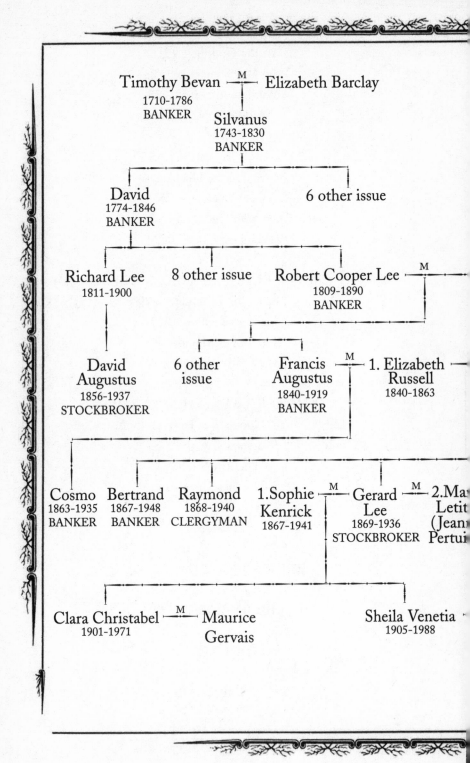

Timothy Bevan ─M─ Elizabeth Barclay
1710-1786
BANKER
                        Silvanus
                        1743-1830
                        BANKER

David   6 other issue
1774-1846
BANKER

Richard Lee   8 other issue   Robert Cooper Lee ─M
1811-1900   1809-1890
                                     BANKER

David   6 other   Francis ─M─ 1. Elizabeth
Augustus   issue   Augustus   Russell
1856-1937   1840-1919   1840-1863
STOCKBROKER   BANKER

Cosmo   Bertrand   Raymond   1.Sophie ─M─ Gerard ─M─ 2.Ma
1863-1935 1867-1948 1868-1940   Kenrick   Lee   Letit
BANKER   BANKER   CLERGYMAN   1867-1941   1869-1936   (Jean
                                             STOCKBROKER Pertui

Clara Christabel ─M─ Maurice   Sheila Venetia
1901-1971   Gervais   1905-1988

THE BEVAN DYNASTY

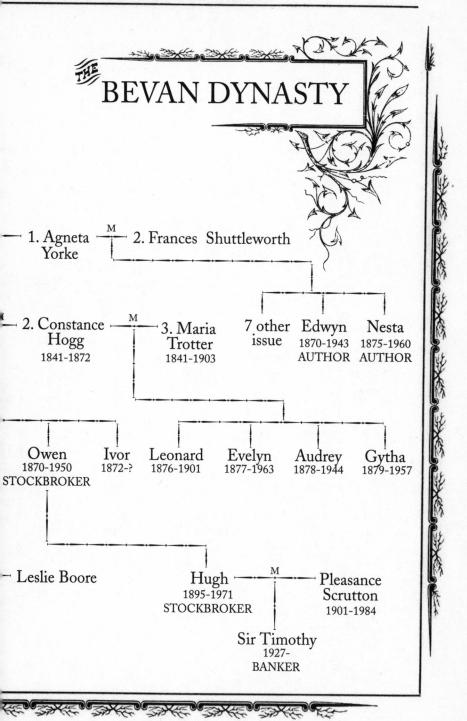

1. Agneta Yorke —M— 2. Frances Shuttleworth

2. Constance Hogg —M— 3. Maria Trotter
1841-1872   1841-1903

7 other issue   Edwyn   Nesta
                1870-1943   1875-1960
                AUTHOR   AUTHOR

Owen   Ivor   Leonard   Evelyn   Audrey   Gytha
1870-1950   1872-?   1876-1901   1877-1963   1878-1944   1879-1957
STOCKBROKER

Leslie Boore   Hugh —M— Pleasance
                      1895-1971   Scrutton
                      STOCKBROKER   1901-1984

Sir Timothy
1927-
BANKER

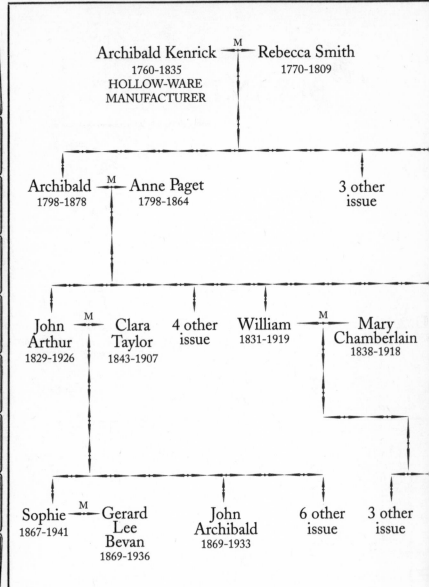

Archibald Kenrick —M— Rebecca Smith
1760-1835   1770-1809
HOLLOW-WARE
MANUFACTURER

Archibald —M— Anne Paget   3 other
1798-1878   1798-1864   issue

John   —M— Clara   4 other   William   —M— Mary
Arthur   Taylor   issue   1831-1919   Chamberlain
1829-1926   1843-1907   1838-1918

Sophie —M— Gerard   John   6 other   3 other
1867-1941   Lee   Archibald   issue   issue
                    Bevan   1869-1933
                    1869-1936

THE KENRICK & CHAMBERLAIN DYNASTY

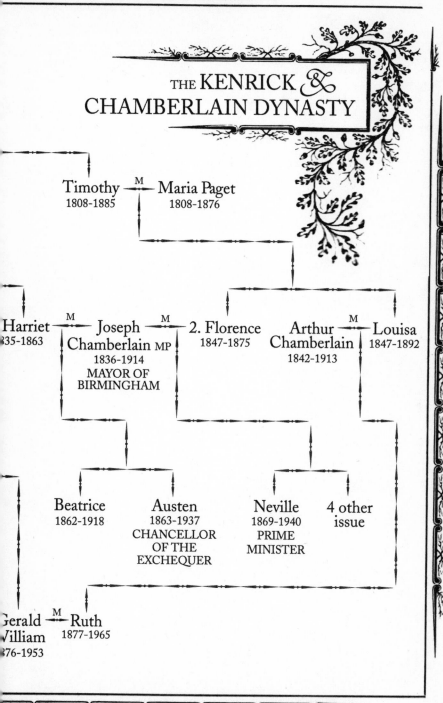

Timothy —^M— Maria Paget
1808-1885   1808-1876

Harriet —^M— Joseph —^M— 2. Florence   Arthur —^M— Louisa
835-1863   Chamberlain MP   1847-1875   Chamberlain   1847-1892
    1836-1914   1842-1913
    MAYOR OF
    BIRMINGHAM

Beatrice   Austen   Neville   4 other
1862-1918   1863-1937   1869-1940   issue
       CHANCELLOR   PRIME
       OF THE   MINISTER
       EXCHEQUER

Gerald —^M— Ruth
William   1877-1965
876-1953

Sonnet II

You do believe I loved you, don't you, Dear?
Since we were swallowed in adversity
It's light enough to read the stranger's sneer,
For fawn and frown are weighed in oboli;
But they're not in accompt: your thought is all.
In the old dancing days when people said
I was in league with fortune, and the scale
Tipped seemingly to humour my least need,
Some friend would stop me in the thoroughfare
Or mart to ask me why I walked so gay:
"Another throw," he'd guess, "With Fortune's spear,"
The whiles my heart was just with you, at play.
And now when almost heaven itself seems vile,
If you can still believe I still can smile.

Gerard Lee Bevan, *Russet and Asp* **(1929)**

The Making of a Fraudster

Havana, Cuba, March 1936

An Englishman old before his time makes his way slowly towards an open-fronted café. He walks painfully, leaning on a silver-topped ebony cane. His breath is short, his shoulders hunched, his pallor sickly beneath the brim of his straw hat.

He reaches his customary table at the front of the café, sits with an audible sigh and a wince of pain, and flaps a hand in greeting to the waiter who will bring his customary coffee. He places the hat carefully on the chair beside him and mops his brow with a handkerchief from the breast pocket of his pale linen suit, stained at collar and cuffs by the humidity and filth of the city. Then he wipes the head of the handsome walking stick — his prized possession, his last beautiful thing, a gift from his beloved wife.

From an inside pocket come a pair of small, wire-rimmed spectacles, which he places on the end of his nose. Anyone watching him closely might observe that he blinks continuously, as though the city's dust is perpetually troubling his eyes. But it is a nervous tic brought on by stress; these days he worries constantly — about making ends meet, about small debts owed here and there, about the state of his own health and the future for his wife.

He has a newspaper with him, a fortnight-old copy of *The Times* of London, well thumbed by previous readers. He has acquired it from the concierge of a hotel that he passes on his morning walk. It carries a report of King Edward VIII's first broadcast to his subjects, in which the new monarch has spoken eloquently about the death of his father, George V, and his own dedication to his subjects.

But our man has never had much interest in the doings of royalty — or politicians, for that matter. For old times sake he turns to the City page, scanning it for the names of companies and their chairmen whom he might once have known in London. He looks for news of Wall Street too, because his wife still owns a handful of shares there.

Then he sees her — small, dark, animated, pretty, many years his junior — crossing the bustling street between slow-moving cabs and bicycles. She carries a basket of fruit and flowers from the market. His eyes light up as he struggles to rise from his seat, a vestige of past gallantry.

'Don't be silly, *chéri*,' she says. Her accent and body language are unmistakably French. She kisses him on the cheek and moves his hat from the chair so she can sit beside him. 'Here,' she takes a flower from her basket, passes it under his nose, trims the stem and places it in his buttonhole. 'That's better. How are you feeling now? At least it's a little cooler today.'

Suddenly ill at ease, he reaches for his hat and pulls it low over his brow. A well-heeled tourist couple, evidently English, the woman showing the agitation of one who thinks she is lost in a foreign place, are coming into the café to ask for directions. Our man shuffles his chair slightly, turning his shoulder away from them. But the husband notices him and stares.

'I say,' he whispers, nudging. 'That chap looks awfully familiar. I'd swear I used to know him in the City.' And a few moments later, glancing over his shoulder as they leave the café: 'It's that chap in the City Equitable business, I'm sure it is. Used to be rich as Croesus and frightfully respectable. Ran off across Europe disguised as a Frenchman and ended up in jail. All over the 'papers in '22. God, doesn't he look old? What *was* his name?'

His name, in fact, was Gerard Lee Bevan, and his wife's name — his second wife and former mistress, that is — was Jeanne. At the time of this imaginary encounter he had no more than six weeks to live. He had indeed been rich as Croesus, and a man of great reputation in the Square Mile and beyond as chairman of the City Equitable Fire Insurance Company, senior partner of the old-established stockbroking firm of Ellis & Co, son of the founder-chairman of Barclays Bank and scion of a great banking dynasty.

How and why he fell from that plinth to end his days a broken man in a rackety Caribbean watering hole is the subject of this enquiry.

But this is not a whodunit. There is no doubt that Gerard Lee Bevan committed the offences for which he was sentenced by Mr Justice Avory in December 1922 to seven years' penal servitude, nor that those offences constituted serious episodes of fraud. There might be a question as to whether any of his associates ought to have gone to prison with him, but only one — Edmund Mansell, general manager of the City Equitable — was ever charged with related criminal offences, and he was acquitted.

Likewise, it is important to ask whether Bevan's fellow directors of the City Equitable were culpable in a non-criminal sense for allowing him to get away with the things that he did, over a period of several years; they too were let off the hook, in a court case which for many years defined the limits of directors' responsibilities. But that Gerard Bevan was guilty as charged is a matter of fact, and since there is not much mystery involved in reaching that conclusion it is probably helpful to the reader to begin with a simple summary of what his offences were and how they came about, so that the detail makes more sense as it unfolds.

Bevan spent the bulk of his City career, which began in 1894, as a stockbroker. Ellis & Co had always been conservative in its way of doing business, but when Bevan succeeded as its senior partner in 1912 he had ambitions to make it much less so. In particular, he wanted it to play a more aggressive role in flotations of stocks and bonds. He also had his eyes on international markets, and was developing growing networks of contacts in North and South America and continental Europe.

The outbreak of the first world war forced him to put his aspirations for Ellis & Co on hold, but brought him a different opportunity.

A young man called Clarence Hatry offered to sell him a controlling stake in a fire reinsurance company, the City Equitable, which was poised for expansion because the war had forced the withdrawal from the London market of the previously dominant German and Austrian reinsurers.

Bevan grabbed that opportunity with both hands and made a great success of it. He led the City Equitable into marine reinsurance as well as fire, and watched the upward march of its premium income, profits and dividends to shareholders — many of whom were his friends, acquaintances and Ellis & Co clients.

Meanwhile, he formed a close association with Clarence Hatry, who — though he too would later go to prison for fraud — was at this stage emerging as a brilliantly creative corporate financier despite the constraints of wartime capital markets.

When the war ended, the stockmarket came spectacularly back to life. In the post-Armistice boom of 1919–20, Bevan, Hatry and a rather unlikely and comical third associate, the celebrated Boat Race rowing coach Peter Haig-Thomas, worked together on a series of lucrative corporate mergers and flotations.

In each case Hatry's Commercial Bank of London did most of the brainwork, while Ellis & Co was the appointed broker to the issue. Bevan frequently took a seat on the board of the floated company and recommended its shares to his stockbroking clients, who were happy to follow his advice. The City Equitable came in on the deals as an underwriter — and sometimes as an eager investor in its own right.

It was conventional for reinsurance companies to hold most of their capital and reserves in the form of highly liquid British government 'gilt-edged' stock — that is what their shareholders and the insurance companies who were their chief clients would have expected to see in reinsurers' balance sheets. But the City Equitable under Bevan's leadership reduced the proportion of its assets held in gilts in favour of acquiring a portfolio of far more exciting investments elsewhere.

So far so good. The reinsurance company's investment policy was far from transparent, but no one was complaining about the results. Some people in the City may have thought Bevan's way of doing business rather cavalier, but that was often the reputation of successful stockbrokers of that era. Hatry was getting rich, and Bevan was getting even richer than he already was, while his clients and fellow City Equitable shareholders were prospering too.

At successive annual general meetings, praise was showered on Bevan as a titan of the modern City, a financier with the Midas touch. But when the stockmarket became more turbulent and prices started to fall in 1920, new issues became much harder to place. Securities created by Hatry and placed by Bevan were often unmarketable — that is, there were no genuine buyers in the market to match against sellers.

To maintain the impression of an active market, Bevan would buy the shares that clients of Ellis & Co wanted to sell, and either sell them to the City Equitable or make loans from the City Equitable to Ellis & Co to provide the stockbroking firm with sufficient cash to pay its clients and hold on to the shares until new buyers turned up in the market.

In flotations, he would sometimes encourage the original family shareholders of the company being floated to buy more shares in the market, thus encouraging the impression of healthy demand for the issue, against a guarantee that Ellis & Co would buy the shares from them if there were no other willing buyers.

He was able to do these things at will, without protest from his partners at Ellis & Co or his fellow directors at the City Equitable, because he had complete personal control of both businesses, and neither had the sort of internal controls that might have stopped him. Nor was there any challenge from their auditors, and most of his directors and partners genuinely had no idea what he was up to.

At the City Equitable, a small committee to which the board of directors delegated all investment decisions did no more than rubber-stamp whatever Bevan chose to do with the company's cash and borrowings — often after the fact and in breach of the committee's own limits. At Ellis & Co, Bevan's four junior partners had little or no knowledge of how he financed their business or invested its capital, which gradually dwindled away as a result. To the extent that Bevan needed the co-operation of the general manager of the City Equitable, Edmund Mansell, he secured it by allowing Mansell to draw extraordinarily large sums of money for himself from the company to fund his own extravagant lifestyle.

As a result, Ellis & Co came to owe the City Equitable almost a million pounds and Mansell owed it over a hundred thousand, while the City Equitable ended up owning a portfolio of investments wholly unsuitable for any insurance company. Bevan made matters worse by using City Equitable funds alongside his own to invest in other ventures which caught his fancy, including Claridge's Hotel in Paris and a vast Brazilian cattle ranching enterprise.

All this remained opaque to the other partners of Ellis & Co until the point was reached at which Bevan had effectively destroyed their firm. It was hidden from the directors and shareholders of the City Equitable by a sleight of hand in which government stocks, bought and sold within a matter of minutes and never actually held in the City Equitable's custody, appeared in the annual balance sheet where the full extent of the loans to Ellis & Co ought to have been shown.

As market conditions deteriorated against a background of world-wide economic slump in 1921, Bevan's manoeuvres became increasingly desperate and his life began to disintegrate. He gambled in casinos, lived with a succession or possibly a combination of mistresses, and borrowed money wherever and whenever he could.

As his situation failed to improve, Bevan took a distinct step into criminality. Having acquired several smaller reinsurance companies, he asset-stripped them to generate cash that was channelled illicitly to Ellis & Co, at the same time floating them on the stockmarket under a new holding company, City Equitable Associated, with a largely fictional prospectus — and thus scooping more cash from investors with which to hold creditors at bay.

This house of cards was impossible to sustain. The City Equitable could no longer pay its claims, and was besieged by rumours of financial difficulties. By the end of January 1922 — having concealed its insolvency for many months — the City Equitable was bust. Likewise, Ellis & Co was in ruins.

Bevan, rather than facing the music or taking a revolver into his library and 'doing the decent thing', chose to flee the country, probably with the ultimate intention of reaching South America.

We will follow his flight across Europe — complete with fake identity, and slow-witted policemen in pursuit — leading to his violent arrest in Vienna, his extradition to London, his trial and imprisonment and the strange life he led afterwards that ended in Havana. Before that, we will look at his stultifyingly respectable Victorian upper-middle-class upbringing, his first marriage, and his emergence as a City swell.

All this provides a colourful narrative, much of which might have come from the realms of fiction. As we shall see, Bevan's story has many echoes in the novels of his lifetime — from Jules Verne's *Around the World in Eighty Days* (1873), in which Inspector Fix pursues Phileas Fogg across the globe under the misapprehension that he has robbed the Bank of England, to Evelyn Waugh's *A Handful of Dust* (1934), in which the machinations of character and fate cause an English country squire called Tony Last to end his days in the Brazilian jungle, condemned forever to read Dickens to his captor.

Most especially, Bevan and his social circle could have stepped straight from the pages of John Galsworthy's *Forsyte Saga* or from the cast of one of his successful West End plays. We will call upon Galsworthy as our unofficial guide and interpreter at many points in this narrative, and revisit in particular a sub-plot of the Forsyte family story, concerning the affairs of the Providential Premium Reassurance Society and its corrupt general manager, Robert Elderson. Written around the time of Bevan's trial, this richly comic boardroom drama undoubtedly draws on the facts of the City Equitable case, and illuminates many of its moral and psychological lessons.

Besides these diverting cultural resonances, Bevan's downfall also offers an opportunity to contemplate the perennial nature of fraud, and the mind of the fraudster. What is it that turns an apparently reputable financier into an out-and-out villain?

In Bevan's case, it ought to be said, he never actually acknowledged himself to be anything of the latter sort. For the rest of his life he argued that if circumstances had allowed him to wrestle with the City Equitable's finances for long enough, he would have put matters right, and that the deceptions he carried out — particularly the window-dressing of the City Equitable balance sheet — were no worse than what was done daily all over the Square Mile.

If that were so, his was a particularly egregious example of the technique, maintained over an extended period of time. Nor did Bevan's demeanour win him sympathy in court; rather the reverse, since here was a man who had fled abroad in disguise rather than face the consequences of his actions like the gentleman and City professional he purported to be.

One question this book will ask is whether there was always a flaw — a streak of wickedness, moral deficiency or deep unreliability — in Gerard Lee Bevan, or whether his personality actually mutated for the worse as circumstances changed against him. It will ask whether, if there had not been such a severe slump in the stock-market after the post-Armistice boom, he might have ended his days rich, guiltless and contented in his magnificent Wiltshire country house, surrounded by fine art, books and Chinese porcelain, instead of as an ex-jailbird scratching a living as a distillery manager in Cuba.

And it will ask what must it have been like for his first wife Sophie, *née* Kenrick, daughter of a high-minded, low-church Midlands industrial family, to live through the shame and distress of her husband's downfall. Opinionated, demanding, increasingly eccentric as she grew older, Sophie does not emerge from this story as a very lovable character. But Gerard Bevan clearly loved her when they were young, before he started cheating on her and dragging her through the embarrassment of banner headlines and bankruptcy; and when he abandoned her, he largely abandoned also his responsibilities towards their two young daughters. So Sophie Bevan deserves a fair hearing too.

Fraud takes many forms, and involves many kinds of people. In good times, when markets are soaring, the incorrigibly unscrupulous never miss the opportunity to take advantage of the gullible. In bad times, when prices are crashing, the previously straight often resort to deception to try to save themselves from ruin. It is the same in every decade, every turn of the economic cycle. It is a pattern of behavior that no regulatory regime or surveillance system has ever succeeded in eradicating.

And that is because fraud is a special kind of human failing: a crime of the mind rather than the hands. It does not require the dexterity of the pickpocket, the physical courage of the rooftop cat-burglar, the violent psychopathology of the mugger. It requires instead a persuasive tongue, a heightened appetite for risk, a certain degree of numeracy and cunning, and a moral blindness to the effect of selfish actions on other people's lives — attributes which match very closely those of the ruthless financier who makes a successful career by staying just on the right side of the line.

It is the fineness of that line between, on one side, what is permitted by law but is ethically dubious, and on the other, that which is plainly dishonest and actually illegal, that makes fraud such a fascinating field of investigation.

Gerard Lee Bevan worked in the City for almost 30 years and was recognised as one of its most consistently successful money-makers. Those who did business with him for most of those years might have said that he treated risk with arrogant insouciance, that he was vain in admiring his own judgement and failing to acknowledge his own mistakes, that he sometimes sailed close to the wind in his methods, that he was not as clever as he thought he was — but never that he was overtly a rule-breaker.

Meanwhile he lived the opulent life of a post-Edwardian plutocrat, but with taste and restraint. He was not physically greedy, having no interest in the pleasures of the table. He committed adultery, but (if this can be allowed as a mitigating clause) with showgirls rather than the wives of his friends or neighbours. If he had a secret vice, it was for collecting beautiful objects.

In all these respects, anyone passing judgement on Bevan's life up to the time of his fiftieth birthday in August 1919 (anyone, that is, who did not have access to the innermost secrets of his companies' accounts, which even at that stage would have hinted otherwise) might have concluded that he was no worse and no better than a thousand others of his class, time and *métier*.

When boom turned to bust soon after that birthday, however, Bevan resorted to a series of unequivocally dishonest devices and repeated lies — to shareholders, bankers, clients and even to his own brothers — to maintain the impression that all could still come right under his golden touch. He did not enrich himself by behaving in this way: his own fortune, a large portion of which was represented by his equity interest in Ellis & Co and his shareholding in the City Equitable, was by then evaporating at least as fast as that of anyone who was harmed by what he did.

The reinsurance business of the City Equitable, though it too experienced difficult market conditions in 1921, was probably sound enough to have survived. What ruined the company was Bevan's habit of using its reserves to invest in anything he fancied, and to bankroll Ellis & Co's involvement with Hatry in new issues and their aftermath.

As *The Economist* would say after Bevan's conviction, the assets and the potential for future success of the City Equitable had simply been 'muddled away', at a cost to its creditors and shareholders (and those who invested in the City Equitable Associated flotation) of at least £3.75 million, equivalent to £150 million in modern terms.[1]

---

[1] A note on inflation and exchange rates. From time to time during this narrative, sums of money are translated for illustrative purposes into their 2010 equivalent, but it would be tiresome for the reader if that comparison were made too often. Suffice to say that steep inflation during the first world war was followed by a sharp deflation in the post-war slump, with the net effect (according to the Bank of England) that prices roughly doubled over the decade of Bevan's heyday, from 1912–22. Between 1922 and 2010, inflation averaged 4.4 per cent, which makes £100,000 in 1922 the equivalent in purchasing power of £4.4 million in 2010. As a rule of thumb, sums mentioned during the key years of the Bevan scandal from 1919–22 can be multiplied by 40 to give an idea of their equivalent value today.

Again as a rough guide, sums mentioned in French francs, which fluctuated widely against the pound in the early 1920s, can be converted at 50 francs to the pound; this means that 100,000 French francs in 1922 would have been the equivalent of about £80,000 in 2010.

Adding in the unpaid debts of Ellis & Co (but eliminating the over-lap, since the largest of those debts was to the City Equitable) takes the equivalent figure to £200 million or so. Even today, when the scale of public-company balance sheets and of dealings and misdeal-ings in the securities markets runs into many billions, a £200 million fraud would be a major scandal. In 1922 it was colossal: the collapse of the Bevan empire, his flight across Europe and the revelations at his trial filled newspaper pages throughout that year, and had reper-cussions long afterwards.

As such episodes always do, this one caused questions to be asked about financial regulation, accounting standards and the role of directors and auditors. On that last issue, the City Equitable case led eventually to a tightening of company law, so it did ultimately change the game. But in a more general sense the scandal merely reaffirmed what has been observed down the ages about human nature and money; that certain types of people will always be prone to excessive risk-taking and marginal dishonesty when there is a possibility of great riches, and some of that group will give way to greater dishonesty when the tide ebbs and the promised riches are about to be swept away.

That is — you might agree, when you know a little more about him — a fair summary of the character type which Bevan fits, and it raises one further question, or parlour game. Where should we place him on the spectrum of the great fraudsters of all time?

The question is perhaps best answered by identifying what Bevan was not doing. He was not, for example, operating a 'Ponzi scheme' — an outright swindle in which money is collected from savers attracted by the offer of unusually high returns, but those returns are simply paid out from the incoming cash to lull investors into believing all was well, while the capital is siphoned off for the benefit of the swindler.

The originator of this racket was the Italian-American Charles Ponzi who was jailed for 'mail fraud' in 1920; his most notorious modern imitator was Bernard Madoff, a fund manager in New York and Florida who was jailed in 2009 having gathered in no less than $65 billion under false pretences and lost $18 billion of it.

By contrast with Ponzi or Madoff, Bevan was running a genuine business, but in a dangerous and deceitful way. Nor was he the kind of fraudster who is motivated by power and influence as well as, or more than, money itself. Such, in Bevan's own time, were Jabez Balfour and Horatio Bottomley, whose careers as members of parliament and noisome public figures were supported by a pyramid of fraudulent property companies in Balfour's case and a series of imaginative stings on the general public in Bottomley's. Another character in this mould was the fictional Augustus Melmotte MP in Anthony Trollope's *The Way We Live Now* (1875), a crooked financier of railway schemes who ends up poisoning himself.

In more modern times, the sometime Captain Robert Maxwell MP, the megalomaniac proprietor of the *Daily Mirror* who drowned after falling or jumping from his yacht in 1991 before justice could catch up with him, seems to fit the same pattern. In the collapse of Maxwell's group of companies under a mountain of debt, and the way in which he was found to have shuffled money between them to try to keep them afloat, there are clear parallels with Bevan.

Indeed, we may be fairly sure that if the City Equitable had maintained a pension fund for employees in 1921 (in common with all but the most socially progressive public companies of that era, it did not) Bevan would not only have managed it imprudently but would have raided it for cash just as Maxwell stood accused of stealing from the Mirror Group's fund.

But there the similarities end. Unlike these publicity-seeking politician-businessmen, Bevan sought no fame or public platform. He played a high-stakes financial game simply because he believed he had a talent for it, he was stimulated by the game itself, and he enjoyed the lifestyle it brought him.

He does however stand comparison with another modern fraudster who was not remotely like him in personality, background or tastes: Nick Leeson, the Singapore-based 'rogue trader' whose dealings ruined the investment banking house of Baring Brothers in 1995.

Whereas Bevan was a Cambridge-educated City aristocrat of many years' market experience, Leeson was a 27-year-old former settlements clerk from Watford. But the pattern of their behaviour matches. Leeson started out conducting an entirely legitimate trading activity in Japanese equity futures contracts on behalf of his firm. Mistakes were made and covered up, and risks multiplied in the effort to make back the losses. Other directors and executives of the bank failed to scrutinise Leeson's departmental accounts until it was too late. What appeared to be a profitable business was in reality concealing mounting losses, and when market conditions turned adverse (after the Kobe earthquake in January 1995) the losses became catastrophic. Having blown away Barings' entire capital, Leeson fled across several Asian countries before finally being arrested at Frankfurt airport, extradited, convicted of fraud and consigned to Singapore's notorious Changi jail.

As Bevan's story unfolds in detail, the reader will see the validity of this comparison of two miscreants from such very different eras and backgrounds. It is all to do with the universality of human response. Here is Leeson himself commenting in that vein on an early 20th-century fraud case with which Bevan would certainly have been familiar — the case of *The Voysey Inheritance*, a 1905 play by Harley Granville Barker that was revived in 2006 at London's National Theatre, which cleverly invited Leeson to offer a comment:

> We [Leeson and the play's central character Edward Voysey, who perpetuates a fraud conducted by his late father] both clearly knew the difference between right and wrong… I knew that I shouldn't be doing it but continued all the same. The question is: why? Ethically correct in our upbringing, something misfires when we are confronted by the ultimate ethical dilemma. Each day I would do whatever was needed to survive, although I knew that each action contradicted what I knew was right…
>
> Very quickly I became blinkered to all that was happening around me; everyone had bought into the success story and the

important thing was to keep the myth — and in turn the status — alive at all costs. As much as I knew that I was wrong, I rarely paid attention to the impact my actions would have on those around me, or indeed to what the personal cost would ultimately be to me. Very quickly a form of tunnel vision descends that only allows you to see the future in terms of successfully digging yourself out of the situation. However bad it gets, failure is still never an option.

That could easily have been a description of the mind of Gerard Lee Bevan, though it is perhaps a little too frank to have come from the pen of Bevan himself. The species of fraud in which Leeson and Bevan and the fictional Voyseys were involved is the product of the interaction of character flaw and financial circumstance, rather than criminality in its purest, wickedest form.

Within that species are many variants of method and outcome, including those in which the fraudster himself is also, in the end, a loser. But still it is fraud, still it parts innocent people from their savings, still it damages trust in institutions and markets. It is always with us — and as the reader will surely conclude, having weighed all the evidence in the case of Gerard Lee Bevan — there is never a convincing excuse for it.

CHAPTER ONE

A Kensington Wedding

'... They were all what is called 'of a certain position'. They had shares in all sorts of things... They collected pictures, too, and were supporters of such charitable institutions as might be beneficial to their sick domestics. Originally, perhaps, members of some primitive sect, they were now in the natural course of things members of the Church of England, and caused their wives and children to attend with some regularity the more fashionable churches of the Metropolis... Their residences, placed at stated intervals round the Park, watched like sentinels lest the fair heart of this London, where their desires were fixed, should slip from their clutches, and leave them lower in their own estimations.'

John Galsworthy, *The Man of Property* 1906

Capital and Industry

The Times of Thursday, 5 October 1893 carried the following announcement in its Marriages column:

BEVAN: KENRICK. On Tuesday, the 3rd Oct., at All Saints, Ennismore Gardens, by the Rev. R. S. Tabor, assisted by the Rev. Gustavus Bosanquet, Rector of Clophill, GERARD LEE BEVAN, son of Francis Augustus Bevan, of Fosbury Manor, Wilts, and Trent Park, New Barnet, Herts, to SOPHIE, eldest daughter of J. ARTHUR KENRICK, of Berrow Court, Edgbaston.

There must have been a certain tension in the air at that wedding. Gerard was about to become a partner in a long-established City stockbroking firm. His father was a leading Lombard Street banker, his late mother the daughter of a baronet. His bride came from a celebrated Midlands industrial dynasty.

The bridegroom's family, with their titled and metropolitan connections, sat a notch higher on the social scale than the bride's, who had always tended to marry within their own provincial community. But in a period of upward mobility for successful Victorian business dynasties of all kinds, that is unlikely to have raised eyebrows, especially as the extended Kenrick clan included the Chamberlains, the most powerful family in Birmingham, which was the late 19th century world's most important industrial city.

Sophie's father, Arthur Kenrick might also have pointed out, if he had made a speech at the wedding breakfast, the happy coincidence that both families traced their ancestry to modest merchant origins in Wales — genealogy being as important to the participants in this story as it is to the reader trying to imagine their world. Over the previous century, Arthur might have added, both families had achieved national prominence in their chosen fields of enterprise. And though it would have been vulgar to say so aloud, no wedding guest could have failed to notice that both families had amassed substantial fortunes.

In fact both bride and groom, born in the late 1860s, belonged to an especially fortunate generation. As the historian A.N. Wilson described them in *The Victorians* (2002): 'this immensely privileged class, probably more comfortable than any human class who had ever existed on the planet.'

The guests that day were witnessing what was in many ways an ideal late-Victorian match of capital and industry, at a moment of high Victorian self-confidence. It was a marriage that would produce two daughters and reach its silver anniversary before it became, rather publicly, a marriage in name only; and almost 30 years before it finally ended in divorce. Ahead of the couple was a path through the most glittering realms of Edwardian society.

Yet something was not quite right. Gerard Bevan, a month before his 24th birthday, was a clever and polished young man, from an eminently respectable stable. But he had already shown himself unsuitable for the family banking partnership after a brief trial there. Instead he had been fixed up with a career in the London Stock Exchange — which suited his nature much better, and was a classic way for the City to accommodate a well-bred black sheep.

As for Sophie, she was two and a half years older than her husband and no oil painting: 'large and plain and tiresome,' according to one description, 'with a rather low voice and a very decisive manner of speaking.' And she was 'marrying out'. That is, she was about to go down the aisle of an Anglican church — albeit one favoured by folk of what John Galsworthy called 'a certain position' — that was a long way in every sense from her own family's preferred place of worship, the Unitarian Church of the Messiah in Broad Street, Birmingham.

According to legend in the Bevan family, Sophie's father and brother had both warned the bridegroom that she was, in some unspecified ways, 'difficult'. But her forceful personality, rather than her looks, was evidently the very thing that most attracted Gerard, and these interventions only made him more keen to lead her down the aisle.

Perhaps in return, someone on the Bevan side had tried to warn the Kenricks that Gerard was unreliable. Those who took a dim view of him might have speculated that he could only be so determined to pluck Sophie off the shelf because she brought a substantial dowry. As a fourth son, he could not expect much inheritance of his own.

But the marriage settlement discreetly fixed between bewhiskered family solicitors must have protected Sophie's interests pretty effectively, since they turned out to be well separated from her husband's when he eventually went bankrupt. And if money was really Gerard's motivation he could easily have aimed richer and higher. He was, in any case, about to make a great deal of it by his own efforts.

Such reports as we have of his personality do not suggest a play-boy or an idle wastrel, but a young man who was just as serious as his wife-to-be. He was abstemious when it came to food and drink. He did not smoke cigars. He had been a regular attender at the chapel of his Cambridge college. He had a delicate aesthetic sense that would later emerge in poetry and connoisseurship.

He was perhaps a bit intense, with an unattractive hint of arro-gance in his manner. But there is no obvious reason why anyone should have thought him, on his wedding day, the 'daring and unprincipled scoundrel' he was judged to be many years later.

So let us begin by giving Gerard the benefit of the doubt, as well as feeling some sympathy for Sophie. Let us assume there was a quotient of love in the match, even if we imagine we can hear aunts and dowagers on both sides of the congregation whispering doubts.

Let us try to sketch the scene that morning — and in doing so, create a collage of the worlds in which Gerard and Sophie were brought up, and the way their characters were formed.

Pillars of Society

All Saints Church in Ennismore Gardens, South Kensington, was built in the late 1840s in the ornate, 12th century 'Lombardic' style that was enjoying a revival at the time. It was a short stroll from Prince's Gate, where the Bevan family had successively owned or leased several large townhouses since the area had first been rede-veloped by a builder called Freake in the late 1850s.[1]

To be precise — since mapping offers a clue as to how the bridal couple first met — Prince's Gate is an L-shaped stucco terrace, of which one section faces Hyde Park and the other forms the eastern side of Exhibition Road, leading towards South Kensington station. Gerard's grandfather Robert Cooper Lee Bevan was the first lease-holder, in 1857, of No 31 Prince's Gate, on the corner of the 'L' with

---

[1] The church became redundant in 1955 and is now — cleared of pews and richly adorned with icons — the Russian Orthodox Cathedral of the Dormition of the Mother of God and All Saints. The Anglican parish merged with that of Holy Trinity, Prince Consort Road.

its front door opening onto Exhibition Road but its principal rooms overlooking the park; it is now the embassy of Afghanistan.

In 1866 Robert Bevan — whose principal home was a large estate in Hertfordshire called Trent Park — bought the exceptionally opulent No 25 Prince's Gate, in the middle of the parkside terrace. The seller was his distant relation Samuel Gurney Junior, an MP (and promoter of the project to lay a transatlantic telegraph cable) who was a sleeping partner in the discount house of Overend & Gurney — the collapse of which shook the City of London a couple of months after this house sale was completed.

We might wonder whether the hugely wealthy Robert had done this deal privately to provide Samuel with liquidity when trouble was looming. In any event, when Overend & Gurney went down, Robert publicly opposed the idea that he and other leading London bankers should get together to rescue it. Perhaps he felt he had already done his bit for cousinhood. He sold the house, to another banker, in 1884.

As for Gerard's father, Francis Augustus Bevan, generally known as Frank, he first owned No 72 Prince's Gate at the end of the Exhibition Road terrace, adjoining what was then the South Kensington Museum but would become much more famous as the Victoria & Albert. Later he owned No 59, a few doors to the north on the corner of Prince's Gardens, and this was most probably where Gerard Lee Bevan was born on 9 November 1869. But since Gerard's records at Trinity College, Cambridge show his home address as No 60 Prince's Gate, we can assume that Frank had in fact acquired two adjacent houses (now demolished) to accommodate his very large family. And that establishment was barely more than a hundred yards from a house which provided a London base for Sophie Kenrick's family, of which more in a moment.

Meanwhile back to All Saints, where the vicar was the genial Ravenscroft Stewart, a Scot who had been a parish priest in Derbyshire before arriving in Ennismore Gardens in 1884. Passionate about the fabric of his church and adept — almost to the point of aggression, by some accounts — at fundraising, we might guess that he had made himself a regular caller at the Bevans, who were very typical of his parishioners.

All Saints was not as high, liturgically or socially, as the likes of St Paul's Knightsbridge, just down the road, or the fashionable churches of Mayfair. It served a well-heeled but unflamboyant middle-class district south of the park between Knightsbridge to the east and Exhibition Road to the west. Some of the householders in Prince's Gate, Prince's Gardens and Ennismore Gardens were members of the old landed aristocracy, but most were representatives of relatively new money: industrialists, shipowners, bankers like the Bevans, or simply inheritors of wealth accumulated by their fathers and grandfathers.

The most plutocratic neighbour, when he was in town, was the great American financier John Pierpont Morgan at No 14 Prince's Gate, a mansion even larger than its neighbours which is now the Royal College of General Practitioners. But as a foreign grandee, he was the exception.

Most of the local residents were 'Forsytes', in the generic definition offered by Galsworthy's tongue-in-cheek family commentator, Young Jolyon:

> A Forsyte takes a practical — one might say a commonplace — view of things, and a practical view of things is based fundamentally on a sense of property…. My dear sir, the Forsytes are the middlemen, the commercials, the pillars of society, the corner stones of convention; everything that is admirable!

Jolyon might indeed have had in mind his uncle Roger Forsyte, whom Galsworthy placed in Prince's Gardens, a stone's throw from the Bevans, and encapsulated as a 'collector of house property'.

This was, then, a comfortable and comfortably-off enclave of the capital. And it was the ladies of these households, no doubt all of rather fixed views as to how they liked their religion dished up, who predominated in the All Saints congregation — to the extent that Stewart sought to balance matters by welcoming soldiers from the nearby Knightsbridge Barracks and hosting a regular get-together called a 'Husbands' Supper'.

One contemporary letter from a parishioner said of Stewart that he 'was very good at getting money, though he was not a scholar or even a very good preacher… His sermons were dull.' That may be one reason why he was not a named celebrant at the Bevan-Kenrick wedding, though it is very likely that he was present and robed for the occasion. A more interesting question is whether the Kenricks had brought with them their Unitarian minister from the Church of the Messiah in Birmingham, James Crossley. If so he, like Stewart, was relegated to a subsidiary role, while the service was led by two priests who were closely associated with the Bevans.

The first was 74-year-old Robert Tabor, former headmaster of Cheam School in Surrey,[2] where Gerard had been a pupil from 1878–83. Tabor's first connection to the family was that as a young man he had been a priest at Enfield in the parish that included Robert Bevan's Trent Park, and where the Bevans had paid for the building in 1839 of a new church, Christ Church Cockfosters.

Tabor tutored Robert Bevan's older children, including Frank, at his parsonage. In 1855 (by which time Frank was at Harrow), Bevan provided Tabor with funds to buy Cheam and turn it into England's most famous preparatory school — a boarding school which took boys from the age of seven or eight up to 13, to prepare them for the next stage of their education at establishments such as Harrow, Eton or Winchester.

Robert Bevan sent several of his younger sons to Cheam and was said to have been so fond of both the place and its headmaster that on his deathbed in July 1890 (just as Tabor was retiring) he murmured last regrets that he could not attend the Parents' Day cricket match. Frank followed his father's example and sent six of his seven sons to the school.

Assisting Tabor in the wedding ceremony was the Rev. Gustavus Bosanquet, rector of Clophill in Bedfordshire, whose family had

---

[2] The school, which traces its origins to 1645, left the town of Cheam in 1934 and is now sited near Newbury in Berkshire.

several connections to the Bevans — Gustavus's wife was Frank's first cousin. And Frank himself was the dignified *paterfamilias* in the front pew. Beside him would have been his wife Maria, and ranged behind them the groom's brothers, half-brothers and half-sisters, plus a dozen or more of Frank's own brothers and sisters (some of them younger than the groom) and innumerable first and second cousins.

The scale, complexity and religious tone of the Bevan contingent at All Saints that morning requires quite some explaining. Although their antecedents were Quakers, the family and many of their ilk had shifted to various persuasions of the Church of England as their wealth and social position evolved.

Robert Bevan, a devout Anglican who held daily prayer meetings in his banking parlour, fathered seven children by his first wife, Lady Agneta Yorke, sister of the fourth Earl of Hardwicke. After her death he had nine more with his second wife, Frances Shuttleworth, daughter of a bishop of Chichester.

Frances Shuttleworth first met Robert Bevan when she attended bible-readings at Trent Park. Originally an Anglican like her husband, she transferred her adherence, with his support, to the low-church Plymouth Brethren, who sought to shun the trappings of the material world. She was noted for her translations of mediaeval German hymns and she prevailed on Robert to give up hunting as a matter of conscience. Even by Victorian standards, she must have been grim company.

Frank Bevan, in turn, fathered ten children by three wives — but the fact that the first and third of those marriages had taken place only 13 years apart was not a matter of which the starched ladies of the All Saints congregation, or even his austere stepmother, might have disapproved.

Frank was at least as devout and high-minded as his father, though Evangelical rather than high Anglican. And it should not, of course, be inferred that Gerard's later infidelity to Sophie was a trait inherited through paternal genes. Rather, the prolific pattern of fatherhood displayed by both Robert and Frank tells us of the negligible state of early and mid Victorian family planning even among the privileged classes, and their belief that procreation was both a duty to and a gift from God.

If John Galsworthy (a close contemporary of Gerard Bevan) is to be believed, it also illuminates an aspect of Victorian thinking about dynastic fortunes. *In Chancery* (1920), the volume of *The Forsyte Saga* which picks up Galsworthy's epic family story in the late 1890s, tells us:

> A student of statistics must have noticed that the birth rate varied in accordance with the rate of interest on your money. Grandfather Forsyte in the early 19th century had been getting ten per cent for his, hence ten children. Those ten… had averaged from four to five per cent of theirs, and produced accordingly. The 21 whom they produced were now getting barely three per cent in the Consols[3] to which their fathers had tied the Settlements they made to avoid death duties, and the six of them who had been reproduced had seventeen children, or just the proper two and five-sixths per stem.

The principle seems much the same for the Bevans. In short, the prolific birth rate of these two Victorian generations was unconstrained by considerations of income — and their ability to pay for doctors and midwives meant that their infant mortality rate was lower than was the case among the less privileged classes. It was only towards the end of the century that forms of contraceptive practice and abstinence were more widely adopted, with the intention and effect of producing smaller families with births at wider intervals.

Meanwhile the mothers still suffered, whatever their station. Frank had already had the misfortune to become a widower twice. His first wife Elizabeth had been the daughter of Lord Charles James Fox Russell, the Serjeant at Arms of the House of Commons,

---

[3] Consols (originally 'consolidated annuities') are a form of interest-bearing British government stock first introduced in the 18th century. They are 'perpetual', meaning they carry no fixed repayment date; they may be redeemed by the government at any time, but rarely have been.

and grand-daughter of the sixth Duke of Bedford. She died in 1863 a few days after giving birth to Frank's first son, Cosmo.

His second wife, Constance, was a daughter of Sir James Hogg, first baronet, sometime member of parliament and chairman of the East India Company. Constance gave Frank five sons in little more than five years — Gerard was the middle one — and died in 1872 a few months after the arrival of the youngest.

Undiscouraged — indeed, anxious to find a new mother for his boys — Frank married for the third time in 1875, to Maria Trotter from a Hertfordshire landed family. They had a son and three daughters, again at short intervals.

Gerard was still a toddler when Constance died, so unlikely to have had any memory of his natural mother, and five and a half when Maria became his stepmother. Maria was constantly occupied with her own pregnancies and infants, and can have had little time or energy for the rabble of small boys corralled upstairs by nannies and nursemaids. She was remembered by the family as 'a very nice woman who had a ghastly time with the five very pert boys'. The younger three, Gerard, Owen and Ivor, were particularly troublesome, and teased her mercilessly.

But they did not get much discipline from their father, who reportedly could not control them at all — and who, in the Victorian manner, would in any event have seen his offspring, selectively or *en masse*, for no more than a few minutes each day.

One way or another, therefore, Gerard had little parental influence in the years before he was sent away first to Cheam and then to Eton. There is always an element of chance in how human character develops: most of Gerard's siblings led blameless lives. But in any large family one or two are made different from the rest, and it is hardly surprising that Gerard turned out so completely unlike his father.

Frank Bevan really was a pillar of Victorian virtue and the City establishment, bred from a mix of mercantile and aristocratic antecedents. On the paternal side, Bevans claim descent from Jestyn-ap-Gwrgant, the last Prince of Glamorgan, who lived in

Cardiff Castle in the eleventh century. More certainly, they descend from a Quaker merchant family in Swansea, of which two sons came to London in the early 18th century to become pharmacists in Plough Court, off Lombard Street in the City. The turning point in Bevan dynastic history came when Timothy, one of the pharmacist brothers, married Elizabeth Barclay, daughter of a partner in a Lombard Street banking house.

Silvanus Bevan, son of Timothy and Elizabeth, joined the Lombard Street bank in 1767. The name of the bank changed from time to time according to the make-up of a partnership drawn from several related families, but by the time Silvanus's great-grandson Frank joined in 1861, it had settled as Barclay, Bevan, Tritton & Co. The Trittons (whose dynastic founder also married a Miss Barclay) were about to play a guiding role in Gerard's Stock Exchange career, and we can be sure that they too were represented at his wedding.

Frank had succeeded as senior partner of the Lombard Street bank when Robert died in 1890. It was a time of change in the cosy world of private banking, in much more than name. This brought heavy responsibilities on Frank's shoulders — and all the more so a few years later when he became the first chairman of the modern Barclays Bank after a bold multiple merger. More of that and how it affected Gerard in the next chapter. But apart from being a busy banker and an energetic husband, what sort of person was Frank Bevan?

Full-bearded and stocky, his photograph suggests benign solidity. The first official history of Barclays, published not long after his death, eulogises his 'wisdom and sagacity' and credits him with diplomatic skills that made Barclays a happy and successful ship in its early years.

That suggests quite a formidable business leader. But less deferential modern historians tell us that Frank 'did not inherit either the rugged physical strength or the decisiveness of his father [Robert]. He also lacked imagination and had a rather limited outlook.' The writers concede, however, that these qualities strongly recommended him to other bankers who were contemplating merging their own firms with his, while not wishing to give up their traditional ways of business. 'His relaxed, easy-going temperament, his charitable instincts and his strong sense of humour perfectly fitted the delicate task of soothing the process of integration.'

A kindly fellow then, a natural conciliator — and a man of wide-ranging commitments and preoccupations. He gave his time outside the bank to the treasurership of St Peter's Hospital in Covent Garden, and was active on behalf of the London City Mission, the Church Patronage Trust and Christ's Hospital. He was a magistrate and a lieutenant of the City of London. He liked music, art, cricket and horses, and in his later years he developed a pioneering interest in motoring.

Frank was also 'a man of property' (another Galsworthian phrase) on a substantial scale. Fosbury and Trent Park, the two homes that were given as his addresses in *The Times* announcement of Gerard and Sophie's marriage, extended to 4,000 acres between them. When these properties passed to him on his father's death, he also received the lion's share of Robert's chattels, which were valued at almost a million pounds.

Fosbury Manor in Wiltshire had first been acquired by Silvanus Bevan in 1810, at the end of his banking career, and had passed down through three generations. Trent Park was bought as a wedding present for Robert in 1833 by his father David (Silvanus's eldest son), allegedly achieved by nodding in his sleep at the crucial moment of the auction.

Sited on what had once been the royal hunting grounds of Enfield Chase, the mansion of Trent Park was designed by the architect Sir William Chambers for George III's physician Sir Richard Jebb, who is believed to have had the grounds landscaped by Humphrey Repton. The Bevans' chief contribution to its development was to plant a double avenue of lime trees and some 30,000 oaks. Perhaps tiresomely expensive to run as a family home even by the standards of the 1890s, it required a domestic staff of 14 men and 11 women.

Though Frank moved to Trent Park, we might guess that it did not particularly suit him, with his many commitments in central

London, to change the habit of three decades in order to make it his home during the week, even when the motor car became a possible means of commuter transport a few years later — but long before the arrival on the edge of the park of what is now the Cockfosters terminus of the Piccadilly underground line.

Nor would it have been practicable to take the family and its entourage down to Fosbury, deep in rural Wiltshire, more than a few times a year. His offspring evidently continued to regard South Kensington as home, hence their attachment to All Saints. His son Owen was still living at 59 Prince's Gate in 1894.

Another of Frank's traits was his resilience in the face of family tribulations and sadnesses, of which there were more ahead. Leonard, his oldest child by Maria, would hang himself in 1901; the only surviving description of Leonard says he was 'extremely musical [and] slightly homosexual'. Maria died two years later — and when the undertaker found Frank sitting in his library to tell him that the cortege was ready to move off, Frank replied disconsolately, 'You know I never attend my wives' funerals.'

Thereafter his daughters took it in turns to keep Frank company. In due course, he sold both Trent Park (to Sir Edward Sassoon, a wealthy MP married to a Rothschild)[4] and Fosbury (to a bibliophile by the name of Alfred Huth from another banking family who had been neighbours in Prince's Gate) and moved to a comfortable townhouse in Mayfair, where Gerard and Sophie would become his nearest family neighbours.

The Playing Fields of Eton

If Frank had never been an active disciplinarian or visible presence during his sons' childhood, the young Gerard would have encountered a firmer hand for the first time in Robert Tabor at Cheam and then in the person of another wedding guest: the Revd. Raymond Coxe Radcliffe, a Cambridge scholar who was his housemaster at Eton and taught him mathematics and classics. Bevan was in

---

4 Trent Park is now a campus of Middlesex University.

Radcliffe's house from September 1883 until December 1888, and school records give us a useful picture of what sort of boy he was.

He was not a King's Scholar (in which case he would have been in the elite house called simply College, rather than in Radcliffe's) nor an Oppidan Scholar, and he did not win any of the major school prizes — though he was sufficiently bright to gain a place at Cambridge.

He was, however, quite a good sportsman. That is not to say he was a Corinthian hero like his contemporary Hugh Bromley-Davenport, who went on to play Test cricket for England, or his distant kinsman and later business associate Theodore Barclay, who went on to row for Cambridge and win trophies at Henley. Nor was Bevan mentioned by name in *Eton in the 'Eighties*, a rather ponderous account of the major sporting feats of the decade by one Eric Parker, whose other works included *Highways and Byways in Surrey*.

But Bevan was a useful team player. He 'got his Field' in 1887 — that is, he was a regular member of the first team for Eton's distinctive winter ball game, a form of eleven-a-side football with the addition of a rugby-like scrum called a 'bully' — and was Keeper (or captain) of the Field in 1888.

In the even more arcane Wall Game — a trial of stamina in the form of long, muddy 'bully', played against an ancient wall — he was a member of both the Oppidan and Mixed Wall XIs of 1888. In the traditional St Andrew's Day contest between the Oppidans and the Collegers, Bevan's Oppidans team lost by seven shies to nil, a high score but evidently not so exciting an encounter as the previous year's, in which a boy called Benson wrote himself into Wall Game history by kneeling on the ball without respite for a full twenty minutes at the bottom of the bully.

Sports played at school, however curious their conventions, are supposed to be character-forming. One 20th century Eton 'beak' (or master), Oliver Van Oss, wrote of the Wall Game as a perfect training for difficult situations in the boardroom or public life: 'The unmovable and the irresistible are poised in perfect balance. Nothing is happening and it seems as if nothing will. Then, for two seconds or so, the situation becomes fluid. If one can take one's chance — and there may not be another — the day is won.'

Who knows whether Bevan thought back to his own or Benson's Wall Game experience when he took his chance and fled the country half a lifetime later. What we do know is that Bevan's prowess on and off the sports field was sufficient to win him election to the Eton Society, known as 'Pop', the self-perpetuating social elite of school prefects who were allowed to wear flamboyant variants of the school's tail-coated uniform and do various other things forbidden to ordinary school mortals.

By the time he left Eton in December 1888, Gerard Bevan — Gerry to his friends — was quite a swell, though perhaps not universally popular with his peers. 'We regarded him as a prig,' one old schoolmate told a reporter 34 years later, after Bevan's conviction. 'He was punctilious to a degree.' A house photograph in his final year, in which he sits next to Radcliffe's rather pretty wife, Mary, shows an intelligent, self-confident, fresh-faced boy, looking straight into the camera. The immaculately combed hair, with a little curl at the left temple, perhaps reveals a hint of vanity.

Eton in the 'Eighties also reminds us, tangentially, of something that Bevan was not, or not inclined to become. The Parker memoir highlights a strong correlation between success on the school's playing fields (where, of course, 'the Battle of Waterloo was won', or so the great Duke of Wellington is supposed to have said) and military service afterwards. The Wall Game hero of '87 became Captain Richard Benson of the Coldstream Guards, and died of dysentery during the South African war.

But then Benson was the son of a colonel: upper-class families with soldiering traditions produced generation after generation of gallant officers throughout the 18th and 19th centuries, but in the relatively peaceful decades immediately before the second Boer War, the sons of mercantile and rentier families were under no social pressure to put on uniform. Like the fictional Forsytes, they and their friends and neighbours were largely occupied with the respectable enjoyment of their accumulated wealth.

Of Frank Bevan's seven sons, one — Gerard's younger full brother Owen — would still be young enough to serve as an army staff officer during the first world war, and win a DSO. But he too made his main career in the Stock Exchange, as a partner in Pember & Boyle, a firm of brokers in gilt-edged stock. One of Frank's daughters, Audrey, married a brigadier, but armed service does not otherwise much feature in the lives of Bevans born in the 19th century.

Another brother, Raymond (who in due course took the younger son's traditional alternative career choice of holy orders) was already an undergraduate at Trinity when Gerard's name was first registered there in May 1889. He matriculated at Michaelmas to embark on the classical tripos and again, college records help us track his development.

Trinity had a large contingent of Old Etonian undergraduates, so there was a well-trodden social path for Bevan to follow — and he did so assiduously in his first year but seems to have become less gregarious, or perhaps more devoted to his studies, thereafter. Though he had not been an oarsman at Eton, he swiftly gained entry to Trinity Boat Club, the social hub for heartier types, as a 'non-rowing member'. He also threw himself into the intellectual cut and thrust of college life, as a member of the Magpie and Stump Debating Society, and the more exclusive Decemviri.

The Magpie and Stump, founded in 1866, was a formal if rumbustious affair, which added about 50 Trinity men to its membership each term. It met half a dozen times a term and liked to debate provocatively offbeat motions such as 'That this house sympathises with Satan in his sorrows' or 'That all handsome men are slightly sunburnt'. It also liked to argue as to whether biscuits should be served with coffee at its meetings; a motion in favour of biscuits found no seconder in 1887, but was carried unanimously three years later.

Bevan was one of the first of the College's 1889 intake to be elected to membership, along with several of his Eton contemporaries, at the 492nd meeting of the society. He immediately made his mark as an active participant, though by no means radical in the views he expressed. Whereas some members relished debate for its own sake, however absurd or contrary the position they were thereby required to support, Bevan seems to have spoken in a consistently conservative direction. In early November he was the second speaker against the motion 'That in the opinion of this house, the present popularity of the Army is a great evil to the country', which was defeated by ten votes to seven.

A week later, he was the first speaker against the proposition 'That in the opinion of this house, state interference with individual liberty should be absolutely discountenanced', holding the floor for an unusually long 14 minutes. On that occasion, his side lost by seven to three, after the word 'absolutely' had been modified to 'strongly'. And he was back the following week with a shorter floor speech which helped defeat the motion 'That this house says Yes to the question, is our Civilisation a Failure?'.

This burst of enthusiasm won him election to the committee of the Magpie and Stump for his second term, but he seems to have soon lost interest. There is no record of him speaking again, and within a short time he had fallen seriously foul of the society's rules. Originally, members had been obliged to speak once in every three debates on pain of a shilling fine; later the fine was two shillings for those who failed to speak for two minutes in the course of a term, and unrepentant non-speakers were ejected from the society.

Such fines were even imposed on the young Bertrand Russell — who arrived at Trinity as an undergraduate in 1890, and whom Gerard might also have met at the Boat Club, where the budding philosopher was an unlikely cox. The humiliation of ejection from the Magpie and Stump had even happened to the future prime minister Stanley Baldwin a few years earlier, as it happened to Bevan at the end of the Easter term in 1890.

But he got back in, at least nominally, as a result of a fiercely contested election for the society's presidency in March 1892 between the reform-minded George Hamilton-Gordon — a grandson of the prime minister Lord Aberdeen and later, as Lord Stanmore, a politician himself — and the candidate for the status quo, Erskine Childers, who was to become famous as the author of *Riddle of the Sands* and as an Irish nationalist politician who would eventually be shot by firing squad.

Large numbers of lapsed or ejected members, Bevan among them, were re-elected in order to pack the ballots — increasing the membership by almost 200 in a single term. This seems to have been a hugely enjoyable episode in Trinity life, culminating in a great dinner after the election: the college was described as being 'united in debate', and the winner, Hamilton-Gordon, cheerfully proposed Childers to succeed him the following term. There is no record of how Bevan voted, but from his debating record we might assume that he was a man for the status quo; in any event, he never attended or spoke at a meeting after his re-election.

The Decemviri was a smaller affair, with fewer than 20 members, and included men from King's as well as Trinity. It was the preserve of serious scholars such as the Trevelyan brothers, Robert and Charles, Harrovian sons of the statesman-historian Sir George, but it was also well stocked with sociable Etonians. Despite its intellectual exclusivity, it too preferred light-hearted motions. It was Bertrand Russell who proposed in November 1891 'That in the matter of the oysters, the Walrus was more to blame than the Carpenter'. Bevan was a member for a while but there is no record of him speaking in Decemviri debates, and by his third year he had dropped out of the membership list.

Was he, meanwhile, a diligent scholar? Again, we don't know — but we can guess that he was, because it is clear that elements of classical learning stayed with him all his life. That much is evident from a tribute in the preface of a 1902 translation of Aeschylus's *Prometheus Bound* by his half-uncle Edwyn Bevan (who was slightly younger than Gerard) thanking him for suggesting 'various improvements'. It is also evident from the archaic style and metric precision of Gerard's own poetry, replete with abstruse references to ancient and mythical worlds, which he would eventually publish after he came out of prison.

These snippets of Gerard Bevan's early life create a portrait of an intelligent, articulate and accomplished young man, straight-laced in his views, conventional in his style, not quite in the first rank of his generation, but always close to the action.

Hollow-ware and Oddwork

On the groom's side of the church, then, we have row upon row of respectable Bevans and their cousins, plus perhaps a peacock selection of Gerard's contemporaries from Eton and Cambridge, and at the back, no doubt, a gaggle of family retainers from Prince's Gate, Trent Park and Fosbury. The bride's side presents a tableau of more muted plumage — representing the non-conformist industrial society of Victorian Birmingham.

To the fore, another *paterfamilias*: John Arthur (hereafter just Arthur) Kenrick, also full bearded, also the father of a large brood, but older, leaner and sterner in appearance than Frank Bevan.

Arthur was a grandson of Archibald Kenrick, whose family owned a small agricultural estate at Ruabon in Denbighshire — at the far end of Wales from the Bevans in Swansea — and whose three brothers were respectively a grocer and chandler, a tobacconist and small-town banker, and a Unitarian minister. Archibald was apprenticed in the iron trade and took himself to Birmingham around 1780. There he found his way among a network of non-conformist families and started his first venture manufacturing buckles for shoes, hats and garments, and livery fittings.

Buckles rapidly went out of fashion, however, and Archibald turned his hand to the more promising field of cast-iron. In 1791, he established a foundry in the village of West Bromwich, beside the Birmingham canal, which grew into one of the great manufacturies of 19th century England. He specialised in 'hollow-ware', which meant receptacles mostly for kitchen use, and 'oddwork', or domestic ironmongery.

The historian of Archibald Kenrick & Sons, R.A. Church, recites the firm's early product range in an almost poetic mode:

Oddwork... included bell pulls, door knobs, handles, knockers, hinges, moletraps and castors, while the production of cast nails was an important special line, as was the manufacture of smoothing irons of every description. The hollow-ware products included round and oval pots, with or without covers and with capacities of up to ten gallons, saucepans, kettles, frypans, teapots, gluepots, grogpots and spittoons.

As the business grew, so did the level of innovation, both in the techniques of enamelling pots and pans (which would otherwise have quickly blackened with use) and in the range of other items and appliances offered in Kenricks' handsome illustrated catalogue. There were coffee mills, American-style waffle-irons, and the 'digester', a large-bellied pot with a steam release valve which was the forerunner of the modern pressure cooker. There was even a 'humane man trap' for apprehending poachers and trespassers without permanently injuring them.

These products were in demand all over the Empire and beyond. 'There are few civilised countries which do not import English hollow-ware,' one of the Kenricks observed in 1866.

Arthur was a major shareholder and the first chairman of this mighty enterprise when it became a limited company in 1883.[5] An archetypal Midlands industrialist of his day, he was a leading figure in the development of West Bromwich as chairman of its Highways Board and Board of Improvement Commissioners, and the chairman of its Liberal Association — though he declined to offer himself to be its member of parliament. He was a director of numerous other metalworking companies as well as the Union Rolling Stock Company, and found time to launch a successful commercial stationery and printing business as well.

Arthur also sat for many years on the board of Lloyds Bank, where one of his uncles had been deputy chairman — a point of minor interest here because Barclay, Bevan, Tritton & Co and the

---

[5] The company still operates on its original site in West Bromwich, principally as a maker of door and window fittings.

provincial banks for which it acted as London agent had little or no foothold in the Birmingham district at that time, so it is unlikely that Kenricks and Bevans had ever done business together. Lloyds and the Birmingham & Midland Bank, founded respectively in 1765 and 1836, dominated the local banking scene.

Meanwhile, comfortably established in what is now the leafy Birmingham suburb of Edgbaston, the Kenrick family also acquired a small shooting estate in Worcestershire, to which was added in the 1880s — indicative of their social advancement — a grouse moor in Scotland.

Arthur and his wife Clara had eight children, of whom Sophie was the eldest. She was followed by four sons and three more daughters. The first son, John Archibald, was the same age as Gerard Bevan, but it seems unlikely that he and his new brother-in-law would have struck up much of a friendship.

John Archibald trained as an engineer in Leeds before joining Kenricks, where he spent four years as a supervisor of the oddwork section and an assistant in the drawing office as preparation for becoming a director, aged 25, in 1894. His wife was a Nettlefold from the family whose screw-making business, Nettlefolds & Chamberlain, became part of the great metal-bashing combine of Guest, Keen and Nettlefolds (now GKN, the vehicle component maker). And like several of his siblings, John Archibald was married in the Church of the Messiah in Broad Street, Birmingham, the centre of worship for all the prominent Unitarian families of the city.

Among that congregation were Birmingham's most important 19th century political dynasty, the Chamberlains — who were related to the Kenricks by marriage several times over. Joseph Chamberlain was a partner in the screw-making business; he later became mayor of Birmingham, a Liberal Unionist MP and Colonial Secretary, and was the first chancellor of Birmingham University. He married, successively, two Kenrick girls; his brother Arthur married another; and his sister married a Kenrick boy.

Joseph's first wife was Sophie's aunt Harriet Kenrick, though she died before Sophie was born, three days after giving birth to their second child, Austen, who spent a portion of his childhood with the Kenricks while his father concentrated on politics. Austen would follow his father into the House of Commons, making an acclaimed maiden speech a few months before Sophie's wedding. He went on to serve as Chancellor of the Exchequer under both Arthur Balfour and David Lloyd George.

Joseph's second wife was Sophie's cousin Florence Kenrick, who died in 1875 after giving birth to the couple's fifth child, who also died. The eldest child of Joseph and Florence was Neville Chamberlain, destined to become prime minister in 1937.

Like John Archibald Kenrick, Neville was exactly the same age as Gerard Bevan, and again it is interesting to wonder how the two got on — for they must have met often over the coming decades. But at the date of the wedding, Neville was managing a sisal plantation Joseph Chamberlain had established (unwisely as it turned out, for it lost him a lot of money) in the Bahamas. So the future prime minister, though very much one of the family, probably wasn't a guest at All Saints.

We can assume that his father Joseph Chamberlain was there, however — with his third wife, the American-born Mary Endicott, daughter of President Grover Cleveland's minister of war. Though he had a 'flint-like, cold demeanour' in public life, his biographer Enoch Powell observed, Joseph was sustained by 'an intensely warm family life of mutual devotion'. The Chamberlains — and this must surely include the Kenrick in-laws — 'were a "clan" in the least derogatory sense of the word. Their family loyalties were total and rendered them emotionally self-sufficient.'

Like the Kenricks and the Bevans, the Chamberlains were also very rich. Their principal home was a *rus in urbis* 100-acre estate at King's Heath in Birmingham — but Joseph also had a London *pied-à-terre*, at No 40 Prince's Gardens (now replaced by a wing of Imperial College), and the bridal party must have come to the church from there. Prior to acquiring that house, indeed, Chamberlain had rented Frank Bevan's previous house, No 72 Prince's Gate, so he would already have been on neighbourly terms with his new relations by marriage.

No photographs of the wedding group are known to survive, but as for the bridesmaids, we can at least identify a clutch of candidates. There were Sophie's unmarried younger sisters, Mabel and Rosa — the wedding of their other sister, Dorothy, having taken place at the Church of the Messiah four months earlier.

Then there were Gerard's teenage half-sisters Audrey, Gytha and Evie, the latter the only one of his siblings who would remain sympathetic to him when he was sent to prison, so perhaps the most suitable to have played a role on his wedding day. Lastly, though a more unlikely candidate, there was Gerard's 17-year-old half-aunt Nesta (Robert's last child) who grew up to be, if not quite a pariah like Gerard after his disgrace, then certainly a family embarrassment. In later life she became the author of books and articles expounding Jewish and Masonic plots for world domination behind every major historical event from the French to the Bolshevik revolutions, and was a member of the British Union of Fascists.

Nesta and her mother may not have attended the wedding at all — after Robert's death they lived for part of the year at his villa in Cannes. If they did so, Nesta would perhaps have been too truculent to be a bridesmaid. But, as we shall discover in Chapter Three, she might have enjoyed engaging Sophie in earnest discussion of their nascent political ideas at the reception afterwards.

Having imagined who was present on that October morning, we still have not answered one fundamental question. How did Sophie and Gerard meet and what attracted them to each other?

A reasonable guess, however, is that Sophie, having passed her mid-twenties without finding a suitable husband among the Unitarian community of Edgbaston and suffered the embarrassment of seeing Dorothy married first, had come to London to lodge at the Chamberlains' house, where the flow of political conversation would have been to her liking. We can imagine that Mary Chamberlain, in the sociable American way, was keen to make neighbourly introductions for Sophie, and would have arranged for her to call on the Bevan household, with its large complement of lively young people.

Perhaps the Rev. Stewart from All Saints (in the manner of Mr Beebe, the ever-eager-to-help clergyman in E.M. Forster's 1908 novel *A Room With A View*) was also a guest at that first tea party. And after an initial spark of attraction had passed between the couple, Frank Bevan and Arthur Kenrick had formed a view that an alliance between the two families made good business sense, which was more than enough reason to ignore any minor nuances of religious or social difference.

We can also guess what the congregation was chattering about as they spilled out onto the pavement of Ennismore Gardens behind the bridal couple and made their way to the breakfast — most probably (on grounds of space for a large party) at the Bevans' rather than the Chamberlains'. Frank and Arthur would, we hope, have agreed politely that Messrs Tabor and Bosanquet had provided a satisfactory service, offending neither the Evangelical nor the Unitarian taste — though to do so would have involved suppression of too much mention of the Holy Trinity, since the essence of Unitarianism, as its name suggests, is a belief in a singular God.

As men of the world, they would have moved swiftly on to discuss the recent downturn of trade and the rise of unemployment, the state of Kenricks' export order book, and the state of the money market as seen from Lombard Street. Others of the party might have tried to open up 'the Irish Question' with Joseph Chamberlain — though they probably didn't get much conversation out of him — or made favourable mention of opposition recently expressed by the prime minister, William Gladstone, now in the last months of his last stint in office, to a proposal for graduated death duties.[6]

The ladies would have been gossiping about other recent weddings — including that of Prince George, Duke of York, the future

---

[6] Death duties were in fact introduced the following year by the Chancellor of the Exchequer, Sir William Harcourt, despite Gladstone's dislike of them. One person who would later write trenchantly in opposition to this tax 'stolen from Capital' was Sophie Bevan: see Chapter Three.

King George V, who in July had married Princess Mary of Teck, an exact contemporary of Sophie's. (As it happened, Maria Bevan was a friend of Princess Mary's mother, the enormously fat Duchess of Teck — and when the future King Edward VIII was born to the Princess the following summer, it was the Bevan family midwife who attended.)

Meanwhile, Gerard's more sophisticated Cambridge friends might have been chattering about what was on offer by way of entertainment in the West End that season: Mrs Patrick Campbell's triumphant role in Pinero's *The Second Mrs Tanqueray* at the St James's Theatre, or Oscar Wilde's *A Woman of No Importance* at the Haymarket.

Some would have been looking forward to the opening at the Prince of Wales Theatre a few days later of *A Gaiety Girl*, a prototype of the kind of light musical comedy that was to keep London society amused for the next two decades. Such shows provided work for an endless bevy of chorus girls who in turn attracted the favours of 'Stage Door Johnnies' — men about town, like the unfaithful Forsyte brother-in-law Montague Dartie and indeed like Gerard Bevan himself, who would take a succession of dancers as his mistresses and eventually abandon Sophie in favour of one of them; and his City Equitable colleague Edmund Mansell, who would leave his own wife for an actress and lose money backing her shows.

Yet others in the wedding party would have been eager to see Gilbert and Sullivan's new Savoy Opera *Utopia, Limited*, opening that very Saturday, though they could not have realised the resonance it also would one day carry for Gerard Bevan's story.

Set in the Kingdom of Utopia, it was in part a satire on the machinations of limited companies and stockmarket flotations, and the idea that a bankrupt company could leave its creditors unpaid without any liability on the part of its promoters. The Kingdom turns itself into a limited company — and Mr Goldbury, the company promoter who becomes Comptroller of the Utopian Royal Household, sings:

Stupendous loans to foreign thrones
I've largely advocated;
In ginger-pops and peppermint-drops
I've freely speculated;
Then mines of gold, of wealth untold,
Successfully I've floated
And sudden falls in apple-stalls
Occasionally quoted.
And soon or late I always call
For Stock Exchange quotation —
No schemes too great and none too small
For Companification!

CHAPTER TWO

On 'Change

'*Think how much sheer barbarism there is around us, from the brutal savage of the gutter to the cunning savage of the Stock Exchange!*'
George Gissing, *The Crown of Life*, 1899

'*Mr Parker is a moneyed man, who happens also to be a stockbroker....
as honest as others, I dare say, but I shouldn't like to trust him much
farther than I could see him.*'
Anthony Trollope, *The Prime Minister*, 1876

The Black Sheep

Gerard Lee Bevan was clearly destined to be a money man, not a vicar like his brother Raymond, or a scholar like his uncle Edwyn. So it seems logical to begin an account of his business career by asking why he became a stockbroker and not a banker like his father Frank, grandfather Robert, great-grandfather David and great-great-grandfather Silvanus.

To be a 'London banker' in the late 19th century was, after all, a calling that carried, as Walter Bagehot wrote in *Lombard Street* (1873), a 'charmed value'. Bagehot went on to offer what sounds a near-perfect job-description for a Cambridge classicist from the very best of banking stables:

He was supposed to represent, and often did represent, a certain union of pecuniary sagacity and educated refinement which was scarcely to be found in any other part of society... The calling is hereditary; the credit of the bank descends from father to son; this inherited wealth soon brings inherited refinement... A certain part of his time, and a considerable part of his thoughts, he can readily devote to other pursuits. And a London banker can also have the most intellectual society in the world if he chooses it.

By the time Gerard graduated in 1893, however, his family bank was in the midst of radical change that impinged on his career prospects. To understand why, we need a potted history of Lombard Street banking.

Partnerships like Barclay, Bevan, Tritton had their roots in the 17th century, when goldsmiths and other tradesmen developed the practice of providing safe custody for the cash and valuables of their wealthy patrons and issuing negotiable notes in exchange for them. Many of these early bankers were Quakers, partly because Quakers tended to combine the qualities of prudence, judgement and courtesy which made for good banking, but partly also because they were excluded by discrimination from other professions which might have suited them, such as the law.

Individual tradesmen-bankers and small partnerships were not equipped to cope with the needs of the rapidly expanding Victorian economy. Bigger corporate customers — industrial enterprises such as Kenricks of West Bromwich, for example, and the leading railway companies — needed bigger banks, and banks needed a scale and continuity of capital which was too often disrupted in private partnerships by issues of inheritance from one generation to the next.

These pressures created a vogue for joint-stock (that is, shareholder-owned) banking, and that trend took a leap forward with the Companies Act of 1862, which introduced the concept of limited liability for shareholders; before that date, their risks were unlimited. The trend was also towards the absorption of weaker partnerships by stronger ones or by up-and-coming joint-stock banks – the Birmingham & Midland, which became the market leader as the London & Midland from 1891, being the prime mover. The Scots also had powerful joint-stock banks, based in Edinburgh, which had begun to encroach into northern English towns and cities.

The advantages of strength through amalgamation were made all the more apparent by the Barings crisis of 1890, when the aristocratic merchant banking house of Baring Brothers nearly ruined itself on an Argentine speculation that would have brought down a number of other City firms if Barings had not been bailed out by the Bank of England.

Barclay, Bevan, Tritton was a reluctant participant in this gradual transition of the banking scene before 1890, partly because Robert Bevan was by nature deeply conservative, but partly for pragmatic reasons. A highly profitable element of the business was its role as London agent for provincial banking firms with which the Lombard Street partners had connections of cousinage and marriage. It was not to Barclay, Bevan, Tritton's advantage to see these provincial banks merging with each other or forming new alliances in London.

But 'the spirit of the age cannot be resisted,' as the *Bankers' Magazine* declared. 'Amalgamation is the order of the day.' And so it was, even in Lombard Street. In 1888, Barclay, Bevan, Tritton had joined forces with Ransom, Bouverie & Co of Pall Mall, whose partners included a Bevan and whose customers had once included Gioachino Rossini and J.W.M. Turner. And in 1894, Barclay, Bevan, Tritton, Ransom & Bouverie (known to City wags by the derogatory nickname 'the long firm') would absorb another Bevan partnership in Sussex, creating the beginning of an out-of-town branch network.

All this was a preliminary to the multiple merger which created — after several years of fraught negotiation — Barclay & Co as a joint-stock bank in June 1896. It was done, as one partner admitted at the time, 'in order to protect our valuable agency business... to some extent an act of self-defence.' But it created a very substantial bank, with a dominant position in East Anglia through various partnerships dominated by the Gurney family, several other strongholds in the Home Counties, and outposts as far north as Darlington. Frank Bevan, the conciliator liked and respected by all the merger parties, was pressed into service as its first chairman.

Why no career opportunity for Gerard in such an expansive organisation, which had already found places for his elder brothers Cosmo and Bertie? The answer is that he simply did not make the grade. He was taken in for a trial period, and either he was judged unsuitable or he found the work and atmosphere not to his liking, or both.

Hubert Meredith, a stockbroker turned author of *The Drama of Money Making* (1931), records that 'by virtue of his family connections, [Gerard] started not on a par with the ordinary bank clerks but as one who had the free entrée to the bank parlour'. That panelled inner sanctum was the room where his father and the bank's other partners sat at large desks facing one another, attended by uniformed waiters or doorkeepers. Every day, according to a fixed routine, they would say prayers together (many decades later, the first morning meeting of senior Barclays directors was still referred to as 'prayers'), review administrative matters and the bank's liquidity position, make decisions on loans to customers, then proceed to lunch in their private dining room. Gerard would have been allowed to sit in on the morning's proceedings, while spending the rest of his day as a ledger clerk.

But this privileged entrée did not persuade him or his seniors that banking was the right career choice for him. Within a year — by the time he was about to be married — it was obvious that he was not cut out to spend the rest of his life in the parlour.

It was not because he was incapable of meeting the intellectual demands of banking. Gerard was probably a lot cleverer than most bankers of his era, but he was simply the wrong sort of personality. And his father, anxious to be even-handed and transparent in his handling of the merger discussions, would not have wanted to burden the bank with a son who was unlikely to measure up to the highest standards.

The fact that the ambitious and rather pompous Cosmo Bevan and the more genial Bertie had already found places in the parlour would have been an argument for not accommodating Gerard as well, rather than the reverse. Indeed, Cosmo is very likely to have been whispering in his father's ear that Gerard was unsuitable, just as he later conspired to keep Bertie off the bank's main board. Another of Frank's sons, Owen, was meanwhile about to start his career in another stockbroking firm, Pember & Boyle.

The official historians of Barclays, Margaret Ackrill and Leslie Hannah, explain:

> Family men who did not make the grade were quickly dropped from the bank. A clearing banker's life did not suit everyone... For those who did want a City career, but lacked the application or aptitude required for banking, there were conveniently arranged alternatives... The bank's commission business with stockbrokers could provide an appropriate entrée to a stock-broking partnership... for family members who chose (or were advised) to leave. The strategy was however, scandalously disastrous for the black sheep of the Bevan family, Gerard...

As we have already noted, none of this suggests that Gerard was, as a young man, inclined to dishonesty. But it does reflect his attitude to risk. Good bankers are cautious on their own behalf and on behalf of their customers. They are also meticulous in record-keeping, and fond of formality and hierarchy. Good stockbrokers, by contrast, are essentially salesman with an inclination to be cavalier both about risk and paperwork, and to regard time spent on administrative detail as time wasted. They are more interested in making money than acquiring the trappings and titles of corporate status.

It must swiftly have become evident that Gerard did not fit the banker archetype. His later career would be marked by blindness to risk — in the bundle of unsuitable investments he made on behalf of the City Equitable, and in his disregard for the rudiments of management control and corporate governance. He had no time for the carefully minuted committee procedures by which bankers ran their businesses, and it would eventually be part of his defence that he was in the habit of signing cheques and contracts with barely a glance at their contents. With these nascent instincts, he must have thought the Stock Exchange looked a far more congenial place to build his career.

The Junior Partner

There were a number of stockbroking partnerships that might have been persuaded to accommodate Gerard, including the one founded by and named after his cousin David Augustus Bevan.[1] But imminent retirements as well as dynastic connections made Ellis & Co a particularly suitable berth.

We do not know the precise date of his arrival there, but it is logical to assume that he started in October 1893, shortly after his wedding, and served the briefest of apprenticeships before taking up the junior partnership that his father had bought for him in January 1894.

The firm had been founded by a young man called Thomas Ellis in 1778. Although few records remain of the early years of the business, it is evident that Thomas prospered from it and that he was closely connected with the Quaker banking community. John Henton Tritton, who married Mary Barclay and became the first of his line to be a partner in the Lombard Street bank, was an executor of Thomas's will.

When the Stock Exchange evolved from its coffee-house origins to become the world's first regulated exchange in its new building in Capel Court at the beginning of the 19th century, Thomas Ellis was a member of its 'general purposes' committee. His two sons took the business forward in the next generation, and Ellis & Co became celebrated for raising £24 million on behalf of the government to pay for Wellington's campaign against Napoleon: a framed charter authorising the negotiation of this loan was displayed in the partners' room.

---

[1] Born in 1856, D. A. Bevan was a son of Gerard's great-uncle Richard Lee Bevan, 'father of the Pytchley Hunt'. His firm eventually became part of de Zoete & Bevan, and was acquired by Barclays in the mid 1980s to form part of a new investment bank, Barclays de Zoete Wedd — of which the author was a director.

By mid-century, when the firm moved to the Royal Exchange Buildings off Threadneedle Street, there were still three Ellises in the partnership, plus Ford Barclay, of the banking family, who was senior partner from 1855 until his death in 1859. In the mid-1880s, Arthur Henry Tritton (a great-grandson of John Henton Tritton) joined the firm, but it remained principally an Ellis family concern until the last of them, Edward and Richard, retired at the end of 1893.

This made space for the admission in January 1894 of Gerard Bevan and Vincent Biscoe Tritton Junior. The latter, a first cousin of Arthur Henry and the older of the two new entrants by several years, took the more senior position on the letterhead. There were still Ellis family members in the Stock Exchange — one of them, Richard Ellis's son Welbore, ran his own firm for a few years — but the 116-year-old Ellis & Co itself was now wholly in the hands of the Tritton-Bevan axis.

Bevan would many years later tell another new entrant at Ellis & Co that 'the first eighteen months are hell'. According to one modern historian of the London Stock Exchange, Ranald C. Michie in *The London Stock Exchange* (1999), 'with no formal qualification required, or apprenticeship to serve, [the Exchange in the generations before Bevan] appeared to be the last bastion of the British amateur'. But like the banking scene, the securities market was rapidly developing in scale and sophistication, and beginning to demand a new kind of professionalism.

The bread and butter of the 19th-century Stock Exchange was its trade in British government stock, which still accounted for 70 per cent of all quoted securities at the mid century. But railway shares and loan stocks had become an important (and sometimes all too exciting) segment of the market since then. Beginning in the 1880s, an increasing number of established companies in other sectors converted to joint-stock ownership and issued shares to the public.

The client base was growing too. The Forsytean middle-classes now held their nest-eggs in portfolios of shares as well as the ubiquitous Consols, and largely lived off their dividends. 'It is possible to see the growth of comfortable seaside towns like Eastbourne and Bournemouth and Torquay as being partly due to people who lived there on the interest from their investments,' wrote Alan Jenkins in *The Stock Exchange Story* (1973).

The London exchange was also beginning to poach business from its provincial rivals: the Manchester bourse specialised in cotton company shares, Liverpool in insurance, Glasgow in shipping and Cardiff in coal, but London jobbers were increasingly essential to their trade. Between 1883 and 1903, the nominal volume of quoted domestic industrial and commercial securities (including brewing, distilling, coal, iron, steel and shipping stocks) in London grew from £43 million to almost £700 million.

Meanwhile, increased use of the telegraph and the tickertape facilitated trade in foreign stocks, including those of American railways, South African mines and a variety of South American ventures. In the early 1890s, the American sector of the market was particularly lively — and for brokers with an eye on continental stocks there was now a telephone connection to Paris. Overall, the number of securities of all kinds quoted in London multiplied approximately tenfold between the mid century and the outbreak of the first world war.

But no member firm was big enough to deal in every listed share. Jobbers often specialised by sector. Brokers did much of their business in shares which they had helped to bring to market, plus those few in which there was continuous, active buying and selling. But there were a great many shares in which there was almost no trade at all — in 1877 it was estimated that 1,082 out of 1,367 listed issues were 'unmarketable'.

For all these reasons, admission to listing had much more to do with the question of whether a share might trade actively, thereby providing a flow of business for members, than whether the issuing company was sound. On that point, although trust between members was essential and there was a mutual self-interest in keeping shadier company promoters at bay, it was not part of the Exchange's role to vet companies coming forward for listing or to give potential investors any reassurance as to their value.

Nor were brokers expected to provide investing clients with any information or analysis beyond the issuing companies' published balance sheets and broad, often unsubstantiated, statements about their prospects. Indeed, most private investors would have had no idea how to interpret detailed financial information if it had been provided to them. 'The overwhelming tendency of investors was to believe all that their directors told them,' says George Robb in *White Collar Crime in Modern England* (1992). Little had changed in the decades since Herbert Spencer, writing in the *Edinburgh Review* in 1854 about the boom in railway shares, had declared that:

> a great proportion [of investors] are incompetent to judge of the questions that come before them…maiden ladies, alike nervous and innocent of all business knowledge; clergymen whose daily discipline has been little calculated to make them acute men of the world; retired tradesmen whose retail transactions has given them small ability of grasping larger considerations; servants possessed of accumulated savings and cramped notions… all of them rendered more or less conservative by ignorance or timidity, and proportionately inclined to support those in authority.

But even with these provisos, far greater expertise was expected of members in the 1890s than had been expected of their forebears, and it was routine for new entrants to serve a period of training in the back office. Having already discovered in Lombard Street how unsuited he was to clerical routine, a second stint on the ledgers must have been particularly tedious to Bevan. But when he entered the Exchange itself, he found an exhilaratingly upbeat mood.

The lean period that had followed the Baring crisis and the downturn of the economy in the early part of the decade was coming to an end. 'A change of feeling is becoming apparent, not only in the Stock Exchange but all over the City,' wrote one financial correspondent in November 1893, 'people giving up talking so much of what they have lost, and beginning to speak about how they may best regain it.'

The Exchange was in fact a very entertaining milieu for sociable young men, and a place that never took itself too seriously — except in matters of dress and headgear, in which any deviation from the norm provoked choruses of protest and derision. There had always been a good deal of japery and larking about, but by the autumn of 1894, it was giving way to more serious excitement. Bevan was about to experience his first boom — in South African mining shares.

The Kaffir Circus, as it was known, was provoked in part by the efforts of an American mining engineer, John Hays Hammond, who set about providing jobbers and brokers with a variety of informative material about claims made for South Africa's deep-level gold mines — a subject on which there had previously been a good deal of scepticism.

Pretty soon, 'everyone was eager for a slice of the Kaffir[2] action', as the historian David Kynaston wrote, even though the shares concerned were (unlike American railway stocks, for example) not officially recognised and listed by the Stock Exchange committee. That meant they had to be traded in the streets outside the Exchange itself, in an increasingly excitable hubbub.

By the end of the year, a full-scale boom was in progress, with settlement clerks working all night in some broking firms, and even on Christmas Day. Rising prices were fuelled by short-term buying and selling of large blocks of shares by professionals who were able to fund themselves in the money market, while at the retail end, 'in clubs and trains, in drawing rooms and boudoirs, people are discussing "Rands",' wrote another reporter, S.F. Van Oss. 'Even tradesmen and old ladies have taken to studying the *Mining Manual.*'

The boom was to last, and become increasingly frenzied, until the autumn of 1895. In August, *The Economist* recorded that 'within the recollection of the oldest member of the Stock Exchange, there has been no speculative movement at all comparable.' New stocks

---

[2] 'Kaffir', derived from an Arabic word for 'unbeliever', was adopted by British and Dutch Cape settlers as both a noun and an adjective meaning 'indigenous', whether of people or of flora and fauna. Always somewhat derogatory, it acquired highly charged connotations during the apartheid era, and its use now constitutes a 'hate crime' in South Africa.

of increasingly dubious merit flooded onto the market. Overall, it was reckoned that British investment in South Africa shares during the year amounted to some £40 million.

Quick fortunes were made, and the arrival of many new players in the stockmarket changed its tone and over-rode some of its old conventions and manners. The stand-offishness of the Committee — whose refusal to recognise Kaffir stocks was a contributory factor in the chaos which often prevailed on the settlement side — was much criticised.

'In the great boom of the mid-Nineties which culminated in the glitter of the 1897 Diamond Jubilee, money had been in the air; Forsytean England reeked of it.' wrote Aylmer Vallance in *Very Private Enterprise* (1955), his 'anatomy of fraud and high finance'. We do not know the extent to which Bevan enriched himself and his first clients in the Kaffir Circus — or the parallel surge of activity in Western Australian gold stocks, known as Westralians — but he must certainly have learned cautionary tales both from the boom and the bust that followed it. And he was able to observe the fate of some of the headline-makers whose rogues' gallery he was later destined to join.

A remarkable number of chancers and scoundrels were at work in the financial world during the first decade of Bevan's career, a fact that underlines two points essential to this story. The first is the unregulated nature of the stockmarket, the primitive state of corporate governance and the minimal nature of company accounts and reporting in those days. The second is a more universal observation of what happens during periods of boom and bust, best summed up by the homespun American billionaire Warren Buffett, the most successful investor of the late 20th and early 21st centuries, who famously remarked that 'when the tide goes out you can see who's been swimming naked'.

The rollercoaster of the 1890s stockmarket was an opportunity for all kinds of misbehaviour, ranging from common forms of aggressive dealing to outright fraud. Five players in particular must have caught Bevan's attention, and deserve a few moments of ours: Barnato, Hooley, Balfour, Bottomley and Wright.

Bad Examples

By far the biggest name in the market during Bevan's first couple of years as a broker was Barney Barnato, the 'ringmaster of the Kaffir Circus'. This pugnacious grandson of an East End rabbi made his first fortune diamond-dealing in South Africa and became a dominant figure in the Johannesburg Stock Exchange. He went on to float a series of gold-mining companies, offering them to investors on the basis of unproven claims rather than actual production, each company equipped with minimal working capital but large numbers of shares in issue. In 1894 he came to London to set up Barnato Bank, Mining, and Estates Company to promote these doubtful stocks which — though Barnato himself was never a member of the Exchange — were avidly taken up by investors during the boom.

While the Kaffir Circus was at its most frenzied, Barnato and his bank prospered mightily. He commissioned a small palace for himself in Park Lane, London (described by one historian as 'early Metro-Goldwyn-Mayer' in style), shared a racing manager with the Prince of Wales, and was reckoned to be worth £4 million. When the crash came in the autumn of 1895, he injected £3 million of that fortune into the market in an ultimately doomed attempt to sustain the prices of mining shares.

He was rewarded with an appointment as a lieutenant of the City of London and a banquet at the Mansion House. But as the South African political situation deteriorated towards war after the Jamieson Raid at the end of 1895 (a failed attempt to stir insurrection among British expatriates in the Transvaal) and his resources dwindled, Barnato hit the bottle and showed increasing signs of paranoia. Sailing to England on the mail steamer *Star* in June 1897 — apparently to take part in the celebrations for Queen Victoria's diamond jubilee — his mind gave way and he threw himself overboard somewhere south of Madeira. The Johannesburg Stock Exchange closed for a day as a mark of respect.

Another wheeler-dealer whose borderline methods Bevan could not have failed to observe was the company promoter Ernest Terah

Hooley, whose greatest coup was to buy the Dunlop Pneumatic Tyre Company for £3 million in 1896 and immediately float it for £5 million, in an issue that was heavily over-subscribed. He brought numerous other famous names to market, including the Humber and Raleigh bicycle companies, and pocketed huge profits each time, living in the grandest style on a large estate near Cambridge. He was even celebrated in music hall song:

> *He walks into the Stock Exchange, and everybody there*
> *Cries 'Look out! Here comes Hooley, the famous millionaire!'*
> *He can buy a share for tuppence and sell it for a pound*
> *When he's bought St Paul's Cathedral, he'll buy the Underground.*

But by 1898 he was bankrupt — the first of four bankruptcies, and the precursor of a long record of encounters with the law. A genial figure who bounced back every time, Hooley would still be active when Bevan was at his zenith 25 years later, and would be jailed for fraud, in relation to the flotation of the Jubilee Mills cotton company, in 1921.

Then there were two men who made names for themselves in public life alongside long careers in financial chicanery. Jabez Balfour, the Liberal MP first for Tamworth and later for Burnley, created a string of property development companies and what became the country's biggest building society, the Liberator. But the recession of the early 1890s brought them all down, revealing a pattern of false accounting, inter-company money shuffling and petty fraud which cost many small investors their life savings.

Balfour fled to Argentina, where he was eventually seized by a Scotland Yard detective and bundled on to a ship for England, thus neatly circumventing the bureaucracy of extradition proceedings that would in due course delay Bevan's own encounter with justice. Balfour received a 14-year sentence at the Old Bailey in 1895.

Next came Horatio Bottomley, a larger-than-life recidivist with a wide-ranging repertoire of misdeeds. The son of an East End tailor's cutter, Bottomley had set out to make his fortune in printing and publishing: he had briefly been chairman of the *Financial Times* in its early days, and in 1889 he floated the Hansard Publishing Union, which was known on the Stock Exchange as 'Bottomley's swindle' and which went bust within two years.

But so brilliantly did Bottomley conduct his own defence in court against fraud charges that he was acquitted – and advised by the judge afterwards to take up a career at the criminal bar, where he might make all the money he wanted. 'But if you go into the City,' said Mr Justice Hawkins, 'you will end with a long term of penal servitude.'

Undeterred, Bottomley went on to promote — and scoop cash from — some 20 West Australian gold-mining and finance companies during the mid-nineties boom, almost all of which were destined to fail. When that stream of opportunity dried up, he returned to publishing, first owning an evening paper called *The Sun* and then a populist tabloid of his own invention, *John Bull*, which the historian A.J.P. Taylor would call 'a cheap organ of hate' and which served as a vehicle for a variety of Bottomley schemes to take money off gullible readers.

He also repeatedly stood for parliament. At his third attempt he won the Hackney South seat as a Liberal in 1906 — hanging on to it despite another set of fraud charges in 1908, forfeiting it when he went bankrupt in 1912, and regaining it as an independent in 1918.

Pathologically incapable of straight dealing, devoted to the pleasures of the cellar, the table and the boudoir, surrounded by a harem of chorus girls, backer of West End theatricals, owner of a string of racehorses, short and stout, Bottomley was a richly comic figure. As *The Spectator* would comment after his fall, there was 'some gaiety about Bottomley's rogueries'. R.A. Haldane, in *With Intent to Deceive* (1970) notes that 'he wore suits which even in those days cost him sixty guineas and revolting as it may seem, he washed down his breakfast kippers with champagne.'

The sensualist Bottomley and the fastidious Bevan were in no sense alike in personality, and very different in the nature of their dishonesty — which in Bottomley's case was habitual, life-long, and designed to feed greedy appetites rather than hide past misjudgements. But the two men would nevertheless one day find themselves fellow prisoners in Maidstone jail, serving identical sentences for the same category of crime.

In making this set of comparisons, we should remember that Bevan himself was a stockbroker rather than a 'company promoter' as such. That latter label applied to a category of financier who specialised in bringing new companies to market — and if unscrupulous, specialised in over-capitalising and over-valuing them, while skimming off as much as possible of the proceeds.

To be over-capitalised meant that a company had more shares in issue than the underlying business was capable of rewarding adequately by way of dividend. The skimming of cash was achieved by selling shares which had cost the promoters very little to acquire before the company came to market, rather than arranging for the company to issue new shares, the sale of which would have brought working capital into the business to fund its development.

This abuse of the flotation mechanism was prevalent to a greater or lesser degree throughout Bevan's era in the City, when there was little scrutiny of new issues, and investors were relatively uninformed and undiscerning. Though Bevan was not a promoter himself, he was destined to co-operate very closely with Clarence Hatry, the most successful of that breed in the immediate post first world war years.

Much of Bevan's fortune before it evaporated, and most of the fraudulent activity for which he was responsible, was connected to dealings in the shares of companies that were brought to market by Hatry and subsequently failed. So if we need a label for Bevan in this context, he was the company promoter's accomplice.

Having clarified that nuance, we can still usefully compare Bevan to another turn-of-the-century celebrity in the company promotion field, Whitaker Wright, who made his first career in the American mining business. Wright returned to England in 1889 and, like Bottomley, took to promoting West Australian mining companies, which he consolidated into the London & Globe Finance Corporation. He also launched the British America Corporation to acquire mining interests in Canada.

The mines were real, and many of those who invested alongside him made money with him. The Marquess of Dufferin and Ava, a former Viceroy of India, became chairman of London & Globe. Wright himself became so rich that he could afford a private theatre, a hospital suite, an observatory and a glass-roofed billiard room under a lake on his Surrey estate. But manipulating the market in his companies' shares, juggling their finances and speculating in new projects — London & Globe put £600,000 into the development of the underground Baker Street and Waterloo Railway, now the Bakerloo line — brought his empire to grief.

London & Globe went under in December 1900, ruining many investors and some 20 Stock Exchange members as it did so. Subsequent investigations revealed fraudulent accounts, false balance sheets, £3 million of debts, and dividends payments that had been covered only by pillaging cash from Wright's other companies.

Exactly as Bevan would do 20 years later, Wright left for France as soon as prosecution threatened. In the company of a young woman who was not his wife, he then sailed to America, where he was arrested in New York in March 1903 and resisted extradition for several months. He was eventually brought back for trial — and was found guilty in January 1904 of 'publishing false statements in respect to the London & Globe Finance Corporation and other companies and making false entries in the books of those companies'. He was sentenced by Mr Justice Bigham to seven years' penal servitude — the same sentence as would later be handed down to Bottomley and Bevan.

Unlike the other two, however, Wright evaded justice. When the court rose he was conducted to a consultation room to see his solicitor and a friend, a Mr Eyre, who had put up part of his bail money. Wright gave Eyre his watch and chain, saying 'I shall have no use for them where I'm going', and accepted from the solicitor a cigar on which he puffed for a few seconds.

Then he bit on a capsule of cyanide which he had secreted in his pocket (he had not been searched before going into court) and slumped, dying, into a chair — being a man with a mind for detail, he had also taken the precaution of secreting a loaded pistol into his pocket, though he did not need to use it. *The Times* called it 'a miserable end and one which pleads powerfully for a pitiful judgement on the culprit.'

Finally, if Bevan was an observer of other practitioners' methods of financial chicanery during the formative phase of his career, he might have found a colourful example on the West End stage, where one of the greatest successes of the Edwardian era was Harley Granville Barker's play *The Voysey Inheritance*, about a crooked solicitor.

The play captures the essence of the 'white-collar crime' which depends for its success on the perpetrator's ability to look respectable, competent and even financially brilliant for as long as he can keep the game running: very much how it would be for Bevan. It contains this exchange between the solicitor's son Edward Voysey, who finds himself with no option but to perpetuate his father's fraud, and George Booth, a family friend:

> Booth: *Now just explain to me… Of what did this defrauding consist?*
> Edward: *Speculating with a client's capital… pocketing the gains, cutting the losses; meanwhile paying the client his ordinary income.*
> Booth: *So that he didn't find out.*
> Edward: *Quite so.*
> Booth: *In point of fact he doesn't suffer?*
> Edward: *He doesn't suffer until he finds out.*
> Booth: *What is the ah — deficit?*
> Edward: *Anything between two and three hundred thousand pounds.*
> Booth: *Dear me… This is a big affair!*

The Senior Partner

A glimpse of Bevan in his pomp at Ellis & Co is to be found in the published diaries of Sir Alan 'Tommy' Lascelles, a courtier who was private secretary to King George VI and, for the first year of her reign, Queen Elizabeth II — but who briefly worked in the City before his army service in the first world war.

Lascelles was a grandson of the 4th Earl of Harewood; his cousin, the 6th earl, would marry Mary, Princess Royal, only daughter of King George V, in February 1922 — just as Bevan was fleeing across Europe, as it happened, and in a ceremony that was coincidentally stage-managed by another City Equitable director, the courtier Sir Douglas Dawson.

In his mid-twenties, having failed to pass the entrance exam for the diplomatic service, Tommy Lascelles seems to have done little except hunt, shoot and attend grand parties for a couple of years after leaving Oxford in the summer of 1909.

On 9 November 1911 Lascelles recorded that he went to see a banker friend, Ronnie Norman (brother of the future Governor of the Bank of England, Montagu Norman), who had overlapped with Bevan at Trinity and moved in similar circles. Norman had news of a job that he thought might suit Lascelles.

> It proved to be City, as I expected. Gerry Bevan, a partner in Ellis's, wants men to go into the office on half-commission. I went round to see him at 1 Cornhill, and liked him, and he said I could think about it till the end of the year. Which I shall do. I have always told myself that I would never go into the City. But it might not be a bad thing, temporarily at any rate. Bevan did not disguise the fact that the first eighteen months are hell.

Half-commission men were not employees or partners of Stock Exchange firms, but freelance brokers, buying and selling securities on their own clients' behalf and splitting the commission with the firm in return for the use of a desk, a telephone and clerical support. They were useful to the firms because they increased deal-flow and the ability to place new stock, without adding to risk exposures or overheads. But if the stockbroker was generally held in low esteem — that 'cunning savage', as the novelist George Gissing put it — the half-commission man stood even lower in the social order. 'West End clubs seemed a particular haunt of these men,' recalled Ranald

C. Michie, 'where they "preyed" on relatives, old school friends and the like for business.'

Having sought advice on 'the effect of the City on the Soul', Lascelles did his best to put off the evil day and toyed briefly with the idea of a career in journalism instead. But at the end of February he 'went down to Ellis's, where Bevan introduced me to one of his partners, [Vincent] Tritton, a rather repellent little man, but said to be very successful'.

Finally, on April Fool's Day 1912, he actually started work, under Tritton's supervision, in the transfer department, 'the lowest rung of the ladder... I was bored and bewildered, understanding little of what I saw and nothing of what I heard.' It all sounded rather like the office initiation of Lupin, son of the fictional diarist Charles Pooter in *The Diary of a Nobody* (1892), George and Weedon Grossmith's classic evocation of late-19th-century London life: 'With respect to the Bank, there's not a clerk who is a gentleman and the "boss" is a cad.'

By Lascelles's fourth day, however, things were looking up:

Light begins to break through the mephitic vapours of Finance. My fellow-clerks are perfectly charming to me, and love me. They spare no pains to explain everything, and in return I think I am beginning to make myself quite useful. It excites me very much. Both sides of this elementary office work appeal to me — the dashing-about with stock to deliver against time, and the book-keeping... And I find myself taking an absorbing interest in the affairs of our various clients — most of them mere names to me, every now and then notabilities, and more rarely friends and acquaintances... It is amazingly satisfactory; and even though I am not earning anything as yet, I feel that the work I do is necessary, and helps the machine on.

Lascelles' positive reference to helping 'the machine' makes an interesting contrast to George Gissing, who expressed in *The Crown of Life* the outsiders' suspicious view of the financial world in the same metaphor but with a very different tone:

> The brute force of money; the negation of the individual—these, the evils of our time, found there supreme expression in the City of London... The smooth working of the huge machine made it only the more sinister; one had but to remember what cold tyranny, what elaborate fraud, were served by its manifold ingenuities, only to think of the cries of anguish stifled by its monotonous roar.

But then Lascelles was by birth and connections a natural insider — and was at least Bevan's social equal, which was perhaps why he found him easier to like than Hubert Meredith, who began his own career in the Exchange in 1906 and was probably treated by Bevan with the hauteur of a member of 'Pop' towards an Eton new boy: 'Although I realised his intelligence and never suspected that his career would be anything other than brilliant,' Meredith wrote, 'I can truthfully say that I disliked him — a sentiment which, I believe, was mutual.'

Nevertheless, Gissing-like sentiments were gnawing away inside Lascelles. It was rapidly dawning on him that he was not cut out for a career in a stockbroking office — he took to referring to Ellis's as 'Nibelheim', the deep Wagnerian cavern inhabited by metalworking dwarves.

His clerical apprenticeship continued — interrupted on the Monday of his third week by news that the *Titanic* had hit an iceberg. The City's rumour mill initially got the story completely wrong: 'It was put about — no one yet knows by whom, that all the passengers were saved and that the ship was being towed into Halifax by one of the rescuing liners, and we all went to bed regarding it as a good joke.'

Business was extremely subdued the following morning when the truth emerged that 1,500 souls were feared drowned, among them a couple of members of the Exchange itself.

Lascelles buckled down to his work, but its incursions into his social calendar began to chafe. He preferred to leave the office at five, even though the clerks around him sometimes worked much later. Writing in October (on office stationery) to Lady Guendolen Osborne, daughter of the Duke of Leeds, to tell her he could not join a Saturday-to-Monday house-party at her father's castle in Yorkshire, he complains that 'Messrs Ellis & Co think I am a confirmed wastrel if I don't come up here [to the office] on Saturdays and at 10.10 on Monday mornings.'

By then he had moved on from the transfer department to join the main office, where dealings with clients took place — but having as yet garnered few clients for himself he had little to do, and he missed his amiable fellow clerks, of whom the firm employed about 50. December found Lascelles enduring 'a terrible dull day in the City'.

By March he had decided to leave Ellis & Co — and his cousin Reggie Lascelles was about to offer him a place, at £100 a year and with the prospect of a partnership, in the jobbing firm of Miller & Lascelles, where both thought the work might suit him better. 'I shook the dust of Ellis's from my feet, with very considerable relief. Bevan is in bed with 'flu, which simplified my leave-taking.'

In a note added to the diary some time after Bevan's criminal conviction a decade later, Lascelles explained that his reason for leaving Ellis & Co when he did was more than just 'general dissatisfaction'. It seems that Bevan the wily market operator had shamelessly played Lascelles the novice, 'having encouraged me to put my few clients into Sopa Diamonds at about £3 1/8, sold his own holding at £3 1/4 and never told me they would shortly be worthless.'

Sopa was a diamond mine in the Minas Geraes region of Brazil, though its shares were dealt alongside other mining stocks in the African section of the Exchange. Sopa's record of producing suitable quantities of gemstones was patchy, to say the least. Later that year, the *South African Mining Journal* reported 'a diamond washing fiasco... Sopa Diamonds have had a gigantic wash, and the result is a gigantic failure.'

The mine's manager had cabled to say that:

> judging from result of work done during month of June and
> two following months there is so much very low grade ore that
> proposition not payable worked with present system. I propose
> to as soon as I can make arrangements return discuss with board
> of directors future policy.

An English broker commented: 'Apparently the manager is
not prepared to abandon the property as worthless', to which the
Journal's editor added, 'Such persistency, however admirable it may
be, is likely to be very costly.'

Before then, of course, Bevan had taken a turn on behalf of himself and his clients, having evidently used Lascelles and the other
half-commission men to support the price until he had done so, to
their own clients' eventual cost.

All in a day's work — and an echo, perhaps, of another passage
in *The Diary of a Nobody*, in which Charles Pooter and a Mr Gowing
have both been induced to buy some shares by the unreliable Lupin,
who has been working for a stockbroker called Job Cleanands:

> FEBRUARY 19... "I say, those Parachikka Chlorates have
> gone an awful smash!" [said Gowing] "You're a nice one,
> Master Lupin, How much did you lose?" Lupin, to my utter
> astonishment, said: "Oh! I had nothing in them. There was
> some informality in my application — I forgot to enclose the
> cheque or something, and I didn't get any."... I said: "I quite
> understood you were in it, or nothing would have induced me
> to speculate." Lupin replied: "Well it can't be helped; you must
> go double on the next tip."

> FEBRUARY 20. The first thing that caught my eye on opening
> the *Standard* was: "Great Failure of Stock and Share Dealers!
> Mr Job Cleanands Absconded!" I handed it to Carrie [Mrs
> Pooter] and she replied: "Oh! Perhaps it's for Lupin's good. I

never did think it a suitable situation for him." I thought the whole affair very shocking.

In 1906 Ellis & Co had moved from Royal Exchange Buildings to No 1 Cornhill, and not long afterwards Arthur Henry Tritton retired as senior partner — no doubt to concentrate on his duties as district council chairman and churchwarden at Leatherhead in Surrey, though his voice was still heard occasionally in Stock Exchange affairs. Vincent Tritton succeeded as senior partner, but like his cousin he opted for semi-retirement in his early fifties, leaving the field open for Bevan in 1912.

A younger Tritton, Arthur Robert, son of Arthur Henry, joined the partnership briefly but left in 1917 — causing some confusion among commentators on later events at Ellis & Co, who assumed the two Arthurs to be one and the same person. Four other partners had come into the firm during the Tritton era — in order of arrival, Neville O'Brien, Harold Gordon, Frederick Tootal and the Hon. Ailwyn Fellowes — but they were all very minor players compared with Bevan.

The Trittons had maintained the superior reputation of Ellis & Co, bolstered by their close personal connections to Barclays. The company promoter H. Osborne O'Hagan called it 'one of the leading firms of London stockbrokers, old-established and prosperous... so old-fashioned was the firm's reputation that I never attempted to secure them for my underwriting list; new undertakings were the last thing I should have expected them to interest themselves in.'

Arthur Henry Tritton himself was a stalwart defender of the status quo. When soundings were taken by an Exchange sub-committee in December 1908 on the question of introducing an authorised scale of brokers' commissions — in part because some brokers were offering reduced commission rates to the banks and other institutions that were becoming dominant investors in the market — it was recorded that Tritton 'objected to any interference between brokers and their clients. If his clients suggested his dealing at rates which he considered unfair, he let them go. He was against the cutting of commissions, but these were days of competition.'

Such conservatism must have been frustrating to Bevan, biding his time at the firm during the first decade of the century and watching other brokers making fat turns on new issues or placements of blocks of shares. But still there was plenty of money to be made, and no doubt he made some in the rubber boom of 1909–10, when rapid rises in both the commodity price of rubber and in the shares of rubber companies, many of them newly floated — all driven by rising demand for pneumatic tyres for motor cars and bicycles — caused a frenzy to match anything seen in the Kaffir Circus.

And Bevan was still building his reputation, good as well as bad. Meredith and Lascelles may not have liked the cut of his jib, but there were other market participants who held Bevan in high esteem. 'In the old dancing days when people said I was in league with fortune', as he put it in the sonnet quoted at the beginning of this book, many were in awe of his money-making touch and his professional mastery.

Baron Émile d'Erlanger, an Anglo-French financier who was, among other things, a keen promoter of an early version of the Channel Tunnel project, recalled: 'Rarely have I known a man able to explain a business in a clearer and more concise form than [Bevan] did. His command of figures and memory were exceptional.'

And after it all went wrong, some of those who had been his clients in palmier days were reluctant to believe Bevan could ever have been dishonest. One such was a Colonel Richmond-Brown, encountered in a hotel in Madeira by a Bevan relation on holiday in the mid-1920s, who declared that he had 'known Gerry for years and I'm quite certain he wouldn't really do anything wrong. He must have just been unfortunate.'

As for Bevan's staff, his long-serving managing clerk Donald Pirie, who had joined Ellis & Co as a teenager not long after Bevan himself, spoke for many when he wrote: 'In common with everyone else connected with Bevan, I trusted him absolutely, and until my eyes were opened at the time of the failure I invariably found him worthy of that trust.'

The new senior partner of Ellis & Co was, then, a man with a high-flying reputation. Some who knew him were wary of his *modus operandi* and his inclination to highhandedness, but many others admired him. His firm had an unblemished 130-year record, his surname was as respected as any in the City, and he himself had been a significant player in Stock Exchange life for almost two decades. But he was by no means the old-fashioned broker that his Ellis and Tritton predecessors had been.

He had a grand idea of himself — his Cornhill office, looking out over the heroic 1844 statue of Wellington by Francis Chantrey towards the great brass doors of the Bank of England, was (according to a *Financial Times* reporter who inspected it after his disgrace) 'expensively furnished... with oak panels decorated with exquisite wood carvings [and] above the fireplace a design of an eagle feeding her young surmounted by the monogram "GLB".' His ambition, we may guess, was to turn Ellis & Co into a different and much grander kind of business.

After a first visit to America in 1909, for example, Bevan was clearly keen to build up his contacts on Wall Street. There may be a clue to the way in which he saw the future in the fact that in August 1912 he sailed to New York on the *Lusitania* with the specific purpose of visiting Goldman Sachs. Indeed, since he gave his address in the ship's manifest as 'c/o Goldman Sachs & Co, 60 Wall Street', it is possible that he was there as a guest of the partners of what would become, in modern times, the world's most powerful investment bank.

That is a curious connection, since the Goldman Sachs of 1912 was by no means the household name it is today. It had just six family partners — similar in scale to Ellis & Co, but operating in a quite different area of the securities markets. Marcus Goldman, a Jewish immigrant from Germany, had set up in 1869 in Pine Street (parallel to Wall Street in Lower Manhattan) as a sole trader buying and selling IOUs from local businessmen.

He prospered and took his son-in-law Sam Sachs into the business with him. The firm of Goldman, Sachs & Co became New

York's leading commercial-paper house — a facilitator of short-term finance for businesses, in negotiable form — and Marcus's son Henry Goldman conceived an ambition to turn it into a powerhouse of securities underwriting as well.

In partnership with another up-and-coming New York firm, Lehman Brothers, that is what he did. The Goldman-Lehman combination could not muscle in on the issues of railway stocks which were the bread and butter of the old Wall Street establishment, led by J.P. Morgan. But there were lucrative opportunities available in flotations of retailers and industrial enterprises which — especially if their owners were Jewish — the establishment firms regarded as beneath their dignity to handle.

Goldman began in 1906 with a $10 million issue of preferred and common stock for the mail order retailer Sears, Roebuck. This was such a market novelty that the issue took several months to place, but the shares afterwards went from strength to strength. After a lull which followed the New York 'Bankers' Panic' of 1907, Goldman and Lehman went on to bring many other big names to market: they included May Department Stores in 1910, Studebaker the car maker in 1911, and F.W. Woolworth in 1912.

Investors were increasingly enthusiastic — Woolworth's common stock jumped from $55 to $80 on its first day's trading — and the syndicate gradually extended its international reach, with Kleinwort, Sons & Co and a smaller London merchant bank, S. Japhet, providing placing power in London and across Europe.

Bevan was probably given an introduction to Henry Goldman by Sir Alexander Kleinwort, with whom he had many dealings over the years and who would have seen him as a broker who could bring extra strengths to this ambitious international operation. This was certainly the kind of circle in which Bevan aspired to move — and the relationship might have flourished had it not been for the impact of war both on the operation of international capital markets and on the standing of Goldman Sachs, which according to its historian Lisa Endlich suffered 'untold damage' to its reputation because of the ardent pro-German stance of Henry Goldman himself.

But Bevan had other strands of international expansion in mind. He had a natural affinity for France, where he spoke the language well. And he had an eye on South American markets; we have already glimpsed his dealings in Brazilian mining shares.

The role of Ellis & Co as broker to the issue of debenture stock in July 1914 of the Southern Brazil Electric Company — a ragbag of small municipal power companies and 'undeveloped waterfalls' with hydro-electric generating potential which Bevan may have had a hand in assembling for flotation — was the kind of business Arthur Tritton would have regarded as quite unsuitable. But it was very much the kind that appealed to Bevan.

The period from 1905 to 1914 had been a heyday of British private investment in Brazil, when some £10 million a year was flowing from London, increasingly towards private-sector ventures. Two-thirds of the total stock of foreign investment in Brazil was British-owned, with holdings in Brazilian railways and utilities each amounting to more than £50 million and lesser sums invested in coffee and rubber plantations, and mines.

Even bigger sums of British money were invested in Argentina, again predominantly in railways. In modern times it is often forgotten that Argentina was the greatest 'emerging market' of the early 20th century: 'All is modern and new; all belongs to the prosperous present and betokens a still more prosperous future,' wrote a British diplomat, James Bryce, in 1912. 'Argentina is like Western North America. The swift and steady increase in its agricultural production, with an increase correspondingly large in means of internal transportation... shows that it will have a great part to play in the world. It is the United States of the Southern Hemisphere.'

As for the capital, Buenos Aires, it was becoming one of the world's destination cities: 'The streets and shoppers present a fine spectacle; the architecture of the buildings is sumptuous, and the pavements are full of life... beautiful women, daintily attired, flit from shop to shop... and the pride of luxury flaunts itself as bravely as in Paris or London,' said another writer, W.A. Hirst, quoted in the publicity for the 1913 launch in Buenos Aires of the only overseas branch of Harrods, the great Knightsbridge department store: this eight-storey emporium with its marble staircases, wrought-iron elevators and jazz orchestras was one of the commercial wonders of the new world — and Bevan would one day take a hand in its fate, a story we shall come to in Chapter Six.

All these exciting fields of development would have to wait, however, because war was on the horizon. The Southern Brazil Electric issue turned out to be a last gasp — and must have been very difficult to get away — coming as it did a few days after the assassination of Archduke Franz Ferdinand of Austria at Sarajevo, the event which precipitated Austria-Hungary's declaration of war against Serbia and the cataclysm that followed.

The London market had already been drifting downwards on thin trading during the early summer. In July, bourses across Europe began to shut down. To begin with, few thought this could happen in London. 'If you ever see that business on the London Stock Exchange has been stopped, you can rest assured that the end of the world has come,' a committee member had told Hubert Meredith when they discussed these ominous happenings in mid July.

But day after day of heavy selling of domestic and foreign stocks was to follow, as investors sought to liquidate their holdings — even 2½ per cent Consols, the premier British government stock, tumbled dramatically. Friday 24 July saw the steepest price falls in a day since 1870, and Wednesday 29 July saw the hammering of several firms which had been unable to receive payments from foreign clients.

After an all-night emergency meeting of the Exchange's general purposes committee, brokers and clerks arrived for work on Friday 31 July to find a notice telling them that the Exchange was closed. Settlements were deferred and some £81 million of debts from brokers and jobbers to British and foreign banks in London were temporarily frozen, or subject to Bank of England support. Britain joined the war four days later.

Thereafter, share bargains continued to be transacted at a very reduced level — in the street, by means of the 'challenge system' which involved advertising a specific offer or bid via the Exchange Telegraph Company's tape, or even through the columns of the *Daily Mail*. Official business on the floor of the Exchange did not recommence until 4 January 1915.

And when it did so, it was only on a highly restrictive, cash-only basis, with minimum prices set by committee for the most widely held 'trustee' stocks to protect the public from sharp falls in response to battlefront setbacks. Brokers had to obtain written declarations from clients that they were not dealing on behalf of enemy aliens — and a combination of factors, including the disapproval of the Bank of England, brought their involvement in international movements of money more or less to a complete halt. The closure of German bank branches in the City removed a major source of short-term funding for member firms.

The priority of the capital market was to meet the government's sudden and ballooning demand for funds to pay for the war effort — as a result of which the national debt would multiply tenfold between 1913 and 1920. Anything that threatened to deflect capital from that priority would henceforth be strictly curtailed.

Thus new issues of shares and bonds, in which Bevan had seen so much scope for profit when he took over the senior partner's desk at Ellis & Co, became subject to Treasury approval in every case. Treasury instructions issued without prior consultation with the Exchange specified that issues for British companies could only be made if they were 'advisable in the national interest'. Issues by non-British companies within the Empire would be permitted only where 'urgent necessity and special circumstances exist'. Issues by governments and companies beyond the Empire — including those of countries which were Britain's wartime allies — were out of the question.

The new regime attracted an initial rush of applications for new issues, some of which were approved. But by 1916 hardly any were coming to market, and the Treasury remained intransigent in the face of all lobbying for relaxation of these rules until the end of the war, by which time the nominal value of British government debt quoted on the London Stock Exchange had risen from just under ten per cent to one third of all securities quoted.

The importance of the London Exchange within the global spectrum of capital markets at home and abroad was severely diminished, as was the volume of stocks listed and traded on it. Conversely, the extent of government intervention in its affairs radically increased.

Far fewer people actually came to work in the Exchange — many had volunteered or been called to fight, but many simply quit stockbroking for other professions — and those that did were often under-occupied. Profits of member firms, if they still made any profits at all, fell to a fraction of pre-war figures.

But at Ellis & Co, Bevan was still keeping his eye on international opportunities for the future. He was to be found in New York again in April 1915, staying at the Plaza Hotel having crossed on the White Star Line's *Adriatic* from Liverpool — a voyage on which the Polish pianist-statesman Jan Paderewski was a fellow passenger. He was there again in May 1916, at the Ritz-Carlton, having arrived on an Italian liner, the *Giuseppe Verdi*, from Buenos Aires — his first visit to South America. But it was all about fact-finding and building networks; there was very little business to be done while the war endured.

So it was little wonder that at about the same time he began looking for a diversification of his interests outside the Stock Exchange. And that is why he was prepared to give a hearing to a young insurance broker, from well outside Bevan's customary circles of acquaintance, who came to him with an investment proposal brilliantly designed to take advantage of wartime disruption in the reinsurance market. The young man was Clarence Hatry, the opportunity was the City Equitable Fire Insurance Company, and their conjunction would be Bevan's downfall.

CHAPTER THREE

At Home

'He was afflicted by the thought that where Beauty was, nothing ever ran quite straight, which, no doubt, was why so many people looked on it as immoral.'

Jolyon Forsyte in John Galsworthy, *In Chancery* (1920)

Upper Grosvenor Street

When the Edwardian era began on 22 January 1901, Sophie Bevan was two months pregnant with her first child. It seems very likely, given that more than seven years had passed since her wedding day and she was well into her thirties, that she had experienced difficulties conceiving, or suffered earlier miscarriages. So it must have been an intensely worrying time for her. But as winter passed into spring and national mourning for the old Queen subsided, the family doctor advised Sophie that she should be capable of carrying this one to term.

This created some urgency for Gerard to find them a suitable new home. They had started their married life at No 18 Connaught Square,[1] just north of Hyde Park near Marble Arch. By 1897 they had moved a short distance eastwards to No 9 Manchester Square,

---

[1] Connaught Square is now best known for the London home of former Prime Minister Tony Blair— a house which was occupied in the Bevans' time by Admiral Sir Erasmus Ommanney, who had served as a 13-year-old in *HMS Albion* at the Battle of Navarino against the Turks in 1827.

a backwater of Marylebone dominated by the palatial Hertford House, where Sir Richard Wallace's great art collection was about to be opened to the public.

These were handsome townhouses, overlooking leafy gardens. Both were well sited on Forsytean London's map of wealth. But the Bevans evidently wanted more space or more prestige, or both — and they found what they were looking for at No 21 Upper Grosvenor Street, Mayfair, as smart an address as Edwardian London could offer.

Their new home, where Clara Christabel Bevan was born in August 1901, was within a few paces of Park Lane and the broad acreage of Hyde Park beyond. It stood almost opposite the colon-naded entrance of Grosvenor House — not the hotel complex on the site today (which dates from 1929) but the 18th century man-sion with Victorian additions which was then the home of Mayfair's landlord and one of Europe's richest men, the second Duke of Westminster, known to his intimates as 'Bendor'.

The terraced house on which the Bevans took a lease had been built in 1732. Since then it had been home to several members of parliament, two generals, a future duke (of Sutherland) and a doctor. In its original design it had a plain but elegantly proportioned brick frontage, and consisted of three storeys plus garrets for the servants. It also had a laundry and stables at the rear in what was then called King Street Mews, now Culross Street, the two buildings being linked by the later addition of a covered passage along the side of the courtyard garden. In the 19th century an extra storey was added, and the servants' accommodation improved.

The grandest feature of Number 21 was an L-shaped first-floor drawing room, with French panelling and a bowed window looking onto the garden. Below, in what was presumably the dining room, another bay window was flanked by Ionic columns under a ceiling of fine decorative plasterwork. The main staircase, rising to the sec-ond floor, boasted a handsome wrought-iron balustrade and a brass handrail 'after the French taste'.

Though not on the scale of the houses in Prince's Gate where Bevan had been brought up, this new home was very ample for a family of three — and then four when Sheila Venetia Bevan was born in April 1905. Again, bearing in mind that Sophie had by then passed her 38th birthday, it was probably a difficult pregnancy, and a stressful time for everyone in the household.

If Sophie was concerned about the nursery arrangements, Gerard must have been particularly pleased with the billiard room at the back of the garden. Panelled in the Jacobean style, with an inglenook fireplace, it was very much the sort of den a fashionable gentleman would have desired when it was added in 1879 for the then lessor, the 10th Earl of Leven and Melville, a partner in the banking firm of Williams, Deacon & Co. We do not know whether Bevan was a keen billiard player but this large space with south-facing windows was most likely earmarked as a home for part of his growing collection of Chinese porcelain and other valuable *objets d'art*. When Sophie was at her most assertive, it must also have been his place of escape.

The most radical change to the house during its first two centuries of existence was commissioned by Gerard and Sophie a few years after they moved in. In 1908, several existing or would-be lessees in Upper Grosvenor Street agreed with the Grosvenor Estate that they would meet the cost of re-fronting their houses and carrying out other refurbishments, in exchange for longer leases. In the Bevans' case, a 'special design' was put forward by a notable pair of architects, Ralph Knott and E. Stone Collins.

This was a new partnership, and Knott, who was not yet 30, was an up-and-coming name in the profession. As an assistant to one of the leading architects of the previous generation, Sir Aston Webb, he had worked on the plans for Admiralty Arch, the Victoria and Albert Museum, and the monument to Queen Victoria in front of Buckingham Palace. Against competition from more established firms, he and Collins had just won the commission to design County Hall, the London County Council building on the south bank of the Thames beside Westminster Bridge.

The grandest 20th-century public building in London, County Hall came to define the ornate style of stonework known as

'Edwardian Baroque', even though it was not opened until 1922 — when it was still missing its north wing, which was not completed until 1933, some years after Knott's death.

The County Hall project was to dominate the careers of Knott and Collins, and their design in Portland stone for the new front at 21 Upper Grosvenor Street contained echoes of it in miniature. It did not, however, please the Grosvenor Estate's surveyor, Eustace Balfour, who felt unable to recommend it to the Duke or even to suggest alterations that might make it less offensive, other than the substitution of smaller window panes. But that proposal was firmly rejected by Sophie, in whose name the new lease was to be — suggesting, incidentally, that it was she rather than her husband who was paying for this expensive project, out of her private means.

Sophie — demonstrating her demanding nature — threatened to abandon the whole contract 'if the small panes are insisted upon', so the matter had to be referred to the Duke himself, who upon reflection saw no objection to larger panes.

Windows were clearly a matter of heated opinion among the ladies of Mayfair at the time. Poor Balfour the surveyor had to contend with the same argument at No 20, where the Countess of Wilton (described by her builder as 'very difficult') also appealed to the Duke, who again gave way.

Balfour lamented that 'if permission is given there is no knowing where such windows will stop'. Thereafter he seems to have given up the unequal struggle, though he did succeed in negotiating minor changes to tone down Knott's scheme for the Bevans. The final result, described by one architectural scholar as 'undoubtedly more enterprising' than other re-frontings in the street, was notable for its oval windows in the fourth storey, and for heavy segmental pediments over the first-floor windows, not unlike those which later appeared at County Hall.

The Estate's board was still not happy, and the Duke himself had reservations about the oval windows, but the scheme was allowed to go ahead — at a cost to Sophie of around £2,000. Three years later, the Bevans had the stables rebuilt too, presumably the better to accommodate motor cars and again to a design by Knott and Collins.[2]

The Veiled Politician

When Gerard Bevan made his first business trip to the United States and Canada in August 1909, Sophie went with him. They crossed the Atlantic on the Cunard liner *Carmania* — the first of a new breed of luxury liners powered by steam turbines, of which *Lusitania* and *Mauretania* would become more famous examples — from Liverpool to New York. Once Bevan had completed a round of business calls in Wall Street, they set off on an extended tour which left a special impression on Sophie.

As wives of wealthy businessmen usually are, Sophie was keen to involve herself in good causes. She was also becoming increasingly interested in eugenics — the then fashionable pseudo-science of preserving or improving 'racial vigour' through selective breeding. As a result of her North American tour, one cause that attracted her support was the encouragement of unmarried women to offer themselves as wives for British men throughout the Empire — an idea that had been promoted by a succession of committees of London worthies since the 1880s, and had gained new momentum in response to high rates of male emigration during the Edwardian years.

In December, not long after their return voyage, she wrote to *The Times*:

Sir: For more than 30 years the young men of the British Isles have found it increasingly difficult to make a living in their native land. Therefore there has been — and still is — a steady exodus of our male population to our Colonies, where they

---

[2] Having housed the Free French Government in Exile during the second world war, 21 Upper Grosvenor Street was later occupied by a dressmaking business on the lower floors, with a maisonette above. But the whole building became empty and apparently neglected by the mid 1990s. Amid extended legal wranglings between commercial lessees and the Grosvenor Estate, the upper floors were reported to have been stripped back to bare brick and joists, and the front door was boarded up.

are unhampered by the many disadvantages prevailing here. Unfortunately they are obliged to leave the corresponding proportion of British women behind. The result is a surplus of 1,000,000 in Great Britain; but let me hasten to add (lest the mistake be laid upon Nature when it is not hers) that there is a proportionate shortage of 1,000,000 in our colonies.

I have recently been on a tour throughout Canada and the States, and was most struck by the scarcity of women in Western Canada — there are about eight men to one woman. And in America the saddest sight of all is the appalling number of half-castes, a blot on the civilization of the States but a blot for which Europeans are responsible. The absence of white women is answerable for the worst type of population, so that in reality there is a very pressing Imperial question; and all those interested in the growth and future of Canada should turn their attention to it. For unless we can induce the right sort of British women to emigrate we shall not have the Colonies peopled with our own race or speaking our mother tongue.

Canada wants unmarried women, her cry is for our marriageable daughters, and each one would find her vocation out there.

Canadian men are one of the finest types of manhood possible, but they are too hard working to be able to return here in search of a wife. How gladly they would welcome the possibility of sharing their homes with a sister or a wife can only be guessed by those who have been there.

I am so greatly impressed with the advisability of encouraging English women to go out there that I strongly urge every suitable, healthy and useful woman between the age of 25 and 35 to depart (if she has nothing to prevent her) and through the British Emigration Society, Imperial Institute, I shall hope to do all that I can to assist them financially.

I am, Sir, yours faithfully,
Sophie K. Bevan

It is an odd little irony that Sophie's elder daughter Christabel, aged eight at the time this letter was written, would grow up to marry, almost certainly against Sophie's wishes, a Canadian who — far from being 'the finest type of manhood' — turned out to be an unspeakable bounder and, like Sophie's own husband, a convicted fraudster. More of him in Chapter Eleven.

Sophie's taste for campaigning soon took her beyond the topic of Englishmen abroad in need of solace towards a much broader patriotic canvas. There is no evidence that she ever took the short stroll up Park Lane to stand on a soapbox at Speakers' Corner, but in 1910 she published a slim volume called *Letters from a Veiled Politician* which was as vehement as anything that might have been heard there at the time.

The author of the letters is 'veiled' because 'the House of Commons has never received me within its honoured walls, and the time is not yet ripe for me to be welcomed by the House of Lords.' But whoever is behind the veil, she (or possibly he) cannot remain silent in the face of the 'grim and gruesome peril' which is 'sapping our national existence'. Addressed to 'My Compatriots', 'All Who Love The British Flag' and other variants of the same theme, the letters are written in what seems to be a partially invented persona, though they include presumably real childhood anecdotes of seeing Gladstone and John Bright visiting 'my native city'.

Her letter to 'Our Greatest Patriot' is addressed to her relation by marriage Joseph Chamberlain, who had by then been severely diminished in mental capacity by a stroke, so presumably never replied. But he might have found much to commend in what she had to say, having himself spoken (in a celebrated speech in 1897) of the responsibility of wielding 'the sceptre of Empire... Great is the task, great is the responsibility, but great is the honour; and I am convinced that the conscience and the spirit of the country will rise to the height of its obligations, and that we shall have the strength to fulfil the mission which our history and our national character have imposed upon us.'

Chamberlain, like Sophie, had a special regard for Canada and other dominions settled by emigrants: 'We want to promote a closer and firmer union between all members of the great British race,' he declared in the same speech. 'If Greater Britain remains united, no empire in the world can ever surpass it...'

Sophie's views would also have been received seriously because her writings show her to be something more than just a drawing-room polemicist. Most unusually for an Edwardian lady, she was interested in the fiscal and demographic detail behind policy-making. She makes ample use of statistics, and when she writes about tax, her proposals always have precise sums of money set against them. She believed that taxes should be taken from income not capital, should be indirect when possible and optional when feasible; that is, based on luxuries rather than essentials. In effect, she is an advocate of Value Added Tax before that name was invented.

She also wants to remove taxes on tea and sugar sourced within the Empire, and replace them with export duties on coal and works of art. Writing to 'The British Sportsman', she tells him he is fundamentally selfish for devoting so much money (£50 million a year, she reckons) to his enjoyment, and should be willing to pay 10 per cent tax on top. Combine that with a 20 per cent tax on horserace betting, yielding £20 million, and it would be possible to 'abolish the Death Duties which are stolen from Capital and impoverish the Nation'.

Elsewhere, the targets of her breathless assaults included the programme of welfare reforms then being enacted by the Asquith government with the support of 'Socialist curs', the accompanying attacks on the powers of the House of Lords, and the notion of Home Rule for Ireland. But the peril to which she addressed herself ran deeper than mere current political issues: it was nothing less than the rotting of the soul of British menfolk.

Rather perversely, Sophie did not think the answer lay in women taking a hand in politics. The veiled one admired the pluck of the Suffragettes, but not their aims. 'Awake, arise, quick march! Ye manhood of the British Isles, ye of the Anglo-Saxon race,' she exhorted,

'Accept your responsibility, shoulder your arms and prepare to be in readiness to protect your country.' As for the women, they should 'remain in tranquility' and let their husbands and brothers step forward: 'No longer need you be viragos for you can respect men who will fight for you and for their country.'

Sophie would not have been regarded as a dangerous crank for holding these views, though her unrestrained public expression of them may have startled her more genteel neighbours in Upper Grosvenor Street and caused some mirth behind Bevan's stiff back on the Stock Exchange. She probably also upset some of her Kenrick relations, who might have thought that she was not only abandoning the family's traditional welfare-minded Liberalism but also getting above her social station.

At a time of fierce national debate, when fundamental aspects of the British polity were under challenge, she was in fact parroting opinions widely held by the Edwardian 'radical Right', which found its voice largely among the upper classes and aristocracy, in response to radical social reforms introduced by the Liberal government after its landslide election victory of 1906.

This included various forms of welfare and the first old age pensions. To pay for it all, plus naval rearmament, Lloyd George's 'People's Budget' of 1909 proposed a range of new taxes, including a tax on land — and was vetoed by Unionists in the House of Lords. This led in turn, after two very close general election results in 1910, to the introduction by the Asquith government of the 1911 Parliament Bill, curbing the Lords' powers to defeat or delay legislation.

Under threat of being swamped by newly appointed Liberal peers, the Unionists caved in and allowed the Bill to pass — but over a hundred peers, known as 'Diehards', voted against it. To the extent that the Diehards had a coherent manifesto, it was the set of ideas to which the 'veiled politician' subscribed in her *Letters* and subsequent volumes.

Only a minority of Diehards were ardent eugenicists, however, and many adherents of eugenics were to be found on the left rather than the right. They included H.G. Wells, George Bernard Shaw (whose 1903 play *Man and Superman* touches on eugenicist themes) and the Fabian Society founder Sidney Webb. But Sophie must have found herself particularly in tune with aristocrats such as the 12th Earl of Meath, who called for measures to promote physical fitness and 'Grit', on the grounds that a strong people would ensure a strong empire; and the 19th Lord Willoughby de Broke, an Eton contemporary of Gerard, who believed that the maintenance of a secure Britain depended upon 'breeding from the best stocks and bringing to maturity the greatest possible number of mentally and physically sound men and women, reared among healthy surroundings, in the ideals of Religion and Patriotism, equipped with a trade education, protected by a Tariff from unfair foreign competition, [and] trained to bear arms.'

She must also have been an admirer of the journalist Arnold White, a protégé of the Diehard 11th Duke of Bedford, who wrote in favour of eugenics and compulsory conscription in a popular weekly called *The Referee*: 'Race improvement today is not a question of philosophy but existence… If the first law of life is self-preservation, England must choose between state suicide and race improvement.'

Apart from offering a curious sidelight on the political differences of the day, do Sophie's writings offer any insights into the Bevan marriage? Something — though it is not obvious what — might be gleaned from this passage:

> In any country, at any period… it may be observed that the two sexes act and react upon each other in such close proximity, such unforeseen ways and with such strange results that —
> – Strong men produce charming women.
> – Cowards create viragos.
> – Clever women educate great leaders.
> – Masculine women encourage effeminate men.

The qualities of one sex, if not dominant in those to whom they by right belong, will be adopted by the other to the detriment of both.

We have had enough of women adopting male attributes and too much of men wearing petticoats. Let us reverse the positions and return to the natural order of things…

The *Letters* attracted replies 'from the uttermost ends of the earth' as well as many invitations to speak at public meetings, or so Sophie said in her introduction to their sequel, *The Parting of the Ways; or Conquest by Purchase* (1911). This was described in advertisements by its London publisher John Murray (it was also published in Toronto) as 'a stirring appeal to all loyal British subjects in the present critical times'.

It was another extended sermon in praise of Imperial ideals and against the decay of British moral fibre provoked by the general thrust of modern life combined with the specific actions of Lloyd George as Chancellor. It preserved the anonymity of the Veiled Politician — unlike the *Letters*, Sophie is not identified as its author, though one reviewer outed her as 'a Mrs Bevan of Birmingham'.

Again a search through *The Parting of the Ways* for glimpses of Bevan family life is largely unrewarding. But one passage does suggest the austere tone of Christabel and Sheila's upbringing, at least as far as their mother was concerned:

Our domestic ideals are that all children should "have a good time" and find the way paved for them, seeing that we have small confidence in their being able to fight for themselves. This is a great mistake, as strength comes from the use of capability, and capability is only found through facing facts.

There was a third and still fiercer volume to come, two years later. *The Path to Peace: A Short Handbook of National Training* argued for a five-point programme to rebuild Britain's national and imperial capabilities:

1. National Service with universal training.

2. Segregation and seclusion under kind care and in suitable environment of the mentally deficient and feeble-minded. Crime springs from this class of unfortunates who are irresponsible for their actions.

3. Enforced notification of all venereal diseases... These diseases are the most deadly and dangerous known to man, and are allowed to go scot-free in our circles like ravening wolves without the slightest prohibition...

4. Rigid legislation for the exclusion of all undesirable aliens belonging to inferior races. These immigrants can never be developed into British patriots, and contaminate our race. England can no longer afford to be the dumping ground for the lowest dregs of humanity, or to receive in her midst the scum of the earth. Future conflicts will be racial ones, and the ingredients which each country accepts for amalgamation with her own breed will play an important part in the struggles for final supremacy.

5. Encouragement for the provision of proper houses for families because homes are the real foundations of an Empire...

What did Gerard thinks of his wife's ideas? As we shall see later, he could spout patriotic rhetoric with the best of them when it suited his purpose to do so at shareholders' meetings during the first world war. But his Cambridge debating record suggests that he was by nature a middle-of-the-road man rather than a radical thinker, and there is no indication anywhere else that he took a deep interest in political ideas.

Nor did he live up to Sophie's ideals of red-blooded but uxorious manliness, ready to fight like a lion for home and country, or Lord Meath's ideal of 'Grit'. In that, as in other respects, he must have been an increasing disappointment to her. He had never worn uniform, and so far as we know he undertook no public service or committee work until the end of the first world war, when he sat on a rather obscure body called the Tobacco and Matches Control Board.

Instead, such of his energies as were not devoted to business were devoted to the pursuit of pleasure — the pleasure of collecting paintings, books, fine furniture and weaponry, Chinese porcelain and Persian rugs, and the pleasure of female company other than that of his opinionated wife.

City Magnate and Don Juan

The extent of Bevan's philandering, and the question of whether it was habitual throughout his marriage or only during a post-war phase when his life was gradually spinning out of control, is a difficult one for the biographer. There must be a suspicion that this aspect of his life was played up by the popular press to make a more lurid story at the time of his trial — just as published comments about his personality from people who had known him before his fall became increasingly derogatory — and that subsequent portraits of him merely echoed this tabloid caricature.

The most detailed account of his amours appeared in *World's Pictorial News*, a lively Saturday illustrated paper, immediately after his conviction in December 1922. Describing him as 'City Magnate and Don Juan', the four-part series was advertised as 'the inner story of Bevan's gay life on the Continent and his love for the ladies'. In the classic style of the salacious exposé down the ages, it is studiously vague as to the actual roll-call and chronology of his sexual partners while suggesting that the specific anecdotes quoted are merely illustrative of a much longer catalogue that might even have matched Mozart's Don Giovanni at *'mille e tre'*.

On close reading, it is possible to infer that the writer had only actually spoken to two former mistresses — one of whom was Jeanne Pertuisot who became his second wife — and had picked up unconfirmed tittle-tattle of a couple more. None of it is especially surprising. In his late thirties and early forties, Bevan was a rich Edwardian with the morals of his class and time and — to be frank — a wife whose attitude to the marital bed was probably driven more by duty than enthusiasm, though we must hope that she did not find him as repulsive as Irene Forsyte found her first husband, Soames.

Bevan travelled abroad often, and it would be surprising if his eye had not occasionally fallen on women who were prepared to make themselves available to him, whether amateur or professional or as, chorus girls of the day tended to be, something in between. The *World's Pictorial News* reporter hints at sightings of Bevan consorting with ladies of the night in Piccadilly and even, in his undergraduate days, in the back streets of Cambridge.

The circumstantial details of the more substantial anecdotes best fit the post-war years; a 'Miss L' is the only one who seems to belong to an earlier phase. She sounds like the archetypal Edwardian floozy — a pretty chorus girl who he met at Brighton, and who fed him a sob story to which he responded with a gift of £1,000. She later accompanied him on trips to Berlin, Vienna and Paris and eventually he was paying her an allowance of £3,000 a year. He also gave her £4,500 worth of jewellery from his favourite *bijoutier* near the Madeleine in Paris. And when he tired of her, he gave her £10,000 worth of shares as a farewell.

Another tale has Bevan spotted in a Parisian nightclub with a girl 'loaded with jewellery of the most costly type'. '*Oh Meester Bevan,*' she is supposedly overheard cooing, '*You are so kind, so clever and so handsome.*' That one sounds as if the *World's Pictorial News* man simply made it up in an effort to bring his piece to the length his editor was demanding.

The other stories all relate to Bevan's post-war life, after he had parted from Sophie in all but name and told her that he regretted ever marrying her; we shall return to them in Chapter Five. But we can safely conclude that even during this earlier era — when, so Sophie would later claim, they had been 'the happiest family in England' — Gerard was regularly and not always discreetly playing away.

A glimpse of the Bevans together in Upper Grosvenor Street is offered in the diary of Alan Lascelles, who found himself dining there in May 1912, shortly after he had been taken into Ellis & Co as a trainee. As we saw in Chapter Two, the rather haughty Lascelles had warmed to Bevan when they first met six months earlier, and Bevan evidently thought well enough of Lascelles to invite him to dinner. But the young protégé already seemed to be taking a dimmer view of his boss, and was not at all impressed by Sophie.

> [Bevan's] walls are hung with Corots, Raeburns, Hoppners, his wife with strings of pearls — everywhere evidence of excessive wealth. She is a gaunt, slouching woman whom I didn't take to, and who began by asking me if I had found my way all right — as if I had walked from Balham.

Lascelles had in fact recently moved to Egerton Gardens, a smart address for a bachelor on the Knightsbridge-South Kensington border, and a pleasant stroll or short cab ride from Mayfair. Perhaps Sophie had also treated him to some robust opinions on political developments, this being the time of the merger of the Conservative Party with Joseph Chamberlain's Liberal Unionists. Anyway, he did not find the encounter convivial.

> It was a Dinner-Party of the sort I rarely see, but which I suppose I shall know only too well in middle age. I took a plump mature sister of Nigel Playfair, the actor, in to dinner, and found her charming; we talked Harrison shop most of the time.

'Harrison shop' referred to two highly gifted musical sisters, May and Baba Harrison, whose playing was the talk of the town at the time — despite being, as Lascelles put it in his dismissive way, daughters of 'a withered Anglo-Indian colonel and his very ordinary wife'. We know from other anecdotes that Bevan had an interest in music as well as collecting, but the high cultural tone of the household evidently did not make up for the social discomfort felt by this particular guest.

No doubt breathing a sigh of relief as he left, Lascelles went on from Upper Grosvenor Street 'to a stately little ball at the Duchess of Northumberland's'.

The Bevans certainly made an odd couple. If others found the atmosphere in their dining room sticky, it must have been all the more so when Gerard and Sophie were alone together.

We might picture them at their elegant breakfast table. At one end, Sophie opens letters to the Veiled Politician forwarded by her publisher and reads aloud the most strident passages of which she approves, interspersed with snippets from *The Times* of the doings of the Liberal government of which she particularly disapproves.

At the other end, Gerard — impatient to get away, his mind on the business day ahead, his expression set in lines of worry — leafs distractedly through the latest saleroom catalogue, or perhaps a continental railway timetable, or a playbill. Occasionally he says 'Yes, my dear… How right you are, my dear', to give the impression that he is listening.

But his mind is on money, and the beautiful objects and women it will buy him.

At Littlecote

In the middle of the war, shortly after the end of the Battle of the Somme and a few months after he had bought into the City Equitable, Gerard Lee Bevan acquired a magnificent country home.

He had previously leased shooting rights over land owned by William Dalziel Mackenzie, a wealthy barrister and railway company director, close to Thetford in Norfolk. But in December 1916 he put his weekend lifestyle on to a very much grander and more expensive footing by taking a 25-year lease on Littlecote House in Wiltshire. We may guess that the lease cost him at least £30,000 (in 1922 he claimed it was still worth £25,000 as security for one of his many debts) and it would be estimated at his trial that the house and estate cost him £10,000 a year to run.

The lessor was 62-year-old Hugh Leyborne-Popham, a noted orni-
thologist and wildfowler who had adventured in remote parts of
Siberia and northern Sweden at the turn of the century. Besides
Littlecote he had inherited another estate, Hunstrete in Somerset,
which was his principal home and where he was, by one account,
'the very best type of landlord, an expert in farming and all country
pursuits, and a most public-spirited Justice of the Peace'.

Leyborne-Popham and his wife Janet had three daughters, but
their only son died in childhood in 1915 — and it was perhaps as a
result of his death that they decided not to keep Littlecote for their
own use. They must have been relieved to find, in the middle of a
war, a tenant rich enough to relieve them of the upkeep of a ram-
bling Elizabethan pile that had last been refurbished more than a
century earlier.

The Leyborne-Pophams descended from Sir John Popham, who
was successively Speaker of the House of Commons, attorney general and Lord Chief Justice of England between 1580 and 1607, and
who had presided over the trials of Mary Queen of Scots, Sir Walter
Raleigh and Guy Fawkes. Littlecote was built for him in the early
1590s on the site of a Tudor house where Henry VIII had wooed his
third wife, Jane Seymour.

Built in mellow brick and flint with stone detailing, the many-
gabled mansion is approached through an idyllic English landscape
of meadow and woodland beside the river Kennet. It is just a couple
of miles from the pleasant market town of Hungerford, across the
county border in Berkshire.[3]

The shape of the house is deceptive. Seen from the front,
Littlecote is grandly proportioned but relatively compact, a range of
ancient and modern buildings to the right-hand side being heavily
screened by trees. But in an unimpeded view from the garden side,
it is elongated and asymmetrical, reminiscent of a wing of an ancient
Oxbridge college.

---

[3] After the Bevans vacated Littlecote, Leyborne-Popham sold it to Sir Ernest Wills, the
tobacco magnate. During the war the house served as headquarters for a battalion of the
US 101st Airborne Division. It remained in the Wills family until 1985, when it was sold
to the entrepreneur Peter de Savary. It is now a hotel and leisure complex.

Inside, it boasts a Great Hall with tall, heraldic stained-glass windows, a charming little Dutch parlour with richly decorated walls and ceiling, and a galleried 'Cromwellian' chapel with a high-roofed pulpit where the altar ought to be, said to be the most complete example of its kind extant. Some of the ground-floor rooms are made gloomy to modern tastes by their dark oak panelling; but the visitor's spirits are lifted on the first floor by light flooding into the Long Gallery that justifies its name by running to 110 feet in length.

The Long Gallery overlooks a formal garden that has changed in design since Bevan's day but must still contain descendants of some of his plantings. To one side of it is the walled vegetable garden, and beyond that the magnificent trees of the park, laid out in the 17th and 18th centuries. In the grounds are the remains of a great Roman villa. In all, it would be hard to conceive of a more perfectly English composition of architecture and landscape.

The historian John Julius Norwich says the house 'whispers insistently of the days of the Civil War' when Alexander Popham, grandson of Sir John, commanded a garrison of parliamentary forces there. Norwich also calls the house 'gruesomely haunted' — by the cries of a distraught mother whose unwanted baby had been born in secret and thrown on to a fire, by the footfall of Cromwellian soldiers, and possibly by Gerard Bevan himself, whose presence has been felt in the Long Gallery.

We may imagine him pacing its length over and over, hands clasped behind his back, eyes cast down, lost in thought as his problems mount — the posture in which he was often seen walking the short distance around the perimeter of the Bank of England between the offices of City Equitable in Lothbury and Ellis & Co in Cornhill. But here at least he had the distractions of his collections of Chinese porcelain and silverware, for which the Long Gallery made a superb setting.

His paintings, books, historic weaponry and fine English furniture, which had long over-filled Upper Grosvenor Street, would all have found space to be seen and admired at Littlecote. He was also able to become what would now be called a hobby farmer, acquiring a herd of pedigree Shorthorn cattle, and to indulge a passion for gardening: he knew the Latin name for everything, and kept nine gardeners fully occupied.

He also fished and played chess — pastimes that suited the contemplative side of his nature — and went to church at nearby St Mary's, Chilton Folliat, or arranged for services to be held in his own chapel. In every respect, as one reporter described it, he played to the hilt the role of 'God-fearing, self-respecting squire'.

With the addition of two adjacent farms bought for the shooting, he now had a splendid place to entertain City friends and clients — a place which made an unequivocal statement about his growing wealth. Littlecote was much grander than the old Bevan house in the same county, Fosbury Manor, a few miles to the south. It was comparable in scale to his father's former home at Trent Park, but considerably more beautiful and more full of history.

'Looking back on my visit I can say without exaggeration that I had one of the happiest times in my life,' one City guest at Littlecote told an interviewer after Bevan's conviction:

> The old-world atmosphere of the place was soothing to the jaded brains of a man who like myself is every day engaged in a battle of wits on the Stock Exchange. Bevan conducted me over the house and grounds. He was extremely proud of it, and told me that though he cared for nothing for rank or title, he was extremely anxious to become one of the leading landed proprietors in the country.
>
> We walked together through the well-wooded park, and stood for several moments staring into the lucid waters of a trout stream. It was there that Bevan spoke of his ambition... to accumulate a much larger fortune, until his riches should approach those of a mighty Rockefeller.

That guest described Sophie as a 'graceful and dignified' hostess, but others found Littlecote's chatelaine as disagreeable as Alan Lascelles had found her in Upper Grosvenor Street a few years earlier. Relations between Gerard and Sophie were increasingly strained — and Sophie, when not on her best behaviour, was becoming increasingly odd.

She wore a combination of jewelled dog-collars and long, trailing dresses — 'all dirt and diamonds' one Bevan family member reported. And she was 'incredibly mean', re-using stained table cloths to avoid the expense of replacing them with clean ones each day, and sometimes failing to offer visitors sufficient to eat.

When Gerard's nephew Desmond (son of Cosmo) visited, he took some biscuits in his luggage as emergency rations and secreted them in a bedroom drawer. The day after his arrival, Sophie challenged him: 'Why did you bring those biscuits with you? Don't you get enough to eat here?'

'No I don't,' Desmond replied, 'That's why I brought them. But you must have looked in the drawer to find them!'

'I *always* go through my visitors' drawers,' said Sophie imperiously.

Sophie was also busy at her writing desk again. *The Home and the War*, published by John Murray in 1918, is an account of how she practiced 'patriotic economy and efficiency' at Littlecote while preaching that the war itself was a kind of purifying force: 'To those who have eyes to see, it has been a resurrection of the national grit and character. We were rapidly becoming too soft, too flabby, too fond of the insidious gospel of comfort.'

She described how she had reduced her household staff to a minimum and encouraged them to enlist, while devoting her own energies to running a dairy, making hayricks, farming rabbits and deer, and growing tomatoes — which she thought particularly good for the health. She also explained the rudiments of goat-keeping — in a passage which finds a comic echo in *Various Reminiscences* (1970), an unpublished family memoir by Pleasance Bevan, widow of Gerard's nephew Hugh: 'At one time, Sophie bred goats. She had a billy goat at stud but so little money came in that she decided the herdsman was robbing her, so she herself led the goat through the village shouting out "Only a guinea a leap!"'

Despite Sophie's eccentricities and her husband's infidelities, there must have been a time at Littlecote — between the spring of 1917 and the end of 1918 — when the family really was happy in its arcadian country retreat. Here Gerard was at his most relaxed, supervising the planting of a new border or the placing of a sapling tree, examining the glaze of a fine Chinese bowl, reading the poems of Shelley or the essays of Walter Pater in the Dutch parlour — then taking up his notebook and starting work on a new poem of his own.

Bevan's published volume of poetry, *Russet and Asp*, which we shall look at more closely in Chapter Twelve, largely occupies a fantasy realm far removed from the real events of his life, and gives no indication as to when each poem was written. So it is impossible to know which of them date from the Littlecote years. But here is part of *You and I*, which might well have been written on a quiet, sunny day there when he was feeling mellow towards Sophie and at ease with the world:

> *If I had been an emperor*
> *And you a beggar-maid,*
> *I should have built an ivory throne*
> *With gold and gem inlaid,*
> *And set a crown upon your head,*
> *And brought you to my halls,*
> *And summoned all my courtiers*
> *To own themselves your thralls.*

> *If I'd been an astronomer*
> *And you that first faint star*
> *That greets us just as Atlas holds*
> *The gates of night ajar,*
> *How free of foil had been my days!*
> *How certain of their hope!*
> *As dusk by dusk I sought your gleam*
> *With Love's sure telescope.*

If I had been — just what I am —
A clumsy, fighting ceorl,
And you had been — just what you are —
A simple, country girl,
And we could wish and wish galore
There's not a thing we'd change;
So long as you and I are one,
Where could we wish to range!

CHAPTER FOUR

The City Equitable

> '*The Providential Premium Reassurance Society was so imposing a concern, and he had been connected with it so short a time, that it seemed presumptuous to smell a rat; especially as he would have to leave the Board and the thousand a year he earned on it if he raised smell of rat without rat or reason. But what if there were a rat?*'
>
> Soames Forsyte in
> John Galsworthy, *The White Monkey* (1924)

A Wartime Opportunity

The City Equitable Fire Insurance Company is a name familiar to every lawyer worth his salt because of the significance of the judgment in the case against its directors for 'misfeasance' which followed Bevan's trial for fraud; we shall revisit both those courtrooms in Chapters Nine and Ten. But in fact the company had a very short life, of only 14 years from beginning to end, and for the first six of those years it was a modest venture which attracted little attention or comment, even in the City.

The City Equitable was founded in January 1908 as a reinsurance vehicle — that is, for the purpose of underwriting fire insurance risks, or portions of them, taken by other companies that were dealing direct with the public, or with businesses seeking insurance for their assets. Its authorised and subscribed capital was £50,000, in a mixture of ordinary and preference shares paid up at four shillings in the pound, which means that its paid-up capital was just £10,000.

And it made a quiet start, gathering in a little over £20,000 in premium income in its first year of operation. By 1913, income still only amounted to £83,433, and the surplus after claims paid and working expenses was just £6,853. But then came the outbreak of war in 1914.

Reinsurance before the first world war was far more widely developed in continental Europe than it was in London. Rather remarkably, there were no British reinsurance companies founded during the second half of the 19th century, though a handful were founded in the first decade of the new century, the City Equitable among them.

In the same 60-year period, at least 45 new reinsurers opened for business in the major business centres of the continent, with the Germans outgunning the rest in both numbers and capital strength. Leading German firms such as Münchener Rückversicherungs-Gesellschaft (founded in 1880, known in London as Munich Re, and one of the few insurance companies that had proved capable of paying out all its claims after the 1906 San Francisco earthquake) accounted for as much as 60 per cent of the market.

When German and Austrian reinsurers' activities in London were curtailed by the war, however, 'British underwriters were left practically without the reinsurance facilities upon which they had previously relied,' wrote one historian of the industry, Edwin W. Kopf. A surge of new opportunities became available to British companies. At the same time, war risks pushed premiums in the marine sector higher than ever before.

The City Equitable operated at this stage purely in the fire reinsurance sector, rather than marine, but even so the prospects of picking up business left behind by the Germans suddenly looked exciting — and attracted the attention of Clarence Hatry.

This clever young man was to be revealed, 15 years later, as a fraudster on a considerably bigger scale than Bevan. He would be described by the economic historian J.K. Galbraith in *The Great Crash 1929* (New edition 1992) as 'one of those curiously un-English figures with whom the English periodically find themselves unable to cope'. Although Hatry's early career had been 'anything but reassuring', wrote Galbraith, he went on to build 'an industrial and financial empire of truly impressive proportions'.

Hatry would also be accorded the barbed accolade of inclusion in Dorothy L. Sayers's list of people (in the introduction to her 1949 translation of *The Divine Comedy*) who might have been assigned to various circles of Hell or Purgatory in a contemporary English version of Dante's masterpiece — a distinction he would have shared with Horatio Bottomley and a murderer called 'Brides in the Bath' Smith,[1] among other contemporaries.

Hatry is a pivotal player in the Bevan drama, and the City Equitable was the first stepping stone of his career in high finance.

Born in Belsize Park, north London, in 1888, the son of a Jewish trader in silk and velvet for top hats and of a half-Hungarian mother, Clarence Hatry had found himself in charge of the family business after his father's death in 1908. It failed with debts of £8,000 which Hatry had guaranteed, and both he and his mother were made bankrupt.

Hatry found the means to pay off their creditors within two years and established himself as an insurance broker, specialising in the negotiation of loans from insurance companies to personal borrowers who were prospective beneficiaries under wills and settlements. The insurers generally required that every loan should have two guarantors, but many potential borrowers could only offer one — so Hatry's smart solution was to put them together in pairs or small syndicates, pooling their guarantors.

More important to this story, he also spotted a niche opportunity arising from the number of Austrian migrants passing through England to take passage from Liverpool for America. There was

---

[1] George Joseph Smith (1872–1915) married and murdered Bessie Williams in 1912, Alice Burnham in 1913 and Margaret Elizabeth Lofty in 1914. All three were found dead in their baths. Smith's motive was money every time, but we must hope that he occupies a lower circle of Hell than either Hatry or Bevan.

no certainty that these travellers would be allowed into the United States when they reached Ellis Island, off New York — so Hatry created the Austrian Immigrants Insurance Association, which sold policies guaranteeing a return passage in the event that the policy-holder was denied entry. Hatry laid off the risk by means of reinsurance, taking the margin as his commission. By the outbreak of war, which put an end to the flow of migrants, he had accumulated profits on this business of about £35,000.

With this in hand, plus money borrowed from a friend, Hatry was in due course able to put together £60,000 to make his first ambitious move into the field of corporate finance. We may guess that the City Equitable had come to his attention as one of the reinsurers with which he had been placing his Austrian migrant business. Spotting the potential for British reinsurers to profit from the withdrawal of their continental competitors, soon after the beginning of the war he bought a controlling interest in the City Equitable from a German shareholder looking for an exit from the market. He then reorganised the company and brought about an increase in its authorised and subscribed (but not paid-up) capital, before selling his stake for some £250,000 to Gerard Bevan and Peter Haig-Thomas in June 1916.

How the connection between Bevan and Hatry came about, we do not know. In social terms they were unlikely collaborators. We might imagine their first encounter in Bevan's grand Cornhill office, Hatry having talked his way in with the promise of putting some useful business Bevan's way.

At his desk is the Old Etonian senior partner of a highly reputable stockbroking firm — known, as we have already gathered, for barely offering the time of day to those he regarded as small fry in his market. Opposite him, waiting to be invited to sit down, is a 26-year-old Jewish wheeler-dealer with a short track record that includes an encounter with bankruptcy: a small, bird-like man with prematurely receding hair, a close-cropped moustache and (according to the literary agent George Greenfield, who worked for Hatry in later life) 'an enormous scimitar of a nose… and the strangest pale blue eyes.'

'He had a soft, sibilant voice,' Greenfield wrote in *The Author* in 1993, 'and a laugh that was a cross between a chuckle and a giggle. He had the quickest of minds and innate charm. A meeting with CCH, as he was known... was like drinking champagne on an empty stomach.'

If doubts were raised about whatever proposition was in hand, 'in quarter of an hour he had plucked out figures, juggled with them and then proved conclusively that the problems did not exist. Of course, when the bubbles subsided, you realised that the problems had not gone away — but while you were the target of CCH's battery of wit and charm, everything seemed not only possible but likely as well.'

That persuasive fizz won the attention of Bevan — who if he subscribed to the casual anti-Semitism and suspicion of parvenus that would have been rife in his circles, never let it put him off the scent of profit, as his pre-war connection with Goldman Sachs in New York confirms. After this first deal together they were to work as partners for six years — with the much less clever but cash-rich Peter Haig-Thomas along for the ride — in a series of hugely lucrative company promotions.

Lords on the Board

Hatry had in any case foreseen the prejudices he might need to overcome in respect of his own background and relative inexperience, and had ensured that the City Equitable already had a very Establishment tone to its board of directors.

Its chairman was Sir David Burnett, first baronet, who had been Lord Mayor of London in 1912. He was honorary colonel of a City territorial regiment, and was best known for organising the public subscription to save the Crystal Palace at Sydenham for the nation. He was joined in April 1915 by several other titled gentlemen — and since they all play walk-on parts in the later Bevan drama, it is worth pausing for a few moments to establish their personae.

The most notable, in his way, was the fourth and last Lord Ribblesdale, aged 61, who was perhaps the ultimate example of the 'lord on the board' — the kind of token boardroom grandee described in a later generation by Tiny Rowland, the autocratic chief executive of the Lonrho mining conglomerate from 1961 to 1993, as 'Christmas-tree decoration'. A rather sad figure, Ribblesdale is remembered not for his business acumen, of which there was no evidence, but chiefly as the subject of a striking portrait, known as 'The Ancestor', by John Singer Sargent.

The picture was painted in Sargent's studio in 1902 at the suggestion of King Edward VII — who had nicknamed Ribblesdale 'the Ancestor' because he felt that the Lancashire peer's ancient lineage, imposing presence and archaic mannerisms of speech and dress encapsulated everything a true Englishman ought to be.

Ribblesdale's life was at its zenith in those early Edwardian days, but became progressively darker: his eldest son died in Somaliland in 1904; his first wife Charlotte died in 1911; his second son Charles died at Gallipolli in August 1915; and in their memory he gave Sargent's painting to the National Gallery, of which he was a trustee.

This tall, gaunt, unmistakably aristocratic figure, whom Sargent painted in Victorian hunting garb, had been a soldier, a Lord in Waiting to Queen Victoria and Master of the Royal Buckhounds (which was, bizarrely, a Cabinet appointment). He was also a celebrated amateur boxer — capable, it was said, of knocking out any man in the House of Lords.

Prone to deep depression and violent temper, Ribblesdale took refuge after Charlotte's death as a semi-permanent resident of the Cavendish Hotel in Jermyn Street — a short stroll from Bevan's later bolthole at the Carlton Hotel in Haymarket. During his time at the Cavendish, Ribblesdale became an unlikely companion of Rosa Lewis, the former shilling-a-week maidservant turned cook who ran the place as a haven of discreet, upper-crust misbehaviour.

Rosa and her hotel were brought back to life in a popular 1970s television drama series, *The Duchess of Duke Street*. During her own lifetime, much to her irritation, she was caricatured by Evelyn Waugh in *Vile Bodies* (1930) as: 'Lottie Crump, proprietess of Shepheard's Hotel in Dover Street, invariably attended by two Cairn terriers...

One can go to Shepheard's parched with modernity any day, if Lottie likes one's face, and still draw up, cool and uncontaminated, great healing draughts from the well of Edwardian certainty.' As to her preferred clientele, as illustrated by the 'Spy' cartoons and old photographs displayed in her parlour, 'there are very few writers or painters and no actors, for Lottie is true to the sound old snobbery of pound sterling and strawberry leaves.'

Strictly speaking, strawberry leaves belong on the coronets of dukes, marquesses and earls, above Ribblesdale's lordly rank. But Waugh's phrase must have been an oblique reference to Ribblesdale and his fellow Cavendish resident Sir William Eden, a choleric Durham baronet (father of the future prime minister Anthony) who stayed there to escape from his wife and family. Waugh's face was not one of those that Rosa liked — in fact she referred to him as 'that little swine' — but he brilliantly captured the eccentric milieu in which Ribblesdale found comfort.

There are a couple of other curious facts about Ribblesdale. George Bernard Shaw is believed to have used him as the model for Professor Higgins in *Pygmalion*. And he astonished London society in 1919 by emerging from his widower's gloom to marry the glamorous Philadelphia-born former Mrs John Jacob Astor, née Ava Willing — a name which provoked a stream of ribald jokes from Rosa Lewis.

Ava had divorced the multimillionaire Astor a couple of years before he went down with the *Titanic*, but had managed to hold on to part of his fortune — a settlement worth £50,000 a year, so it was said — and a house in Grosvenor Square. Gossips said it was a marriage of convenience, title for her, money for Ribblesdale, and Ava showed little interest in becoming chatelaine of Gisburn, the cold, damp family seat in rural Lancashire which she visited only once. But married life would certainly distract the peer's attention from the growing troubles of the City Equitable — as would his own health problems, as a result of which he was a director in name only during the months leading up to its collapse.

Those troubles were still a long way off when Ribblesdale joined what looked like — indeed, actually was — a company whose prospects had been miraculously transformed by the outbreak of war. Ribblesdale took his seat alongside his old friend Colonel (later Brigadier-General) Sir Douglas Dawson GCVO CMG, another quintessentially Victorian figure who might have been invented by George Macdonald Fraser for a walk-on part in the *Flashman* novels.

Like Ribblesdale, Dawson was lean and ramrod-straight; like other grand patriots of the era — Field Marshal Sir Douglas Haig and the composer Sir Edward Elgar, for example — he wore an enormous, drooping moustache. He was the nephew of an Irish earl and the son of an officer who was killed at the battle of Inkerman in the Crimea in 1854. A celebrated slow bowler at Eton, he had gone on to serve with distinction in the Egyptian war of 1882 — despite having his horse shot from under him at the battle of Kassassin — and in the Guards Camel Corps in the Sudan. He then became a military attaché in Vienna, and was so well liked at the court of Emperor Franz Josef that he was allowed to break etiquette and host a ball in his bachelor apartments.

Dawson went on to serve as attaché in Paris, Brussels and Bern before returning to join the Royal Household as master of ceremonies to King Edward VII and secretary of both the Order of the Garter and the Order of Merit. During his years on the City Equitable board, his day job, as it were, was as Comptroller of the Lord Chamberlain's department and subsequently State Chamberlain — and he also held a War Office post as 'Inspector of Vulnerable Points at the Horse Guards'.

The youngest director of the City Equitable — a less significant figure in this story because he left the board before the troubles began — was another Old Etonian professional soldier. He was Captain the Honourable Arthur Bingham of the 5th Lancers, a former aide-de-camp to the governor general of New Zealand. He would shortly inherit the title of Lord Clanmorris of Newbrook.

Dawson later said of Ribblesdale that he was 'very keen' and far from silent at the board table. Ribblesdale would attend 39 board meetings before his health gave way. Dawson himself would eventually clock up no fewer than 67, and would also become a director of a controversial sister company, City Equitable Associated, and of Amalgamated Industrials, one of the conglomerates created by Clarence Hatry.

As officers and courtiers, these three gentlemen would all have been sticklers for correct form and administrative good order. Outside the Bevan-Hatry ambit, Dawson was also a director of the National Bank of Ireland and the Norwich Union insurance company, so he was not a complete stranger to the money world. But he took a modest view of his capabilities, admitting that he 'never professed to be a judge of finance or investments'. It is quite probable that none of the trio had the foggiest clue about the deeper intricacies of reinsurance or investment — and neither did their next colleague, the 45-year-old Earl of March, heir to the Duke of Richmond.

Lord March had served in the army in the South African war and returned to uniform during the first world war, commanding the Sussex Yeomanry. His only other experience of the business world had been a short stint as a director of the Liverpool London & Globe insurance company before he was asked by Hatry to join the City Equitable.

He had been due to sail with his regiment for Gallipoli in September 1915 when he was seized by an infection which caused paralysis and wasting of the leg muscles and left him disabled for the rest of his life. Doctors advised him to spend as much time as possible in the country, and photographs invariably show him using a wheelchair or crutches. As well as ending his military career, this misfortune rendered him almost completely ineffective as a director.

Though Lord March acquired other directorships, including Hatry's Commercial Bank of London, he rarely attended City Equitable meetings after the end of 1915; he offered to resign in 1917 but was persuaded by Bevan to stay on. He finally reappeared in October 1918 only to suffer another dreadful setback when his eldest son, Lord Settrington, died from the after-effects of war wounds in August 1919. March started attending again in July 1920, and finally resigned just before Christmas 1921, apparently unaware of any impending problems.

To be a director of a public company (the distinction 'non-executive' did not come into common corporate parlance until much later) a century ago was not the well defined quasi-professional role it is today. Just as the distinction was made (and persisted until 1962) between 'gentlemen' amateurs and professional 'players' in first-class cricket, so it was also made in business. And it was invariably the gentlemen, perceived as officers and leaders, who provided the team captains.

For the titled and decorated classes, often rich in land but poor in cash, boardroom appointments offered a useful additional source of income — anything from £250 to £1,000 per directorship — in return for a handful of meetings per year and no very onerous responsibilities. It was a modest recompense for the late-Victorian shift of power from the old aristocracy to the new plutocracy of business.

As one City Equitable investor said from the floor at a shareholders' meeting, there were 'three qualifications for directors. The first of these is unquestionably integrity, the second an exalted position, and the third, sound business judgement.' That third attribute, we might add, was only expected to be exercised in a very broad, non-technical way, all matters of detail being left to managers and clerks.

Not every boardroom was stuffed with gentlemen whose business judgement was unproven. The directors of well-established insurers such as the British General (a forerunner of Commercial Union) and the Prudential (which listed on the Stock Exchange in 1924) were for the most part men of long experience in the insurance world or the accountancy profession. Other reputable companies such as the Westminster Bank, by contrast, chose a high proportion of their directors from the pages of the *Peerage*. But as a broad rule, the newer and more speculative the company, the more likely it was to boast what the fraudulent promoter Ernest Terah Hooley called 'front sheeters' — directors whose names in the prospectus might attract investors' attention and lend respectability. 'The average Briton dearly loves a lord, or if he is not to be had, a baronet, knight, or hon. will serve, while colonels and majors have their special uses,' said the *Journal of Finance* in 1898.

Were there any City professionals at the City Equitable table? There was a solicitor, Henry Grenside, in his late thirties, with an office at Dean's Yard, Westminster (suggesting that there might have been an ecclesiastical element to his practice) and a wife and two children at Weybridge in Surrey. He sounds a decent middle-class chap, but he turned out to be little better than a stooge for Bevan.

Grenside was right at the heart of the City Equitable's affairs, but exhibited little or no grasp of what was really going on in the company. And his legal expertise failed to impede the most outrageous of Bevan's abuses of company funds — his decision to allow the company's general manager, Edmund Mansell, to help himself to an enormous overdraft facility. We shall meet Mr Mansell in a moment.

A more effective contributor to the board was a second lawyer who joined in August 1915. This was a sharp-pencilled Aberdonian, Moir Milligan, senior partner of a firm of advocates called Davidson and Garton and director of a small Scottish bank; it was he who eventually made the crucial intervention that would lead to Bevan's downfall.

But until that climactic moment several years hence, the business was run from day to day by its general manager, Edmund George Mansell. He had been with the City Equitable since it first opened its doors, having previously worked in a more junior position in a large insurance company, and having been promoted in 1915, at the age of 42, from the lower executive rank of 'manager and secretary'. He was a genuine expert in the field of fire insurance as well as an avid business-getter, and was probably the only one in the boardroom with a complete grasp of the City Equitable's portfolio of risks.

This, then, was the make-up of the company after Hatry's intervention but before Bevan came over the horizon. At its sixth annual general meeting, on 20 May 1915, Sir David Burnett had reported 'steady progress'. Premium income over the 14-month period in review (the year-end had just been moved from December to February) had amounted to £154,086 — almost double the 12-month figure for 1913 — and profits after allowing for directors' fees were £12,279, enabling the payment of a dividend of nine pence per share.

The company held ample reserves and some £51,000 worth of 'high-class' investments. A recent rearrangement of the capital had created a better balance between the interests of ordinary and preference shareholders. The chairman and his fellow directors thought 'the future of the company would be a bright one… At all events, they would do what they could to render it so.'

Mansell the general manager was more specific, and his report was more confident about the future:

This very substantial increase in the income and profit is due to the opportunity which has been afforded to this company by the unfortunate European war, of obtaining valuable treaty[2] interests which had previously been held by German and Austrian companies.

To meet the further expansion of the business it was necessary that fresh capital should be raised, and it is with extreme gratification that I am in a position today to inform you that, since the subscribed capital of the company was increased from £50,000 to £250,000, further valuable contracts are already being entered into which will have the effect of very considerably increasing the income of the company, and I feel sure that at future annual meetings your directors will be able to report a constant and substantial increase in the company's annual income and corresponding profits.

The position of the City Equitable in the insurance world is now…very firmly established, and with the larger resources which it now has I have every reason to anticipate that … the company will continue to grow both in size and importance, and be recognised as the principal reinsurance office in the kingdom.

Perhaps it is unfair to contrast these self-congratulatory pronouncements with what was happening at that very moment in the war

---

[2] 'Treaty' here means a continuing contract with an insurance company, under which a series of reinsurance risks were accepted by the City Equitable.

across the Channel, from which the company was gaining such advantage. The soldierly element of the board would have been acutely aware of the reality behind Mansell's carefully chosen 'unfortunate'. Both March and Clanmorris served in the army during the war, and Clanmorris would resign from the board in 1918 to concentrate on his military duties. Clanmorris's younger brother would win a VC at Jutland; March had already lost a brother in France; Ribblesdale would lose a son at Gallipoli. Every member of the board and staff of the company would have had relatives, friends or neighbours serving (or already killed) on the Western Front.

So it was impossible for anyone to be blasé about the war and we should not imagine a whiff of cynicism in Mansell's words. Business was business, but to put matters in context, suffice to say that both Mansell and Burnett were speaking shortly after the second battle of Ypres, in which the Germans had used mustard gas as a weapon for the first time, and on the day that the less well-known battle of Festubert began. Launched to assist a French offensive near Arras, this week-long British attack culminated in the capture of the village of Festubert, but in doing so gained a single kilometre of ground at a cost of 16,000 casualties.

Another year on, and the City Equitable's progress was still very much in the right direction. Its portfolio was becoming more international, reaching right across Europe though not yet into the American market. Giving his report at the Cannon Street Hotel on 29 May 1916 (coinciding, as it happened, with the battle of Verdun), Burnett — still in the chair but due to hand over to Bevan four weeks later — sounded positively smug.

Premiums had risen to £363,498 and profits to £22,600 after writing off almost £5,000 of expenses in connection with a new issue of preference shares. Investments stood at £106,000, and cash in hand or on deposit at almost £30,000. On the other side of the balance sheet, the fire insurance fund reserve for unexpired risks stood at more than £145,000. Handsome dividends were proposed on both classes of shares.

'Well, gentlemen,' Burnett said, before inviting Mansell to speak, 'I think you may regard the future of the company with every reasonable hope. It possesses undoubted potentialities which in the opinion of the board are likely to be brought to fruition by a combination of a bold and cautious policy, especially as regards the building up of substantial reserves.'

Mansell then went on to reiterate what he had said the previous year about the 'unfortunate' war, and to address himself to the company's future. It was his aim, he said, to make the City Equitable 'one of the strongest reinsurance companies, if not the strongest, in the world', expanding 'gradually and surely' while maintaining the confidence of the leading British fire insurance companies which were the major source of business. But there were opportunities also 'in different parts of the world' which would assist the company to maintain 'the elementary principle of both insurance and reinsurance — namely spread of risk'.

For all these purposes, a further increase of the company's capital might shortly be needed, though it was a feature of the City Equitable's spectacular performance as an investment during these years that the paid-up portion of its capital remained relatively — or as *The Economist* would later say, 'ridiculously' — small, rising only to £75,000 (£15,000 in ordinary shares and £60,000 in 6 per cent preference shares) while the authorised and subscribed capital was increased to £375,000.

The unpaid but callable £300,000 difference represented a margin of safety from the viewpoint of the insurance companies that bought reinsurance cover from the company. But City Equitable investors could never have imagined the catastrophic circumstances in which it would eventually be called up.

'I think it will be agreed,' Mansell concluded, 'that the position of the City Equitable is a unique one in the annals of reinsurance, and with a continuance of the energy combined with the utmost caution which has been exercised in the past, we not only hope but intend... eventually to make the leading reinsurance company in the world a British institution.'

The shareholders were so pleased by this patriotic sentiment that they voted a £1,000 bonus fund to be divided between Mansell and his staff.

Crack Oarsmen

And so the progress of the City Equitable towards the goal articulated by Mansell continued year by year. The next annual meeting, on 12 June 1917, came at the time of the British advance at Messines on the Western Front. The new chairman and major shareholder, Gerard Lee Bevan, opened by saying, 'With your leave, I do not propose to offer any remarks as regards the change in occupation of the chair', which sounds ungracious towards his predecessor but was perhaps merely an example of old-fashioned understatement, intended to sound modest in relation to himself.

Bevan made greater fanfare of the fact that the company now had more shareholders than ever before — many of his associates and Ellis & Co clients having followed him in: 'the list will bear favourable comparison with that of many a larger company'. He was also pleased to announce that two other new directors had joined the board with him, Charles Theodore Barclay and Peter Haig-Thomas.

> These two gentlemen are so well known in business circles that they require no praise from me. In their younger days, as some of you may remember, they were both crack oarsmen, so let us hope that they will renew their triumphs and help year by year to row us past the winning post.

Theodore Barclay, known to his friends as 'Pubbles', had been a friend of Bevan since childhood. They were distant cousins with multiple connections. Theodore's grandfather Ford Barclay had been senior partner of Ellis & Co, and his father Henry Ford Barclay, who married a Miss Gurney, had been a partner both in the Gurney bank in Norwich and in Overend & Gurney, the City discount house which had collapsed so scandalously in 1866 — though its partners, incidentally, were all acquitted of fraud.

The Overend crash had consumed a slice of the family fortune, but the Barclay coffers had been restored by the success of the Gutta Percha Company, whose resinous product was used for insulating underwater telegraph cables and of which Henry Ford Barclay was a director. Theodore's eldest brother Hugh was vice-chairman of Barclays Bank.

A couple of years older than Bevan, Theodore too had made a successful career in the Stock Exchange, beginning as a 'railway jobber' (a market maker in railway stocks) with the firm of Hensley and Aston — where he was believed to be the first Etonian ever to become a jobber, an occupation that was sometimes likened to being a barrow-boy at the Covent Garden fruit and vegetable market. In 1909 he had moved upmarket, as it were, to join the broking firm of Sheppards & Co, which had a strong Gurney family connection. There he had swiftly risen to senior partner.

Barclay had been a great athlete in his youth, having been captain of boats at Eton, rowing twice for Cambridge in the Boat Race against Oxford, and winning the Silver Goblets at Henley Royal Regatta in a record time. But by the time he reached the height of his business career his health was poor, a bout of typhoid having weakened his heart.

Peter Haig-Thomas — a big, colourful character in this story — was still very much involved in rowing as a coach, and in full vigour in every way when he joined the City Equitable board aged 34. He came from a family of Welsh coal-owners in Aberdare, and brought useful political connections as well as industrial experience and a distinctly gung-ho spirit.

An only child, he had inherited a big pile of money with which to dabble in the world of investment. He was the most bullish of all Bevan's associates, investing personally on a large scale in several of his high-risk propositions. With a powerful physique — at his peak he weighed in at 18 stone on a five-foot-ten-inch frame — came the personality of what would be called in modern parlance an Alpha Male, and a tendency to leap before he looked.

Haig-Thomas's family came from modest farming antecedents. But his uncle, David Alfred Thomas, a former MP for Merthyr Tydfil, had emerged as one of the most successful entrepreneurs in the South Wales coalfields, where for many years he managed the huge Cambrian Colliery in the Rhondda, scene of a terrible explosion in 1905 which killed 33 miners.

In 1913 David Thomas secured the family fortune by merging Cambrian with three adjacent collieries — operating between them 19 mines, and producing more than three million tons of coal per annum. The new grouping was then floated on the Stock Exchange as Consolidated Cambrian Ltd, with a capital of £2 million.

Peter Haig-Thomas was a director (later managing director, and eventually chairman) of Consolidated Cambrian. Ellis & Co was the broker for the flotation, which may explain how he and Bevan first met. They were also involved together — presumably at Bevan's instigation — in the flotation in 1914 of Southern Brazil Electric, of which both became directors.

Uncle David Thomas meanwhile went on to become an important public figure as Lord (later Viscount) Rhondda, Lloyd George's emissary to the United States at the beginning of the first world war. He survived the sinking of the *Lusitania* in May 1915, and was later president of the local government board and minister of food control.

The three key elements of Peter Haig-Thomas's life story are money, rowing and women. He had first married Maud Nelson (whose brother Roland had rowed with him at Eton and Cambridge) but she died from complications following the birth of their third child. He was married for the second time in 1917 to Lady Alexandra Agar, eldest daughter of the wealthy 4th Earl of Normanton.

It was characteristic of Peter that their honeymoon was combined with his favourite hobby of big-game hunting. They spent it shooting lions in the Sudan, and the family photograph album showed the couple, both wearing long shorts and carrying heavy rifles, lodged up a tree as they waited for their prey. It was equally characteristic of the era that when Lady Alexandra found her head-gear unsatisfactory, a lady's maid was despatched from London via Suez laden with hatboxes.

The Haig-Thomas surname requires brief explanation. Haig was the maiden name of Peter's mother Rose — she was a cousin of Sir Douglas Haig, the commander of British forces in France throughout much of the first world war — and there was a double family link because her sister Sybil had married Peter's uncle David. At the insistence of Rose, who evidently thought Thomases were too common in both senses, Peter hyphenated his middle name to make it part of his surname, just before his second wedding.

Peter had been the first of his family to enjoy an expensive private education, and like Barclay it was at Eton that he began to distinguish himself as an oarsman. He went on to gain a blue in his freshman year at Cambridge in 1902, rowed in three winning Cambridge boats, was president of the university boat club in 1904, and made a late return to the crew for a rare fourth blue in 1905, when Cambridge lost by three lengths. No intellectual, he failed to achieve a degree but went on to win numerous rowing trophies at Henley, and for the Leander club in international competition.

Though his own top-class rowing career ended in his mid twenties, Haig-Thomas was a physical fitness fanatic for the rest of his life, so competitive that he could not bear to be overtaken in the street by anyone walking faster than him. As we shall later see, it was for his contribution to rowing, as a veteran Boat Race coach with very forceful opinions, that he would ultimately be remembered.

As a businessman, his record was rather less impressive. He would collect a clutch of directorships as a result of his connection with Bevan and Hatry — and lose a substantial portion of his fortune investing in the companies concerned — in addition to his leading role in Consolidated Cambrian, which itself came to grief in the 1920s.

According to his grandson Tony Haig-Thomas, who knew him well in his last years and was fond of him for all his faults and foibles, 'he really didn't know a debit from a credit... You'd have to say he had no financial acumen at all.'

The fact that both these new directors were Old Etonians, giving Bevan's old school an almost clean sweep of the City Equitable boardroom, must have made it easier for him to commit his later deceits unchallenged. In such a socially homogeneous group, who would ever want to rock the boat? It was a point picked up by Galsworthy in the fictionalised version of the City Equitable story into which we shall dip in Chapter Twelve, though the novelist chose a different school: 'On the Board they had all, as it were, been at Winchester together!'

A Nine Years' Wonder

Back to the business in hand at the 1917 annual general meeting of the City Equitable. Premium income had risen to £618,000, despite relatively little growth in fire reinsurance, Bevan told the assembled shareholders. The difference had come in the marine sector: British insurers had been writing more marine business as a result of the war — and, after 'our most careful and painstaking consideration', not to mention 'exhaustive enquiries' and 'strong recommendations from various influential sources', the new City Equitable regime had decided to plunge in after them. Such was the initial success of this diversification that £36,000 had been set aside against a potential tax charge on 'excess profits'.

Once again, the strength of the balance sheet was heavily advertised. British government stocks accounted for more than four-fifths of investments held, and £100,000 had been subscribed to a British War Loan. Reserves now amounted to £363,000, and the directors intended to make the year-by-year building of reserves 'our chief aim... so that we may as rapidly as possible reach the high standard of financial stability which forms such a striking feature of the great British insurance companies, and is a household word throughout the world'.

'As to the future outlook, gentlemen,' Bevan concluded, 'I can see no cause for other than confidence.' The shareholders evidently thought so too, and one of them, a Mr Monro, proposed additional remuneration of £200 a year for the chairman and £50 for each of the directors, in addition to their entitlement under the company's articles of association — which had been fixed at £250 a year at a time when the shareholders 'did not dream of having such figures presented to them' as had been tabled today.

The motion was passed, and Bevan acknowledged the shareholders' generosity — pointing out that several of the directors, including himself, were now also significant investors in the City Equitable for the simple reason that they felt they were 'backing a winner'.

'A hearty vote of thanks to the chairman' concluded the meeting. It was, we may guess, followed by a suitably hearty lunch.

And so to the next annual meeting, on 28 May 1918, when war was still raging: the Germans were advancing across the Aisne, north-east of Paris, and bombarding the capital, while the RAF was mounting bombing raids into Germany. But at Winchester House in Old Broad Street, Bevan was again able to announce 'very satisfactory' financial results and good news on almost all fronts.

He began by welcoming the appointment to the board of Henry (later Sir Henry) Grayson, managing director of a long-established family shipbuilding and repairing business on the Mersey and the Admiralty's wartime director of ship repairs, an appointment which carried a colonel's commission in the Royal Marines. Grayson was 'a household name' in his industry, according to Bevan, and he clearly brought serious expertise to the marine side of the City Equitable portfolio.

And it was indeed the marine department that was driving the company's growth: marine premiums amounted to £740,000 for the year gone by, while on the fire account, premium income had risen from £358,000 to £458,000. In real terms (that is, allowing for the high level of wartime inflation) the company had multiplied its income seven times over since the start of the war, and its profits for the year stood at almost £97,000.

Bevan acknowledged, however, (in the very first hint from anyone that market conditions might ever turn against the City Equitable) that the war-risk element of the surge on the marine side was 'a purely temporary business and may lapse at any moment'. But he also reckoned the company now had 'such a valuable and far-reaching marine connection that even when we revert to normal times we believe we can not only maintain but even improve upon the figures in this year's balance sheet.'

What he did not say, until a year later, was that the City Equitable and other war-risk insurers and reinsurers had been having a pretty torrid time during the early months of 1917 when German U-boats resumed a campaign of unrestricted attacks against merchant and civilian passenger vessels. The German strategy, conceived by Admiral von Holzendorff, was to sink so much British tonnage that Britain would simply run out of ships and sue for peace before the Americans could intervene.

In the course of February and March 1917, U-boats torpedoed a million tons of shipping; in April, another 880,000 tons, with an 'actual loss ratio' for the insurers involved of 93 per cent; in May and June, another 1.3 million tons. So it seems odd that Bevan did not choose to allude to these horrific events in his speech covering the year in which they would certainly have impacted on the City Equitable's claims record.

It was never his way to linger over bad news. Instead, he emphasised the good shape of the balance sheet: investments now stood at £337,000, double the previous year's figure, and cash in hand had also almost doubled to £123,000. What he did not talk about was the way he was now handling the company's liquid assets.

Soon after his arrival in 1916, he had established a 'finance committee' consisting of himself, Peter Haig-Thomas and Henry Grenside, with complete discretion to act as they thought wise within a limit of £5,000 per investment. That limit had in fact been brushed aside right from the start, and there had been fundamental confusion about the committee's role: Haig-Thomas and Grenside apparently believed it existed only to decide on long-term investments, while the rest of the board assumed it was also looking after short-term placement of surplus funds.

In practice, the committee rarely did anything other than rubber-stamp decisions already taken by Bevan, and the pattern of its investments would become imprudent to the point of utter folly. Yet neither the board nor the shareholders of the Company would have an inkling of what was going on until it was too late; more of all that shortly.

Bevan did address one problem at the 1918 meeting, however, albeit of an administrative nature. There was a rather large current asset in the form of uncollected premiums, £626,000, which attracted some comment from the floor — but Bevan attributed it in part to insurance companies being understaffed because of the war rather than 'any lack of care... It takes many months to collect them but we are always jogging along, and we hope after the war we shall be able to reduce that figure substantially in proportion to the other figures in the balance sheet.'

And he had a couple of hiccups to report in the foreign portfolio. 'The Russian business'— embarked upon after a visit two years earlier to Petrograd[3] — had been thrown into turmoil by the Bolshevik revolution. The volume of the City Equitable's Russian accounts was quite small, but it had become impossible to obtain up-to-date information from Petrograd, and with the concurrence of the auditors, a provision of £21,000 had been made against the company's Russian exposure.

Ever the optimist — and increasingly fond of striking statesman-like poses — Bevan expressed the hope that 'the better elements in Russia' would rally against the Bolsheviks, and that the western allies would not abandon them. 'Then when the time comes — as come it must — that the Russian people reawaken to a sense of their

---

[3] Petrograd was the name given to St Petersburg in 1914, until it became Leningrad in 1924.

greatness, they will surely turn with especial gratitude to those who have never lost faith in them or forsaken them in the darkest hour of their calamity.'

Meanwhile, the biggest hit to the fire account had been 'the conflagration at Salonika', better known today as the Great Thessaloniki Fire which swept through Greece's second largest city on 18 August 1917. Some 9,500 houses and 4,000 shops were burned to the ground, and those that had insurance had mostly obtained it from British companies, led by the North British & Mercantile (later part of Commercial Union) which paid out on no less than 3,000 claims. Bevan was pleased to report, however, that thanks to Mansell's 'sound principles and correct methods', the impact of reinsurance claims passed through to the City Equitable for this disaster 'did not exceed three or four weeks' ordinary losses'.

And the chairman was by no means discouraged from looking for more foreign business, though his latest initiative was a little closer to home — and, as we shall see in the next chapter, closer to his heart in a more personal sense:

It may interest you to know that the manager and myself have visited Paris on more than one occasion and have succeeded in securing treaties with several of the leading French companies... Every fresh link forged in unison with those marvellous Allies of ours is a matter for reciprocal congratulation and we cordially hope that the relations which we have opened up there will prove to be of a permanent character and to our mutual advantage.

As had by now become traditional, the meeting concluded with a round of back-slapping for all concerned. The most enthusiastic shareholder was again Mr Monro: 'wonderful' was his word for the progress of the company, and it was echoed back to him, along with 'a very high degree of excellence', in Mansell's response on behalf of himself and his staff.

'We have heard of a nine days' wonder,' quipped Monro to cap everyone, 'but we have in this company a nine years' wonder.'

CHAPTER FIVE

The Post-Armistice Boom

'I've got ambitions — I'm a serious man. Suppose I was to consider this and that, and every potty objection — where should I get to? Nowhere!... I've got the guts, and I've got the money; and I don't sit still on it. I'm going ahead because I believe in myself.'

The unprincipled industrialist Hornblower,
in John Galsworthy, *The Skin Game* (1920 play)

The Lucky Englishman

By the time the war was nearing its end, many things were changing in Gerard Bevan's life.

No one ever directly accused him of being, in Stanley Baldwin's resonant phrase, one of those 'hard-faced men who look as if they had done well out of the war'. But the truth was that he had: his bold move into the reinsurance business combined with the success he had made of Ellis & Co despite wartime capital-market restrictions had turned his already substantial wealth into a seven-figure paper fortune.

And his lifestyle had become correspondingly opulent. It would be said later that he was spending £50,000 a year on his homes, his collections, his travels and his mistresses — of whom there seem to have been at least three in the immediate post-war years. 'So long as I had plenty of money,' Bevan told his Austrian captors, 'There were many women who were prepared to link their fate with mine.'

The one whose fate was destined to be linked with his until his death was a young dancer called Maria Letitia Pertuisot, always known as Jeanne, whose family came from the Burgundy region of France. According to one account he first met her in 1916 at the elegant spa town of Vichy in the Auvergne, when she was in her early twenties and he was 47. Hugely fashionable during the 'Belle Epoque' for its thermal baths and its opera house, Vichy was a much quieter place in the middle of the war. Perhaps Bevan had gone there to take the waters for his incipient rheumatism.

However they met, Jeanne gradually became a semi-permanent fixture of his life. From June 1919 — so it would be said at his divorce hearing — she was staying regularly with him in Paris, whenever he was there on business. But that did not mean he was faithful to her, any more than he was faithful to his wife.

There was, for example, a petite dancer from the famous Folies Bergere music hall in Paris, known only (to readers of *World's Pictorial News*, that is) as Madame F. Having eyed her in the floorshow, Bevan had sent his card to her dressing room in classic Stage Door Johnny style. All had gone well, and he took her with him for a weekend in Monte Carlo — another of his regular haunts — where she lost some of his money at the casino tables.

Bevan enjoyed casino gambling, even though he once described betting on horses as 'the verge of madness'. He preferred high-stakes roulette and baccarat, and was known (though perhaps not always) as 'the lucky Englishman'. A story was told of him being approached as he left the Monte Carlo casino with his winnings one night by a man in evening dress who claimed to know him from London. 'If you'll give me some of the money you have won tonight, I shall thank you to my last hour,' the man pleaded. 'If not, there is only one way out.'

Without comment, Bevan thrust the whole of his winnings into the man's hand and strode off towards his hotel. He was evidently more capable of sudden acts of kindness than of forgiveness: when 'Madame F.' started flirting with another man, he gave her 80,000 francs and told her to get lost.

Some time later, however, she turned up at his office in Cornhill and demanded to see him. She knew he was married, she told him, and she would make trouble unless he paid her off. 'What you suggest has the ugly sound of blackmail,' Bevan responded. 'I don't suppose you want to see the inside of an English prison, but that's where you'll go if you come to me again with such a proposition. Now go.'

She went — but Bevan sent £100 to her hotel later that day, presumably to be sure she had enough to settle her bill and catch the boat-train back to Paris.

Undeterred by that experience, Bevan also took up with a beautiful Belgian girl, yet another dancer, called Meddy Fabry, who he met at Nice and brought to London. (Since we are in the realm of tabloid muckraking here, the reader might wonder whether Meddy Fabry and 'Madame F.' might have been one person, made to appear as two to add substance to the 'Don Juan' story — but the detail of their circumstances differs sufficiently to suggest that the letter F was coincidental in their names.)

While Meddy was with Bevan some time in 1921 — so she told the dogged newshound — he went off to Scotland to complete a deal, presumably connected with Jute Industries in Dundee, of which we shall learn more later in this chapter. He told her he was going to make 'millions', though he was presumably talking in francs rather than pounds. He had said he would give her 'a handsome present' from the proceeds: 'Would 200,000 francs set you up?' But the deal fell through, and the present was never delivered — though there is a suggestion that Bevan eventually gave Meddy enough to leave the stage and start a little business of her own in Brussels.

Lavish presents offered but not delivered, or given but taken back, are an incidental feature of stories about Bevan. We shall hear later of a block of shares he gave first to his daughter Sheila, then reclaimed and gave to Jeanne instead. And Pleasance Bevan recorded this anecdote:

Once when in Paris and in one of his recurring low-ebb financial moments, he asked [Jeanne] to let him look at the pearls he had given her (magnificent, I always heard) as he thought something was wrong with the clasp, or some such excuse. So she handed them to him and he rushed off before she could stop him and took them to a jeweller and sold them. A quick worker, our Gerard!

With such a complicated private life, there was little wonder that Bevan had begun to spend less time with Sophie and their daughters. Though a thin semblance of marital respectability was maintained in Upper Grosvenor Street, and rather more so at Littlecote, Bevan actually lived apart from his wife, at least during the working week, from sometime around the end of 1918. His real London home was a suite of rooms in the Carlton Hotel at the corner of Haymarket and Pall Mall, and he also kept a suite at Claridge's in Paris.

The Carlton — opened in 1899 by the great hotelier Cézar Ritz and the chef Georges Auguste Escoffier after both had been sacked from the Savoy for fiddling the books and, in the chef's case, taking bribes from suppliers — was designed to outmatch the Savoy in luxury and elegance. Built in the French Empire style, it was more or less symmetrical with Her Majesty's Theatre (by the same architect, C. J. Phipps, though he died before the hotel was completed) which it adjoined, and which survives today.[1]

Winston Churchill dined regularly at the Carlton, and was doing so on the evening war was declared in 1914. The young Mae West stayed there, and once hinted that she had a brief encounter with one of the hotel's pastry chefs, 'Ho… Ho… Ho… Something', who had 'the slinkiest eyes'. If true, this was none other than Ho Chi Minh, the future Vietnamese communist leader, who worked at the hotel from 1913 to 1917.

---

[1] Badly bombed during the second world war, the Carlton remained semi-derelict until it was demolished in 1959, to be replaced by New Zealand House, an 18-storey block in the charmless 1960s style.

When Bevan moved in, Escoffier — though much occupied as a consultant to other hotels and a designer of kitchens for ocean liners — was still the Carlton's figurehead and *maître de cuisine*. We can picture him touring the dining room in spotless chef's whites, receiving the acclaim of his plutocratic clientele: '*Ah, bonsoir, Monsieur Bevan. Mademoiselle, enchanté. I trust everything is to your satisfaction...*'

The Carlton was as grand a London *pied-à-terre* as it would be possible to imagine. Bevan's suite cost him £2,000 a year, and he had it fitted out with his own fine furniture and works of art. Given his habit of buying expensive jewellery for his lady friends and relations, he was no doubt also an important customer of the Mappin & Webb kiosk in the hotel's foyer.

He continued to travel a great deal, most regularly to Paris — where he acquired not only a suite of rooms (and a dedicated manservant when he was in residence) but also a substantial personal shareholding in Claridge's on the Champs Elysées, a palatial hotel opened in 1914 which advertised itself as 'the most modern in Europe', with a grill room, tea rooms and 'Swimming Pool with Hammam'.

It was a sophisticated and raffish place. The setting for murder in one of Georges Simenon's Maigret detective stories, *Les Caves du Majestic* (1939), it would also become the home of another fraudster, Alexandre Stavisky, who (not dissimilar to Clarence Hatry in the later phase of his career) made himself notorious by issuing hundreds of millions of francs worth of fake bonds in the name of the municipal pawnshop of the city of Bayonne.

One way or another, Bevan was beginning to live a life removed from the familial influences that might have kept him on the straight and narrow. If the severity of Sophie's demeanour and personal philosophy had ever constrained his behaviour, it had surely ceased to do so. As for paternal influence, Bevan's father Frank was by now in his late seventies and in declining health, having at last vacated the chair of Barclays (though he kept a seat on the board) and having modestly refused a peerage — much to the chagrin of his eldest son Cosmo, who would have inherited it.

Frank spent his sunset years at his Mayfair house doing jigsaw puzzles under the solicitous care of his daughters and his butler. As we have seen, he was never a stern influence on his sons at any stage of their lives. But if his status as a great man of the City had occasionally caused Gerard to temper the way he did business, for fear of causing family embarrassment, that factor too was now fading.

Cosmo Bevan, who was vice-chairman of Barclays for a short period after Frank retired from the chair, certainly kept an eye on what Gerard was up to in the stockmarket and elsewhere, and is said to have once told their ailing father, 'Your son is a blackguard.' Greatly upset, the old man told Cosmo not to talk that way about his own half-brother. 'Well, he is,' Cosmo retorted sharply, and it was perhaps a blessing that Frank died in August 1919, well before that opinion was confirmed by Gerard's criminal conviction.

This was, then, a period in which Bevan was at the zenith of his City rise, but beginning to yield to temptation and folly in a variety of ways. His respectability and eminence were confirmed by a string of directorships and his appointment to the Tobacco and Matches Control Board — his only venture into public service — which, so it was later said in court, 'occupied some hours of his time daily'. Yet his inclination towards sharp dealing and ill-judged risk-taking was about to be given fuller rein than ever before, in the post-Armistice stockmarket boom.

A Craze for Speculation

On the day the war ended — Monday, 11 November 1918 — the National Anthem was sung in the Stock Exchange, where business had been suspended. In front of the Mansion House, the official residence of the Lord Mayor of London, the Old Hundredth hymn — the one that begins 'All people that on earth do dwell' — rang out from a flag-waving crowd of 100,000 gathered in the rain. It was the end of the most terrible conflict in human history, and the beginning of a peculiarly febrile post-Armistice phase in the financial markets and elsewhere.

Inflation was rampant, Bolshevism in Russia had created new international tensions, trade unionism was on the rise, strikes were widespread. But the Exchange was suddenly busier than it had been at any time since 1914, and most of the action was in industrial stocks.

'The changing over of the world from war to peace called for a general re-stocking of merchandise and goods of every description,' wrote Hubert Meredith. 'Company promoters did not miss this golden opportunity.' *The Economist* called it 'a craze for speculation': the surge of industrial activity to meet pent-up consumer demand was matched by a parallel surge in mergers, flotations and recapitalisations which seemed suddenly to be 'part of the order of nature'.

Under wartime capital controls, an inactive market had prevented owners from realising anything but a war-depressed value for businesses they wanted or needed to sell; now there were many company owners waiting for an opportunity to sell at a more reasonable price, or to raise capital for investment in new factory capacity to meet an anticipated surge in orders. In addition, the experience of the war had made it plain that many of Britain's industrial companies were too small to compete successfully in international markets.

As a result, there was a need to restructure entire industries, bringing together smaller firms, usually family owned and managed, to form new conglomerates with economies of scale in their operations and access through the stockmarket to capital for further development. But the flotation mechanism was more often used to generate cash for family shareholders and promoters rather than to fund expansion of the companies themselves.

The peak of this boom — £170 million of new issues in six months — came in the last quarter of 1919 and the first of 1920. From start to finish, about £400 million of new issues would come to the market before the boom was over. Most were amalgamations of businesses in mining, steel, textiles and the rapidly growing car and motor-component manufacturing sector. Others were capital raisings for established names such as Vickers, Dunlop and J. Lyons, the operator of Corner House restaurants.

In the midst of it all was Bevan's clever collaborator Clarence Hatry, who had invested some of the profit from his City Equitable coup in 1916 into a new vehicle for his undoubted talents, the Commercial Bank of London, what might now be called a 'corporate finance boutique' which he created out of the shell of an unhappy little venture called the Anglo-Japanese Bank.

The Anglo-Japanese story is a diversion at this point, but it offers its own interesting sidelight on the early-20th-century international business scene. It had been launched in 1906 to carry on 'all descriptions of banking business in the large field now open and rapidly extending in Japan, its Dependencies, Korea and the Far East and elsewhere'. Its chairman was Sir Westby Perceval KCMG, a director of the Union Bank of Australia, and the board included the Tyneside industrialist Lord Armstrong and Baron George de Reuter, son of the founder of the telegraph company. Its subscribing shareholders included a number of Japanese banks and trading houses, and its aim was to emulate the success in the Japanese market of established competitors, led by the Hong Kong and Shanghai Bank and the Chartered Bank.

But that proved more of a challenge than its founders anticipated. For the first few years, the bank benefited from abnormally cheap money in Japan, and from Japanese goodwill towards Britain as a result of Anglo-Japanese intelligence co-operation during Japan's naval war with Russia in 1905.

By 1913 losses had accumulated on Japanese government bonds, the business was going nowhere and the dividend had been cancelled. Perceval had resigned and a new chairman, 35-year-old Alexander Roger, was obliged to admit that the original business plan no longer looked viable: 'The difficulties in the way of an English bank's doing business in Japan are very great, owing among other things to the necessity of relying in a great measure on Japanese advice and, to a certain extent, losing English control.'

So adverse were conditions in the East, he went on, that the bank was now trying to build a new portfolio of business in London, and was thinking of changing its name. It might be three years before the dividend was restored, and in the meantime the shares stood at a miserable tuppence three-farthings. 'You can have mine at that price,' one angry shareholder shouted, to which Roger replied, 'I'll take them.'

Roger was a junior partner of the powerful financier Viscount St Davids, whose investment trusts had bought out the remaining Japanese shareholders. The Japanese business was gradually unwound, the name was changed to the Commercial Bank of London, and in March 1914 the capital was reorganised at a substantial loss to original subscribers.

The chairman declared that he hoped this rebirth would be accompanied by 'a fair measure of good fortune' — but then war broke out, and the results announced in May 1915 were 'so discouraging as to make it scarcely worthwhile endeavouring further to make the company a success'. The shareholders resolved to carry on, but only on a very cautious basis. A year later Roger had to tell them that 'until the war is over I cannot conscientiously hold out much hope of any improvement in our earning capacity'.

Then along came Hatry, flushed with cash from his sale of the controlling stake in the City Equitable to Bevan and Haig-Thomas, and full of ideas. He needed a base from which to do deals — and this small bank, reduced to being run on a 'care and maintenance' basis, offered a platform which enabled him to get around the wartime capital control which prevented incorporation of new companies.

In October 1916, Hatry and his fellow investors bought out the existing shareholders of the Commercial Bank at £2 17s 6d per share, a price which Roger — who was serving at the time as director-general of trench warfare supplies at the Ministry of Munitions — felt able to recommend, no doubt with some relief. Haig-Thomas, who still had ample cash in hand, came in for a big stake, and Bevan was probably an investor too, though for reasons we shall see in a moment he did not join the Commercial Bank board.

Roger handed over the chair to Sir Charles Hobhouse, a Bristol MP and former postmaster general who is best remembered for his political diaries, published as *Inside Asquith's Cabinet* (1977).

The newly constituted board included Hatry, Haig-Thomas and a survivor from the previous regime, Captain Cecil Higgins MC, a South American specialist who sat on the board of Southern Brazil Electric with Haig-Thomas and Bevan. A few months later, *The Times* commented:

> The board... is now a strong one. The bank recently moved to new premises at 6 Austin Friars, where it has for some time been actively engaged in the development of British trade and industry. At the present time it is paying special attention to the work of financing shipbuilding and ship repairing.

It was also paying attention to its own capital arrangements. In November 1917, Hatry acquired the British Commercial Bank (formerly Reuter's Bank, an offshoot of the telegraph company) and merged it with the Commercial Bank of London to create a merchant bank that was well poised to take advantage of an upturn in market conditions when the war at last came to an end.

In the course of 1918, reorganisations and flotations were carried out by the Commercial Bank for, among others, the marine engineering firm of Clarke Chapman, the food wholesaling business of Burton, Son and Sanders in Ipswich (Bevan was for a time on the board of both) and G.H. Hirst, one of the oldest names in the Bradford woollen trade. All of this, said Hobhouse, was a credit to the 'brilliant abilities and indomitable industry' of Clarence Hatry — who, we should remember, was still only 30 years old and had no formal training in law, accountancy or banking.

Things got better and better for Hatry. In July 1919, Hobhouse was able to report that 'since the date of the armistice the business of the bank in every department has increased in a most satisfactory way, and very considerable profits have been made.'

Indeed, a profit of £207,000 for 1918 would almost double to £407,000 for the first nine months of 1919. And in December, when another capital reconstruction was announced — to create a capital base of £2,250,000, of which £975,000 would be issued to existing shareholders and £1,275,000 to the public — the published prospectus declared:

> The business is not only very profitable but sound. With what discrimination these operations have been conducted and how… advantageous they are to the public generally is illustrated by the fact that the shares of almost all of the companies reorganised or founded by the Bank, since it came under its present Management, now stand at a premium — in many cases a very considerable one — above the price at which they were offered to the public.

To which the chairman added, when he next spoke to shareholders:

> The Commercial Bank of London has now developed into an industrial bank combining at once some of the best features of the German system, the elasticity of the old-fashioned private banker, and the latest improvements of joint-stock banking and we have managed to seize and occupy a unique position in the financial world.

The shareholders shouted 'Hear! Hear!' and the prospectus named a dozen more companies on which Hatry had exercised his magic.

They included H. and C. Grayson Ltd, the Merseyside ship-building and repairing business of the same Sir Henry Grayson whom Bevan had recruited as a City Equitable director. Leyland Motors, the bus and lorry maker of which both Bevan and Haig-Thomas became directors, had been bought and sold by Hatry 'within the hour' (by George Greenfield's account) at a personal profit of at least £250,000. Agricultural Industries, yet again with Bevan and Haig-Thomas on the board, was a clever repackaging of a bundle of farming and food trading interests at which we shall look more closely in a moment.

Hatry, we should note, was not in the business of bringing established, mainstream companies to market. Just as the grandest

American companies were clients of J.P. Morgan rather than the upstart Goldman Sachs, so British 'blue-chips' of the era took their financial advice from the City's old-established and often aristocratically managed merchant banks and issuing houses, which in turn preferred to deal only with the most reputable stockbroking firms — whose partners moved in the same circle as the banks' directors, or were their brothers and cousins.

As the accountant, regulator and Hatry expert Chris Swinson notes, Hatry's corporate clients were more likely to be 'marginal or "odd" businesses, offering high potential returns'. Or as W.S. Gilbert put it to Sir Arthur Sullivan's tune:

> *No schemes too great and none too small*
> *For Companification!*

One of Hatry's techniques for achieving this was to set up a new company which would buy from the old owners the business to be floated, thus guaranteeing them an exit price. The shares in the new company would then be sold to the market at a price higher than had been given to the old owners — and at a substantial profit to Hatry and his associates.

What was Bevan's professional contribution in all this? Right up until the 'Big Bang' City reforms of the 1980s, when banks were permitted for the first time to acquire stockbroking and jobbing firms, a rigid separation was maintained in flotation and share-issuing work between the functions of the sponsoring bank and the function of the appointed broker. The role of the latter was to ensure that Stock Exchange rules were complied with, to place a portion of the new shares with their investor clients, and to ensure a healthy market in them after the issue was complete.

This was a good business for brokers to be in, and many other member firms were at least as active as Ellis & Co in bringing new names to market during the boom. But a useful contrast can be made with the activities of Cazenove & Akroyds (later just Cazenove & Co), the most self-consciously elitist of partnerships, which was busy building a corporate client list and a capacity to place shares with large institutions that would be the envy of the City for decades to come.

Under the leadership of Claud Serocold and Charles Micklem — the former a charming but shrewd door-opener, the latter a frugal man of detail who invariably chose to travel third-class — Cazenove exercised 'admirable restraint at a time when there was easy money to be made', according to its historian David Kynaston. The firm was involved in only nine new issues in 1919–20 — largely for solid industrial names such as the British Cellulose & Chemical Manufacturing Company and Sheffield Steel Products — when other, more bullish operators notched up as many as 25.

Most tellingly, Kynaston records a brief encounter between Cazenove and Clarence Hatry, who presented a 'perfectly respect-able' draft issue prospectus in which he had taken the liberty of inserting the name of Cazenove & Akroyds as broker — only to find himself being haughtily shown the door by Micklem. It was, says the historian, 'a crucial instance of quality control'.

There were no such difficulties in the relationship between Ellis & Co and Hatry's Commercial Bank; they worked together repeatedly, using well-oiled mechanisms. But given this division of functions it would not have been appropriate for Bevan to sit on the Commercial Bank board even though he may have been a share-holder in it and was a director of several of the companies whose share issues it managed.

Indeed, the potential conflict of interest that might have attracted attention if the City had been more closely regulated in those days was not between Ellis & Co and the Commercial Bank, but between the latter and the City Equitable. By early 1919 there were three City Equitable directors, Haig-Thomas, Lord March and Henry Grenside, on the seven-man Commercial Bank board, from which Captain Higgins had resigned.

At the City Equitable, the 'investment committee' which was by now regularly backing Commercial Bank share deals consisted of two Commercial Bank directors, Haig-Thomas and Grenside, under the leadership of Bevan, whose links to Hatry could hardly have been closer. It was impossible for this committee to take objective risk decisions on the City Equitable's behalf in relation to Commercial Bank issues. Overall, it was a deeply dangerous connection.

What is certain about it is that Bevan's skills — including the ability to preserve the appearance of a healthy market in any given share even when there wasn't one — were as vital to Hatry's success as Hatry's relentless deal-making was to the rise of Bevan's reputation and fortune.

The duo were in many ways chalk and cheese, but their stories are inseparable. And they were both by now immensely wealthy.

Bevan spent his money elegantly — on beautiful objects for his collection and gifts for his ladies; on his farm and garden at Littlecote and on entertaining business connections there; on travelling abroad and playing the tables at Monte Carlo.

Hatry was flashier, throwing famously lavish parties at his house in Upper Brook Street, Mayfair, round the corner from the Bevans. One of his racehorses, Furious, won the 1920 Lincoln Handicap at Doncaster, the first big event of the flat-racing season. His yacht Westward, built for an American millionaire and requiring a crew of 40, was the largest racing yacht in England in its day, and cost him a reputed £15,000 a year to maintain.

But Bevan's successful contribution to their joint enterprise was often achieved not only to the ultimate cost of City Equitable shareholders and creditors, but at the expense of Ellis & Co clients who took his advice. Typical was Colonel Reginald Grove, a retired officer who had commanded a battalion of the Cheshire Regiment until 1910, returning to service as an assistant adjutant and quartermaster-general during the first world war. According to his grandson, the Colonel 'never had much money... [he] invested little bits in investments that he knew nothing about and then repeated the process until disaster struck.' Bevan evidently encouraged him in that habit, costing him some £2,000 he could ill-afford to lose.

Among the shares Bevan persuaded Grove to buy were those of Agricultural Industries, an archetypal Hatry promotion. This was a company formed to take over a large farming enterprise in Lincolnshire owned by a family called Dennis, with some 9,000 acres under crops at the time of the flotation in November 1919, making it the largest producer of potatoes in the United Kingdom. It had plans to increase that figure to 17,000 acres by 1922 and claimed to farm 'on the most up-to-date scientific principles' using 'the most efficient labour-saving machinery'.

To repackage a farm, however big and advanced, as a listed company, was something of a stockmarket novelty. But the venture was given corporate credibility by the fact that it also owned an import-export trading business in agricultural and orchard produce, conducted at Covent Garden, Spitalfields and King's Cross markets. It had ambitions to build factories 'for the bottling and preserving of small vegetables' and (we can almost hear Bevan's voice in the prospectus here) operated branches of the trading business in Paris and the United States that had 'been greatly hampered by the war but will gradually become normal again'.

Of course it also had the usual impressive board of directors. In the chair was Sir Ailwyn Fellowes KCVO, a Norfolk farmer who had been president of the Board of Agriculture in Arthur Balfour's cabinet and was now deputy chairman of the Great Eastern Railway. He must often have been confused with his nephew, the Hon. Ailwyn Fellowes, the junior partner at Ellis & Co (an Eton and Trinity man like Bevan, as it happened, and the husband of a French princess) who probably had a hand in bringing all the parties together for the flotation.

At the table with Sir Ailwyn were Viscount Wolmer, the MP for Aldershot; Colonel Archibald Weigall, MP for Horncastle in Lincolnshire; and a prominent hotelier, Sir Francis Towle, who was a director of the Commercial Bank. When Weigall resigned a few months after the flotation to become governor of South Australia, he was replaced by two more grandees: Charles Adeane, a distant Bevan relation who was the lord lieutenant of Cambridgeshire, and Captain the Hon. Algernon Fitzroy, MP for Daventry and chairman of the House of Commons agriculture committee.

If all those Establishment names reassured would-be investors that the proposition was reputable, the last three on the list underlined the possibility of rich returns to come: Bevan, Haig-Thomas and Hatry.

'The company opens up a comparatively fresh field for the company shareholder,' commented *The Economist* at the time of the flotation, 'and for that reason is hardly suitable for the small investor, who will be well advised to wait and watch progress.' But under Bevan's guidance, Colonel Grove did not wait or watch for long. Early in 1920, he bought 1,380 shares at six shillings per share, followed by another 400 at 19 shillings and fourpence ha'penny, making a total investment of a little over £800.

There is no record of whether Grove lost money on Agricultural Industries — which had some difficulties but was not one of the Hatry companies that failed in 1922–23. The fact that he was still an active Ellis & Co client in 1920 shows how persuasive Bevan could be, however: the colonel had already experienced something of a rollercoaster ride with his investments.

In the previous autumn, Grove had expressed concern about two other shares Ellis & Co had put him into. Bevan's reply displays his perpetual bullishness combined with a willingness to resort to technicalities unlikely to be understood by such an unsophisticated client.

The first company referred to, originally called Gath y Chaves but renamed South American Stores when it was restructured for listing in London, was a chain of department stores across Argentina and Chile which had suffered a strike by seamstresses, who were paid a pittance to work in dreadful conditions. Bevan was one of its directors:

13 October 1919

Dear Colonel Grove,

As regards South American Stores, the shares fell a little on the strike that took place in May and June of this year, and have not since recovered, but I look upon this depression as purely temporary. The business is now doing splendidly again, and is rapidly making up for the losses it sustained during the six weeks of the strike.

As regards Amalgamated Industrials, I hope you will not be in any hurry to take your profit. A new and important group have come into the concern, and they are going to have shares issued to them in return for the businesses they are bringing in. When effect has been given to the agreement, the Company will have a capital of £5,000,000, of which £4,000,000 will be issued, and it will own something like 12 different industrial concerns, principally Cotton, Shipping, and Steel. The net income from these concerns will be at least £1,250,000 … so that the margin over the proposed dividend on the Ordinary, viz., 10 per cent, will be very large indeed.

It will certainly be the most important combination of its kind in the country, and there ought always to be an active market in the shares. Under these circumstances I look forward to very considerable appreciation in the shares, and I strongly advise you to hold them.

Yours sincerely,
G.L. Bevan

The 'new and important group' referred to was that of a ship owner called John Slater, to whom Hatry had sold a controlling interest in Amalgamated Industrials, just four months after the flotation, for a seven-figure profit. There was some industrial sense in a conglomerate that embraced coalmining, iron and steel, Clydeside shipbuilding, trawler owning, fish merchanting, and marine insurance — the combination of which could be described, at a stretch, as a form of vertical integration. If it made less sense to add Lancashire cotton mills into the mix — well, cotton was a growth industry too, so why not? At the height of the boom, investors were not much troubled by questions of organisational logic.

When the Amalgamated Industrials prospectus was issued in June, the *Financial Times* commented:

> There will probably be ample opportunities for the profitable employment of funds in British industry during the peace era on which we are now entering, but in the case of a concern like this it all depends on the experience and wisdom of the Board whether good use is made of the cash entrusted to it. The directors in this instance are connected with well-known concerns of varied character, which should be of benefit to them in the conduct of the new venture, and the bulk of the support which the issue may get will certainly come from those having personal knowledge of their record… those having confidence in the commercial reputation of the directors and willing to back it up will probably get a fair run for their money.

Among the directors the *FT* was referring to was Sir Douglas Dawson from the City Equitable (though in this prospectus one of his other directorships, of the National Bank of Ireland, was shown against his name) and Hon. Ailwyn Fellowes from Ellis & Co. Three other members of the board were recognisable as directors of other companies in which Hatry had a hand.

Although all of these except the younger Fellowes came off the board around the time of Slater's arrival, to be replaced by representatives of various companies within the Amalgamated Industrials group, Hatry followers must have been relieved by the announcement that Hatry and Haig-Thomas had agreed to become joint financial advisers to the new board.

Slater himself said in his chairman's address in October 1919 that the original prospectus of Amalgamated Industrials had offered a distinct lack of 'concrete information' — but 'I think it was largely due to the success which has usually attended Mr Hatry's undertakings that the public readily seized again the opportunity of following his advice and leadership'.

One phrase in Bevan's letter to Grove, 'there ought always to be an active market in the shares', looks ironic in hindsight. As P.S. Manley wrote in an analysis of the City Equitable crash in *Abacus* magazine in 1973:

> At times, [Bevan] repurchased blocks of shares when [clients who had bought shares in new issues] wished to sell and placed them on Ellis & Co's books, thus piling up the firm's holdings in shares in which there was little or no market, then or later... There is a significant parallel with the way in which Hatry in the same period was sowing some of the seeds of his own downfall... He consistently followed a policy of providing a ready market himself for shares he had promoted in order to maintain prices.

In ignorance of how this trick was done, the combination of the names of Hatry, Haig-Thomas and Bevan must have looked gold-plated to the likes of Colonel Grove. In fact it was John Slater who led Amalgamated Industrials to its unhappy fate.

Funded by a £4 million issue of debenture stock in July 1920 to which Ellis & Co was again the broker, Slater bought up a number of ship-owning businesses, including the Ulster and Cork Steamship companies. Two years later, the group was severely over-extended and in trouble. It went into receivership and most of the debenture holders accepted an offer of £30 per £100 of stock.

Rather remarkably, Hatry sued a newspaper called the *National Champion* for suggesting that he rather than Slater was responsible for what had happened — and he won his case.

As for Colonel Grove, he added a rueful hand-written note to the letter from Bevan that he carefully preserved: 'This company went bust and I lost £1,000. I could have made a profit but this letter induced me to hold on.'

Eminently Healthy

Back at the City Equitable, Bevan had another year of 'eminently healthy' performance to tell his shareholders about at their general meeting on 14 May 1919. He reported that net profit for the year to February had climbed to £188,000. Total assets had risen from £1.2 million to £1.8 million, and the problem alluded to the previous year, of a disportionately large volume of uncollected premiums, had been satisfactorily addressed: that figure had been brought down from £625,000, just over half the balance sheet, to £413,000, or less than a quarter of it.

Income growth had followed its customary upward gradient. Fire premiums were up by a third at £613,000, amid such a glut of new business opportunities that 'we have to exercise unusual discrimination in the selection of our treaties'. On the marine front the increase was even more dramatic, from £740,000 to £1.35 million.

'Those of you who study insurance accounts' would have noticed something odd about that last item, the chairman went on. Many marine insurance (as opposed to reinsurance) companies had been showing a marked diminution in their premiums for the year under review, for the simple reason that 'war risk' business had come to an end. The City Equitable's figures would inevitably follow the same trend — but with a time-lag of about six months, so the difference had not shown through by February 1919. But 'the falling off, when it comes, need not in any way disturb your minds. Our marine business is in an extremely healthy and satisfactory condition.'

It was at this point that Bevan waxed eloquent on the subject of war risks and losses of civilian shipping — the missing portion, as it were, of his speech from the previous year. In the first phase of the war, he said, premiums had risen but shipping losses generally had not, so there had been good profits for those who got in early. But then came those terrible months in 1917:

...the time within the memory of us all, and perhaps the gravest in the history of our race, when the enemy flung the last shreds of conscience and humanity to the winds, and respecting neither sex nor child, not even the sacred flag hoist over their hapless victims by the Sisters of Mercy,[2] they became the desperadoes of the sea.

After mid-1917, however, shipping losses steadily declined — and although war-risk premium rates declined also, there were increased profits to be made: 'War underwriting turned out to be better business at two guineas per cent than it had been a few months previously at five or six guineas per cent. All honour to our sailors who made this possible!'

Bevan also raised 'the question of American business', which he and Mansell had looked at but drawn back from, since it would have required a very substantial commitment of the company's capital and management resources to make any impact on the American reinsurance market, whereas 'it is easy to keep in touch with our European friends by periodical visits across the Channel'.

He then gave an entertaining account of how he and the general manager did this, in the course of a section of the meeting which dealt with a rationalisation of the share capital — a proposal to convert the existing ordinary and preference shares into a single class of ordinary shares which would give the company a more conventional profile. The capital structure had hitherto caused confusion, he said, not least when seeking new business abroad, because it was unusual for a reinsurance company (or indeed, he might have added, any public company) to have four times as many preference shares as ordinaries.

You must appreciate that with the growth of our business, Mr Mansell and myself often have to travel to negotiate treaties... We may fairly claim that we have met with a considerable measure of success. In the course of our negotiations we

---

[2] This seems to have been a reference to the sinking in June 1917 of the *Llandovery Castle*, a British merchant vessel serving as a Canadian hospital ship; she was torpedoed while returning to Liverpool from Halifax, Nova Scotia, and among those who perished were 14 Canadian nursing sisters known as 'Angels of Mercy'.

are constantly asked what our capital is, and I assure you it is no easy matter to explain.

Last November, for instance, Mr Mansell and myself visited Italy with the idea of opening up relations there. It was, I may tell you, not exactly a joy ride… our troubles began with our visits to the insurance companies. The smallest dwarf-sized dictionary would easily comprise our joint knowledge of Italian, and the Italians themselves did not seem to us particularly good linguists.

The first question the managers invariably asked was 'What is your capital?' After a few ineffectual struggles, Mr Mansell suggested that it would not be immoral to forget the existence of the Ordinary shares. What happened then I really have not a notion. The fact is we used to say what we could. Anyway, after leaving our photographs and our mother's maiden name at no less than three different Consulates, we managed to return with a treaty or two in our pockets.

Gentlemen, we shall have to make many other similar visits. We have relations with numerous foreign companies, French, Italian, Dutch, Spanish. We are out to get all the business — that is, all the good business — we can for you, but we want you to help us by making it as easy as possible, and that is why I have no hesitation in asking you to consent to the simplification of the capital as submitted to you in this resolution.

The resolution was carried by 202,560 shares against 4,504 — though oddly enough, the change of capital structure was never actually put into effect — as laughter gave way to cheers at the end of a virtuoso performance.

Bevan finished his main address to the meeting with a couple of other witticisms. Paying his customary tribute to the manager and his staff, he complemented them on the 'zeal, insight and intelligence' they had shown during the past year, but noted that 'the seven-hour day — or is it six? — may burrow underground but shows no sign of ascending to the company's office.' That was a reference to a recent miners' strike demanding a reduction in the working day below ground from eight hours to six; in response, a commission chaired by Sir John Sankey had proposed seven.

Bevan's other *bon mot* was perhaps a device to avoid talking about the future direction of the company's business, which was a lot less clear than the past:

> Gentlemen, it has been remarked that optimism only becomes necessary when you get into a hole. It seems to me, therefore, that it would be a work of superogation on my part to indulge in flights of fancy as to our future. You have heard my story of the year's doings, and I propose to let the facts unadorned speak for themselves.

If he had done just that, however, he would have revealed that the balance sheet he had just presented contained a very big lie. It showed as an asset a loan to Ellis & Co of a little over £50,000. But the true figure of Ellis & Co's debt to the City Equitable was nearer £320,000, the bulk of it unsecured. In its place on the balance sheet was a holding of British government stock which had never, in fact, been in the City Equitable's possession.

This was the beginning of the pattern of fraud which would bring the company to ruin: the 'hole' which no amount of optimism on Bevan's part could eventually hide. If the 'facts unadorned' had really been presented to shareholders of the City Equitable in May 1919, instead of the one-man show of comedy and deception they got from Gerard Lee Bevan at the height of his hypnotic powers, they might have resolved to declare their company insolvent there and then.

Wily Dundonians

By mid-1920, the boom was over and stockmarket conditions were deteriorating rapidly. Credit was tight, and Bank Rate had risen to 7 per cent. Industrial and commercial shares lost about a third of their value during the year and the market for new issues had become satiated and unpredictable. Issue volumes fell by around two-thirds compared to the height of the boom, and some issues were undersubscribed (unwanted shares thereby coming to rest with the underwriters) despite supposedly alluring terms.

Hatry, always a shrewd reader of markets rather than a blind optimist, sensed that conditions were changing. When he left his office in February 1920 to undergo abdominal surgery and took an extended period of convalescence, he left instructions at the Commercial Bank (so he said later) to 'sell all speculative holdings and keep the bank's resources liquid'.

His fellow directors — including Haig-Thomas, on whom it would clearly have been a mistake to rely even though he carried the title of 'joint managing director' — failed to do so, and indeed took on additional risky commitments while he was away, obliging him in due course to realise some of his personal assets to prop up the bank when it was unable to meet its current liabilities. It later came to light that around half of the Commercial Bank's capital had been lost by the end of 1920.

It was against this background that Hatry brought one of his most famous companies to market, with Bevan's participation — an involvement which would eventually play a direct role in the downfall of Ellis & Co. This was Jute Industries Limited, a combination of six of the leading family-owned businesses in Dundee, the traditional home of the jute industry.

Jute fibre, from plantations in Bengal, was spun in Dundee into a variety of products including ropes, tarpaulins, sacking and the hessian backing for linoleum flooring. The industry had experienced a boom during the war, helped by the intervention of a government purchasing board which smoothed out the swings in raw jute prices.

After the war, the Dundee firms faced a slump in demand and labour unrest, combined with increased cheap competition from mills in Calcutta and a return to more volatile raw material prices. The leading family firms had been at loggerheads with one another when markets were favourable, but evidently saw the advantage of joining forces to cash in by flotation when conditions started turning against them.

Hatry was invited to help them do so. But his slippery reputation preceded him to the extent that, when he bought the first of the six companies, J. & A.D. Grimond (the family business of the Liberal Party leader Jo Grimond, whose father was a director of the company) in July 1920, at least one shareholder refused to take a Hatry cheque and insisted on being paid in banknotes.

Indeed, Chris Swinson — having made close forensic studies of Hatry's *modus operandi* — believes the jute men or their representatives first approached Hatry precisely because they knew that the realisation of the value of their holdings 'was likely to involve obfuscation if not manipulation' and that they needed a financier on the case who brought those particular skills.

Some of the families still needed persuading, both to work together and to sell up. But Hatry took the train north, interviewed them all, and swiftly won them round. In September, the acquisition of four more companies was announced. In October the biggest name in the industry, Cox Brothers, came aboard to complete a syndicate that employed half of the workforce of the Dundee industry and commanded about a third of the British jute market — though not before advice had been sought from the City financier Robert Fleming (founder of the eponymous merchant bank), a Dundonian who had begun his career as a Cox Brothers clerk. 'I need not repeat what I said to you personally,' Fleming warned in a letter to the new group's chairman designate, Ernest Cox, 'but Hatry promotions are not liked in many places.'

The board of the new group consisted of ten representatives from the acquired companies, plus Hatry, Bevan and Sir Alexander Roger, the former chairman of the Commercial Bank of London.[3] Jute Industries Limited was floated a month later, offering two and half million 9 per cent preference shares at par, of which 500,000 were to be taken up by 'the directors and their friends' and another

---

[3] Untainted by these associations, Roger went on to be chairman of the Birmingham Small Arms Company and, from 1948 to 1958, a deputy chairman of Midland Bank.

million to be sub-underwritten by them. Ellis & Co was, naturally, the broker to the issue, alongside a firm in Glasgow.

The prospectus showed group profits having risen from around £620,000 in the middle years of the war to £1.5 million in the year to 30 September 1920. But the truth was that past profits, particularly those of the war years when the market had been under tight government control, were really no guide at all to future performance. This point was conveyed only by a very guarded warning: 'While the profits... in the immediate future are likely to remain at a high level and may even in some cases exceed those of the past year, it is improbable that this increase will continue or that the profits as shown for 1920 will be fully maintained. On the other hand...'

There followed a list of six reasons to be optimistic, including 'the great economies in operation which are certain to result from the unification of previously conflicting interests' — even though the constituent businesses were in fact maintaining largely separate operations.

The market's appetite for new shares was already at a low ebb and the declining state of the jute trade cannot have been entirely unknown to London investors, even if the wily Dundonians hoped it might be. Despite the rich 9 per cent coupon offered on the preference shares — the average offered in 1920 was 8.1 per cent — and the additional attraction that they were 'cumulative and participating', entitling the holder to an additional slice of dividend if profits permitted, the issue was undersubscribed.

Only 2.15 million shares were taken up, and the rest left with the underwriters. The City Equitable was among them, as was the First National Reinsurance Company, where Bevan was a member of the finance committee — and which had recently resolved to place all its securities business in the hands of Ellis & Co.

At that stage, Bevan appears to have tried to make the issue look more successful than it was by persuading directors of Cox Brothers (and presumably those of other companies in the syndicate) to take large blocks of the preference shares against a guarantee from Ellis & Co to buy the shares if there were no buyers in the market within a specified period. It is not clear whether he delivered on this promise.

Rather curiously, he resigned from the Jute Industries board within three months, but not before he had arranged for a loan of £420,000 from the Midland Bank[4] to Ellis & Co to be passed on to Jute Industries to finance the additional acquisition of another Dundee mill and a merchanting business shortly after the flotation.

This was one of several large loans obtained by Ellis & Co in the same period, including £300,000 from Kleinwort secured against shares in another Hatry company, British Glass Industries. As P.S. Manley put it: 'Ellis & Co had become a borrowing machine through which funds were channelled into speculative investments and amalgamations, a process Bevan's partners knew little or nothing about.' For a stockbroking firm to act like a merchant bank in this way would have seemed extraordinary in modern times, but under the scant regulation of the time it seems to have attracted no attention from the Stock Exchange, the Bank of England or Ellis & Co's own auditors.

By May 1921, Midland was pressing to be repaid, and the inability of Ellis & Co to do so must have been one of the reasons behind Bevan's scheme to asset-strip other reinsurance companies, including First National, under the umbrella of a new vehicle called City Equitable Associated, and pass the cash proceeds across to Ellis & Co. More of that manoeuvre in Chapter Six.

Investors who had contemplated but shunned the Jute Industries offer must have felt a sense of *Schadenfreude* when they saw the results announcement for the year to September 1921, published in February 1922 at the height of the Bevan escape drama. Profits were down to £308,000, after a dramatic write-down of stock valuations — though the chairman claimed that without the write-down they might have exceeded a million pounds. He described 'a year of

---

[4] 'Midland' is used here and later as shorthand for a bank which went through several changes of name as it grew by merger and acquisition. Originally the Birmingham & Midland, then London & Midland, it became London City & Midland Bank in 1898, and London Joint City & Midland Bank in 1918. It finally simplified itself to Midland Bank Limited in 1923.

unparalleled stagnation' in which prices both of raw jute (of which the group had large holdings) and manufactured goods had plunged shortly after the flotation.

Cox fielded criticisms that insufficient information was flowing through from the operating companies in the group to the holding company, and that the group was over-capitalised (at £7 million nominal and £4.5 million issued), meaning that dividends were spread too thin. Unlike numerous other companies in the Hatry-Bevan stable, however, Jute Industries was not heading swiftly for the rocks.

Rather it was destined, year after year, to under-perform the expectations created by the 1920 share issue. In 1922, it reported a severe shortage of orders, with many of its mills working at only two-thirds capacity or worse. 1923 was marred by an extended dispute over spinners' working conditions.

In 1924, the problem was over-supply of yarn spun from jute — and no dividend was paid to ordinary shareholders, although the preference dividend was still met. Raw jute prices continued to swing wildly. And so it went on: in 1926, the chairman reported that trading had been 'the most disastrous in his memory'.

The only positive development was that the company gradually provided its shareholders with more adequate information about the real state of its trade and its balance sheets. Finally, in early 1929, a £2.9 million write-down of the value of the investments in the operating companies had to be matched by a write-down of the company's issued capital from £4.5 million to £1.6 million, in which the preference shareholders took a full share of the pain.

By then, of course, Bevan's brief role in Jute Industries was long forgotten and Hatry had also gone from the board, although one of his London companies continued to look after the register of shareholders. But the shareholders' unhappy ride can be traced straight back to the way in which Hatry put the syndicate of jute companies together, and the terms of the flotation.

In effect, he conspired with the Dundee families to secure a price for them that was not justified by trading prospects. He and

Bevan encouraged new investors to believe that the profits of war-time and the immediate post-war boom were a guide to the future.

Hatry and Bevan knew exactly what they were up to, and they did it very skilfully. If either had any scruples about pushing out shares that were unlikely ever to justify their valuation, they subordinated that consideration to the need for quick profits from this and other deals in the post-boom phase to bolster their own increasingly troubled businesses.

Both would have said that what they were doing was nothing out of the ordinary in the stockmarket of the era; it was all in a day's work. But they were particularly prolific and successful at it, and a small army of investors was eager to follow them over the precipice ahead.

Partners and Directors, 1918–22

Ellis & Co, Stockbrokers *in order of seniority*
Gerard Lee Bevan
Neville O'Brien
Harold Gordon
Frederick Tootal
Hon. Ailwyn Fellowes
Donald Pirie (managing clerk; 'salaried partner' from September 1921)

The City Equitable Fire Insurance Company
Gerard Lee Bevan, Chairman
Theodore Barclay, stockbroker (resigned October 1920,
died March 1921)
Lord Clanmorris of Newbrook, soldier (resigned 1918)
Sir Douglas Dawson, courtier
Sir Henry Grayson, shipbuilder
Henry Grenside, solicitor
Peter Haig-Thomas, coal-owner
Earl of March, landowner and soldier (resigned December 1921)
Moir Milligan, Scottish advocate
Lord Ribblesdale, former courtier
(Edmund Mansell, general manager)

City Equitable Associated Limited *at flotation in July 1921*
Gerard Lee Bevan, Chairman
George Adair, insurance company director
Sir Douglas Dawson
Henry Grenside
(Edmund Mansell, general manager)

Commercial Bank of London *as at April 1919*
Sir Charles Hobhouse MP, Chairman
Clarence Hatry (managing director)
Henry Grenside
Peter Haig-Thomas (later joint managing director)
Rowland Hodge, shipbuilder
Earl of March
Henry Pelham-Clinton, director of gold-mining companies

Gerard Lee Bevan's other directorships
In 'Hatry' companies:
Agricultural Industries Ltd
Burton, Son & Sanders Ltd
Clarke Chapman Ltd
H & C Grayson Ltd
Jute Industries Ltd
Leyland Motors Ltd

In South America:
Gath y Chaves/South American Stores
Harrods (Buenos Aires) Ltd
Southern Brazil Electric Company

CHAPTER SIX

Boom Turns to Bust

'Of course it's pleasant and comfortable to keep within the law…
Then the law will look after you. Otherwise you have to look pretty
sharp after yourself. You have to cultivate your own sense of right and
wrong; deal your own justice. But that makes a bigger man of you, let
me tell you.'

The corrupt solicitor Voysey speaking in
Harley Granville Barker, *The Voysey Inheritance* (1905 play)

Back from Brazil

'I believe this company is one of the most successful in London. None has made more progress in the time under the present management. I am sure we must all feel very well satisfied with the results, and that we shall unite in re-electing these gentlemen.' The speaker was Neville O'Brien of Tunbridge Wells, who happened to be a partner of Ellis & Co but who was speaking on this occasion as a shareholder of the City Equitable, at its annual general meeting on 17 June, 1920 in Winchester House, Old Broad Street. The gentlemen concerned were Bevan, Haig-Thomas and Lord March, who were retiring by rotation and offering themselves for re-election.

Bevan, fresh back from an extended tour of South America, had returned in time to present yet another set of impressive results, with a near doubling of fire premium income. A more modest increase had been achieved in marine premiums, following the giant

leap in 1919, despite difficult market conditions and increased competition — and 'it is a matter for congratulation that our loss ratio is
so moderate'. As to future developments, 'it is quite probable that
within the next few months we shall have decided that the moment
is opportune for us to enter as a reinsurer on a moderate scale in
United States business'.

'On the subject of investments I should like to point out the
large amount that we hold, either in the form of short-dated loans or
Treasury bills. By pursuing this policy, and at the same time exercising discrimination in the choice of our miscellaneous securities,
we have hitherto avoided the depreciation which would otherwise
have resulted...'

That statement contained a clear falsehood, but if challenged
Bevan might have pointed out that he was truthfully describing
the published balance sheet; it was the balance sheet itself that
was lying. In fact, what appeared to be a large holding of Treasury
bills concealed a loan to Ellis & Co of nearly half a million pounds
which was anything but short-dated in the sense that if the City
Equitable had called it in, Ellis & Co could not possibly have found
the cash at short notice to pay it back. And the 'miscellaneous
securities' portfolio was stuffed with shares that were unmarketable and shown only at valuations provided by Ellis & Co, which in
reality meant valuations pencilled in by Bevan himself but bearing no relation to the market's assessment of those shares as dem-
onstrated by investor demand. In many cases, such demand was
non-existent.

But still the positive but cautious tone of Bevan's presentation
was reinforced by what appeared to be a significant strengthening
of the company's reserves: these already stood at 77 per cent of fire
premium income and 80 per cent of marine premiums, but Bevan's
declared intention was that these ratios should continue to grow
year by year until 100 per cent was reached.

All this moved another shareholder, the loquacious Mr Monro,
to new heights:

I was pleased to hear from the chairman that it is proposed to do in this company what, I believe, has never been done in any insurance company — that is, to make the reserve for unexpired risks cent [i.e. 100] per cent... Our directors are not ordinary directors; I think they thoroughly deserve the greatest appreciation we can give them, more especially our chairman. [He] is not the sort of chairman who simply sits in the chair here once a year, but he, with [Mansell] takes the keenest interest in every phase of the business.

That last remark was no doubt true in one sense, since only Bevan and Mansell knew the company's innermost secrets. But it is curious to recall that at this point Bevan had only been in touch with City Equitable affairs by letter and telegram since he sailed for Buenos Aires at the beginning of February. The fact that the chairman had left the general manager to get on with running the City Equitable for more than four months seems to have reassured shareholders such as Monro that all was ticking along smoothly, rather than ringing alarm bells as it might do in a modern company.

The truth was, however, that during his South American sojourn Bevan had conceived one of the investments that would ruin the City Equitable. He became excited about the prospects for cattle ranching in Brazil and on his return he assembled a group of investors to pursue the opportunity in a very big way.

'The Syndicate Inglez' would put upwards of a million pounds together to buy a portfolio of ranches and some 10,000 head of cattle. Bevan and Haig-Thomas each sank over £100,000 into this venture, while Bevan told Grenside, as the third member of the City Equitable investment committee, that the proposition would be 'a first-class lock-up for some of the company's surplus funds'. The City Equitable duly invested £150,000 in the syndicate.

This was as illiquid an investment as it would be possible to imagine. An exit for the syndicate by means of flotation was no doubt contemplated, but would have been several years down the road and in the meantime the cash was completely inaccessible.

What's more — typical of Bevan — the ranch deals were done by skimpy contracts which failed adequately to secure the rights of the syndicate. As an investment for a reinsurance company, the scheme was inappropriate in every possible way.

Meanwhile, Bevan was also doing deals which had nothing to do with the City Equitable, including exercising his financial engineering skills in another vivid parable of boom and bust: the case of Harrods (Buenos Aires) Limited. As we saw in Chapter Two, this offshoot of the great Knightsbridge department store was a flagship of British commercial interests in Argentina. One of its major competitors was South American Stores, about which Bevan had written to his client Colonel Grove a few months earlier and of which he was a director.

He had been involved over the winter, from London, in negotiating a merger between the two department store companies. This was completed in February 1920 just after he arrived in Buenos Aires and as part of the agreement he joined the Harrods board as well. No doubt he participated in lavish celebrations of the new partnership.

'Argentina is now experiencing a wave of prosperity that puts all previous good times in eclipse,' *The Times* had recently declared. Both department store groups had big expansion plans; Harrods ambition was, as its chairman put it, to 'possess the best equipped and most up-to-date store in the world' — nine and a half acres of floorspace offering every kind of luxury item and provision on a prime site in the heart of the booming Argentinian capital.

But before that project could be completed, global economic conditions changed dramatically. Argentina, as a country that thrived on its export trade, suffered a sudden reverse in prosperity. A severe deflation in prices received for Argentinian meat, cereals, wool and hides caused a slump in domestic spending power which took large slices out of the department stores' turnover and profits.

At the end of the year, Bevan would be called upon to make one of his characteristically upbeat speeches at a Harrods shareholders meeting in London. In it he explained the particular temporary difficulties of the Argentinian marketplace, where dock strikes, local political interference and protectionist measures elsewhere had added to the fundamental problem of deflation.

He also spoke of turning a corner and 'looking forward to better times'. The directors would 'spare no effort, leave no stone unturned, to bring renewed prosperity to the company', he declared, to the same sort of plaudits from the floor that he was so accustomed to receiving at City Equitable meetings.

In fact the depressed trading conditions would continue for many months longer, and the company would eventually face a capital reconstruction which included heavy write-downs of the investments it had made during the period of Bevan's involvement.

By the time he made that speech in December 1920, the British economy had also plunged, as had all the markets in which the City Equitable operated. Overseas production of food and raw materials (including that of Argentina) far exceeded European demand, while demand for British manufactured exports from producer countries dwindled in return. Prices tumbled in both directions, and there was a glut of unwanted shipping capacity. At home, unemployment doubled between December 1920 and March 1921, and passed two million by June.

Against such a background, Bevan's upbeat tone and understatement of the downside risks were remarkable. He could have won medals for skating so elegantly over thin ice.

The Twin Bastions

Bevan's performance at the City Equitable's twelfth annual general meeting on 4 June, 1921 was surely an all-time personal best. Both the City Equitable and Ellis & Co, to which the reinsurance company was locked in such a suffocating embrace, were by now under considerable financial pressure — half the capital of the latter had already effectively been lost. But Bevan's speech offered shareholders and fellow directors no inkling of the problems that were beginning to besiege him.

He began with a eulogy for Theodore Barclay, his fellow director and lifelong friend who had died of rheumatic fever exacerbated by a weak heart on 30 March 1921, aged only 53, having resigned from the board in October 1920. His 'singular charm, simplicity of manner [and] high integrity' marked him out as an exceptional person, Bevan said. 'Enemies he had none; of friends a multitude.'

That was followed by Bevan's customary tribute to Mansell and the staff — which would ring hollow some months later when it became clear that during the year on which Bevan was reporting, Mansell had been liberally 'lending' himself large sums from the company's cash account, with Bevan's tacit connivance but without the awareness let alone approval of the rest of the board.

The chairman ended with a supremely pompous peroration, phrases from which were to be thrown back at him for the rest of his life. It deserves to be quoted in full:

Gentlemen, what of the future? Let us face it without vanity and without fear. It has been a year of storm and stress, of fluctuations and upheavals such as no man has ever seen, and even the most experienced pilot has sometimes lost his bearings. But it is not a time to give way to pessimism.

The old trading instinct so deeply engrained in the British character still retains all its potency, and if only those in authority will eschew mandates of adventure, will cease from meddling with industry, and will recognise the necessity — the paramount, the imperative necessity — of readjusting burdens of taxation, not to the demands, not even to the needs, pressing as many of them are, but rather to the actual abilities of the nation to bear them, then I feel convinced that the same spirit which carried us so triumphantly through the war will also enable us to surmount the many difficulties it has left in train.

Banks and insurance are the twin bastions of modern finance, the two main forts that guard the mysterious citadel called "credit". Of their permanence there can be no question, because they render services indispensable to any civilised

community, and inasmuch as we are privileged to belong to one
of these groups, it is our duty, and it will be our fixed and constant endeavour, to play our part, relatively small though it may
be, in a manner not unworthy of the traditions of this great City.

In between these rich slices of ham, he gave a gloss on what had
actually been happening to the business, and what he planned to do
next. He explained first why losses had been more severe than usual
on the marine account, despite his claim in previous years that the
company was unusually skilful in spreading its risks.

There had been a surprisingly high incidence of vessels encoun-
tering uncleared mines. There had been a good deal of pilfering of
cargo in port, reflecting something of a breakdown of order in post-
war society, though 'the dominant characteristic which we possess in
common with the greatest of ancient empires — I mean the respect
of the law — will surely and gradually reassert itself.'

Lastly (and, we might suspect, by far the most important reason, though Bevan did not give it special emphasis) the market in
which the company operated was now suffering an excess of supply
of reinsurance over demand, 'and a great deal of business has been
written at unprofitable rates'.

As to the unusually large figure for 'loans' on the balance sheet,
Bevan described this item as 'for the most part terminable at call'
and higher than usual 'due solely to the expectation of having to
make heavy remittances to America in the near future' for the building up of a reserve fund in US government and municipal securities
to underpin the company's new line of American fire reinsurance,
which offered the promise of substantial growth.

In fact, as we shall see in Chapter Nine, more than £900,000 had
been lent to Ellis & Co and almost £100,000 to Edmund Mansell,
neither of whom were in any position to repay 'at call' — or as it
turned out, ever. And a £200,000 holding of National War Bonds was
entirely fictitious, since the sleight of hand which made it appear
to be in the City Equitable's ownership did not actually take place
until several days after the balance sheet was struck.

We do not know whether Bevan had any real intention to expand the City Equitable's business in the United States, or whether that strategy was largely a bluff — a cover for the fact that his real priority throughout 1921 was simply to generate, by any means available, sufficient cash to keep his businesses afloat.

He had, for example, approached the general manager of the Midland Bank, Frederick Hyde, at the beginning of the year to ask for a £600,000 loan to support the drive into the American market. Some money was advanced as a result, but Bevan failed to adhere to a condition set by Hyde that cash should be accumulated on deposit with the Midland at the same time.

Bevan and Hyde had a difficult meeting in August — the Midland was already pressing for faster repayment of the 'Jute loan', the £420,000 lent to Ellis & Co and passed on to Jute Industries. Hyde now referred sternly to his notes of their previous encounter, while Bevan tried to claim that he had a different understanding of the terms of the loan to the City Equitable; he was given six months in which to pay it off.

But still it was possible to present a broadly positive picture of the reinsurance business. The fire account had taken another 'big stride forward' over the past year, he told the shareholders, with premiums passing the £2 million mark. On the downside, a number of small and in his view under-capitalised reinsurance companies had recently entered the market — and in respect of this development, Bevan had an eloquent masterplan to unveil:

> Acting separately, it will be very uphill work for them to obtain good business, but pulling together, and in conjunction with a well-established concern like our own, there is no reason why they should not be able to build up a sound, well spread premium income. It is the old story of the faggots. A single twig is easily snapped, but several of them bound together can become a really powerful weapon.

A False Prospectus

This, then, was the rationale presented for acquiring control of three smaller reinsurance companies and putting them together under a new holding company. Investors were given to understand that it was all a strategic gambit to strengthen and protect the City Equitable's competitive position — a springboard to the next level of success. But in reality it was an asset-stripping exercise to procure emergency injections of cash for both the City Equitable and Ellis & Co.

Bevan began by taking control of the First National Reinsurance Corporation, where (though not on its board) he had already used his position on the finance committee to steer the company's securities business into Ellis & Co's hands; by various means he was able to extract £137,000 from First National. He moved on in June 1921 to acquire controlling interests in the Greater Britain Insurance Company and the City of London Insurance Company, both of which showed entirely respectable balance sheets (that is, holding conventional levels of gilt-edged stocks) for the previous year-end.

In both cases, the existing boards resigned and were replaced by Bevan's nominees; at both, Bevan and Grenside became the finance committee. At the Greater Britain, this 'committee' promptly resolved to withdraw the company's holdings of securities from bank custody and place them in Bevan's hands for disposal; £412,000 was realised. Likewise, £61,000 was generated by selling War Bonds which belonged to the City of London Insurance.

It is possible to trace where much of this cash went. It was used to reduce Ellis & Co's debts to its bankers: in June, when the asset-stripping exercise was in progress, Ellis & Co repaid £6,000 to Barclays, £25,000 to Kleinwort, Sons & Co, £29,000 on its 'overseas account' with the Midland, and another £200,000 to Midland on the 'Jute loan'; it is not clear whether any of the last amount was funded by a corresponding repayment to Ellis & Co from Jute Industries itself.

In any event, this was still not enough to relieve the overall position of the group, and in July Bevan launched on an even more reckless course. A prospectus was issued for an offer to the public of 250,000 8 per cent participating preference shares of £1 each in City Equitable Associated Limited, a shell company into which had been injected the City Equitable's shareholdings in Greater Britain, City of London and First National.

The directors of City Equitable Associated were Bevan, Grenside, Sir Douglas Dawson and George Adair, a director of the Greater Britain. Minority shareholders in the three smaller companies were persuaded to exchange their shares for those of the new parent, so that the three companies became wholly-owned subsidiaries.

The preference shares, issued at par, were payable in four instalments, of which the last tranche of ten shillings per share would fall due in January 1922. There were several features of this issue which later formed part of the case against Bevan.

Perhaps the most obviously fraudulent aspect was the fact that the assets of the subsidiary companies were shown in the prospectus as they had been at their last balance sheet dates — 31 December 1920 for Greater Britain and First National, 30 September 1920 for City of London — and not as they were at the time of the issue, having already been turned into cash which had been snaffled by Bevan for other purposes.

The prospectus showed the City Equitable Associated companies holding 'cash investments and other interest-bearing assets' of almost £1.2 million between them, while the City Equitable itself had supposedly been holding £2.9 million worth of the same sort of assets as at 28 February 1921. Those numbers bore no relation to the real state of the group in July 1921.

Furthermore, the capital and proposed dividends of the new company were 'guaranteed' by the City Equitable, a promise that could never realistically have been honoured. And the prospectus said that the subsidiary companies of City Equitable Associated had sufficient revenues from their investments to cover the 8 per cent dividend. But they did not, because their investments had already been stripped out.

None of this was plain to investors or the City press. *The Economist* took a cautious view: 'The guaranteeing company has had a profitable career, but the information given in the prospectus is scarcely sufficient to allow the investor to gauge the value of this guarantee... Without more precise information... we cannot advise investment in this issue.'

But the *Financial Times* was bullish — 'the shares have undoubted attractions and potentialities' — and so was the market. The issue was oversubscribed, with Kleinwort, Sons & Co taking up £30,000 worth for its clients. Instalment payments from subscribers during the third quarter of 1921 (including those who chose to subscribe in full immediately and collect 6 per cent interest on their advance payments, rather than wait for the final subscription date) brought in £140,000 to ease the City Equitable's cash position.

It is worth observing that the City Equitable Associated issue took Bevan's wrongdoing to a different level. There is a rather fine distinction involved, but one that is worth making.

Bevan could have been accused, up to that point, of encouraging investors to put their money into the shares of the City Equitable itself on the basis of a falsified picture of the company's strengths. But many who did so were Ellis & Co clients and members of Bevan's social circle who had profited by taking Bevan's advice or following his lead on other investments over the years. Indeed, a huge block of City Equitable shares, worth some £850,000 at the peak, was held by Ellis & Co either as nominees for favoured clients or as an investment of the firm's own capital.

This inner circle of shareholders, including Bevan himself, was reckoned to account for 85 per cent of the City Equitable's preference shares and 95 per cent of the ordinaries. They included Mrs Alice Keppel, the former mistress of Edward VII, who held 3,000 shares; the 13th Earl of Lindsay with 1,000; the widowed Lady Guernsey with 360. Also on the register were Lords Ilchester, Rendlesham and Romilly, and Lady Adelaide Dawnay. Connections of the other directors also invested, including the former Ava Astor, who bought 2,000 shares around the time of her wedding to Lord Ribblesdale in 1919.

But in defence of Bevan's position up to that point, it might have been emphasised both that he was himself the largest individual investor in the City Equitable and that — at least until 1920 or early 1921 — he genuinely believed he was running a successful reinsurance business, albeit one that he was secretly using to bankroll a less successful stockbroking business and to back his own investment hunches elsewhere.

And if anyone had ever seriously criticised his rather cavalier style (there is no evidence that anyone did, though cautious investors who looked askance at his stockmarket reputation would simply have avoided investing with him) he would have been able to remind them that his fellow City Equitable investors had thus far received extraordinary returns.

During the company's rise, the relatively small size of its paid-up capital had been greatly to investors' advantage. As *The Economist* explained: 'The shares authorised and subscribed amount to £375,000 but the capital paid up is only £75,000, which in comparison with the enormous premium income [of £3.5 million in 1921] looks ridiculously small.'

The rate of dividends paid (measured against the paid-up capital rather than the market price of the shares) had risen from 150 per cent in 1919 on the ordinary shares to 250 per cent in 1921, and from 37.5 per cent on the preference shares to 62.5 per cent, *The Economist* continued: 'Returns of this size on so small a capital are very remarkable, and have naturally attracted much attention, both from insurance men and from investors.'

The difference with the City Equitable Associated scheme was that Bevan must have known by mid-1921 that he had a potential disaster on his hands on all fronts. He certainly knew that the prospectus for the preference share issue was false. By advertising the issue throughout the financial press, he was deliberately appealing to a wider investing public rather than the more sophisticated circle of his own market followers.

If his earlier actions had, arguably, occupied a no-man's-land of sharp City practice, the City Equitable Associated gambit took him well over the line into outright fraud.

Hand-to-Mouth

Peter Haig-Thomas was one of the first people to sense that not all was as it should be — or perhaps he just took offence at Bevan's high-handedness in pressing ahead with the formation of the City Equitable Associated without consulting him. He claimed to have known nothing about it until he read about it in the press. Bevan subsequently told him that it had been discussed at a City Equitable board meeting from which Haig-Thomas had been absent, and offered him only a 'fairly satisfactory' explanation of the project.

Haig-Thomas said later that he could see the point of trying to gain control of some of the smaller reinsurance companies that were cutting into the City Equitable's market, but that he was not happy with the 'guarantee' from the City Equitable of the new company's capital and dividends. In early July, without warning Bevan beforehand, he sent a letter resigning his membership of the City Equitable's finance committee.

He gave as his reason the fact that he was not in London as much as he used to be — which was quite true. Consolidated Cambrian, his family coal business in Wales, had been demanding more of his attention. The slump-stricken coal industry had been released from wartime government controls at the end of March and the owners had immediately proposed a cut in miners' wages as well as a return to localised or 'district' pay rates — which meant lower rates for those working in less productive mines. When the miners responded with demands for national equalisation of wages, the owners refused and locked them out.

As a negotiator, Haig-Thomas would have been more inclined to shout than conciliate. Whatever his personal impact on the dispute, which lasted until July, workers across the industry suffered a bitter defeat. Meanwhile, despite his run-in with Bevan, he chose to remain on the board of the City Equitable, no doubt to keep an eye on his own substantial investment there.

The situation he might have observed, as summer turned to autumn — if he looked closely enough — was one of continuing deterioration in the marine business combined with, as P.S. Manley described it in his *Abacus* magazine article, 'a financial hand-to-mouth existence'. Bevan was scrambling around the City, borrowing wherever he could both corporately and personally. As we shall see later, there also appeared to be a collusion with Edmund Mansell to divert City Equitable company funds in order to keep Bevan's own creditors at bay.

Bevan persuaded Sir Henry Grayson to lend £100,000 of War Loan bonds to the City Equitable — and immediately had them turned into cash, presumably to pay outstanding reinsurance claims. He borrowed from banks against the security of the unpaid ten-shilling subscriptions on the City Equitable Associated shares, and used part of the proceeds to pay the first dividend on those shares when it fell due on 1 January 1922, even though the new company had made no profit.

Meanwhile, both the insurance market and the stockmarket were beginning to whisper that the City Equitable was in trouble. Those rumours even reached the north east of Scotland where Moir Milligan, the Aberdonian advocate on the City Equitable board, picked up on them at the beginning of December 1921.

He travelled to London for an urgent meeting with Bevan and Mansell on 8 December, at which he asked Bevan to explain why two writs had been issued against the company in connection with unpaid claims on its marine business. Bevan, so Milligan later testified, replied that 'these difficulties had been overcome and there was no cause for anxiety'.

Having returned to Scotland, Milligan set out in a letter a series of questions which he felt had not been adequately dealt with at the meeting. In a reply dated 29 December, Bevan wrote:

> The rumours that have been started in some quarters are ridiculously exaggerated, and though, of course, we, like others, have suffered heavy losses in the marine field during the last few months, this, we hope, is only a temporary phase, and anyway our marine treaties have now been carefully sorted out and those upon which we had any anxiety were cancelled some time ago.

Questioned about this letter at his trial, Bevan described it as 'a perfectly accurate statement'. But it did not offer Milligan the detailed answers he was seeking. At a tense board meeting early in January, he read out this exchange of letters and followed up with: 'I am not at all satisfied with the situation, and I must insist on having an independent investigation into the affairs of the company.'

Bevan asked Milligan what he would do with the report if he had it. 'Whatever I think proper,' came the prickly reply, which Bevan tried to parry by suggesting that Milligan might have a conflict of interest because he was a director of another insurance company.

Milligan stood his ground. Unless an independent investigation was forthcoming, he would resign, and he was joined in that threat by Sir Henry Grayson and Sir Douglas Dawson. The latter, incidentally, was extremely busy at this juncture organising the forthcoming wedding of the Princess Royal to Viscount Lascelles, so the looming City Equitable crisis must have been particularly embarrassing to him.

'You're not going to give us a stab in the back like that, are you?' said Bevan, to which Milligan replied that he 'would be the last person in the world to give anyone a stab in the back' but that if the chairman did not agree to an independent investigation, he would resign on the spot. Since he clearly could not just put his hands up in time-honoured style and say 'It's a fair cop, gentlemen', Bevan was in no position to raise objections to an investigation.

It was also agreed that Mansell would send the directors a full set of answers to the questions Milligan had set out in his letter to Bevan. Mansell asked for ten days to prepare this material, but it was never circulated. Events moved too fast, and indeed the board never carried through its resolution to appoint an independent investigator because the company's creditors were about to do so for them.

At a further board meeting on 13 January, the true scale of the debt owed by Ellis & Co to the City Equitable was revealed, as was the very large amount owed by Mansell personally, by then well over £100,000. Effectively, the game was up. Milligan moved a resolution that the company's solicitor should present a petition to the Bankruptcy Court asking for the appointment of the Official Receiver. Bevan, from the chair, did not object or vote.

The motion having been passed, Bevan was asked to leave the room and Milligan was asked to take the chair — which he would also occupy at the company's last board meeting, on 30 January.

But before then, several other manoeuvres were afoot. On 16 January, after a meeting with the general managers of several leading London insurance companies which had used the City Equitable as a reinsurer, a well-respected City accountant called Frederick Van de Linde was asked by Sir Arthur Worley of the North British & Mercantile to investigate the City Equitable's accounts. Two days later, the accountant called on Bevan at his office at Ellis & Co to seek his co-operation.

Bevan at first demurred, Van de Linde would later tell the court, 'saying that he didn't think I could do anything more than had been done'. Pressed by Van de Linde, Bevan produced a list of invest-ments dated about October 1921. This contained 'quite a number of liquid assets', causing Van de Linde to express surprise that dif-ficulties had arisen as a result of the supposed non-marketability of the holdings.

Bevan advised him to seek out a more up-to-date list, and with the assistance of the company's auditor, Van de Linde did so. It showed a considerably worse position. Some of the holdings seemed simply to have disappeared while most of what had been a large loan due from Ellis & Co had been replaced by a mixed bag of securities, chiefly industrial, and a further tranche of investment in the Brazilian ranch enterprise.

On 25 January, Van de Linde was asked to present what he had been able to find out in this short time to a meeting of insurance managers and Lloyd's brokers at the Cannon Street Hotel. Bevan chaired the opening of the meeting, but had uncharacteristically few words to offer (and none of his customary ebullient optimism) before he handed over to Sir Arthur Worley, who called on Van de Linde to speak. The accountant told the assembly that the City Equitable's genuine assets were 'sticky'; that is, they would be difficult to realise and there would probably be heavy losses against their book values.

A committee from among those present was appointed to assist Van de Linde. In the discussions that followed, mention was made of a financier known to Bevan who 'might find money in order to help the company'. This was a reference to Hatry, who had been talking to Frederick Hyde at the Midland Bank.

Two weeks earlier, Hatry had asked Hyde to come up with another £50,000 advance for the City Equitable — not a sum that would have made much difference at that stage, but a request which Hyde swiftly declined. Hatry nevertheless told Van de Linde that Hyde's boss, the Midland's chairman Reginald McKenna,[1] might still be prepared to find 'a considerable sum' to save the City Equitable. This was not the case, and Montagu Norman at the Bank of England had by now also indicated that he had no intention of intervening or encouraging others to do so.

Van de Linde was also trying to get to the bottom of a suggestion that a vital transfusion of cash was about to be injected into the City Equitable by a group known as the 'CB Syndicate', which was willing to buy some or all of the unmarketable shares. Henry Grenside gave Van de Linde a list of securities supposedly sold to this group,

---

[1] A former Liberal politician, McKenna had been Home Secretary and Chancellor of the Exchequer in the Asquith administration.

and the accountant was also shown what seemed to be an authentic set of bought-and-sold notes.

Van de Linde pressed Bevan to reveal who was behind the syndicate and where the money was, if it had ever been received. 'The reply... I did not regard as satisfactory.' The mystery of CB Syndicate would occupy many hours of testimony at the subsequent trial.

On 29 January, Bevan tried one last pull of the family strings. He wrote to Frederick Goodenough, his father's successor as chairman of Barclays Bank, asking for a meeting of bankers and insurance company representatives to see whether a rescue could be put together. He explained that the City Equitable needed a cash injection of £600,000 to put it back on a sound footing.

He also explained that £545,000 belonging to the City Equitable Associated companies was in the hands of Ellis & Co in cash and securities. This could not be delivered for the time being, as Ellis & Co itself was overstretched in part by the extent of its support for Hatry's Commercial Bank of London — thus raising the potential threat of a domino collapse that might spread across the banking sector.

'There has been no division of profits for eighteen months,' Bevan's letter continued. 'I have surrendered an endowment policy intended for my children, my fellow directors and myself have given up our cars, and it is not in our power to make any further sacrifices.'

Goodenough, a lawyer by training, had joined Barclays as its company secretary at the time of the 1896 amalgamation and had been Frank Bevan's formidably competent lieutenant for many years. Much feared by his underlings, a tyrant in his own boardroom, Goodenough had no tolerance for human frailty. Loyalty to his old boss's family evidently did not loom large in his reaction to Gerard's letter. He declined to answer it.

As January advanced, dealings in the shares of the City Equitable and City Equitable Associated became, according to one City columnist, 'a matter of somewhat delicate negotiation'. The £1 shares of City Equitable Associated, which had reached 17s 4½d (on a ten-shillings-paid basis) in September 1921, were now worthless, and it is not clear how many investors met the final ten shillings subscription payment that had fallen due on 12 January.

The preference shares of the City Equitable, which had stood at 59 shillings in September, were at 15 shillings by mid-January and three farthings by the end of the month. The ordinary shares had once stood at £12 10s — reflecting their exceptionally rich dividend yield — but now crashed to nothing, and soon both categories of share would actually be worth less than nothing. Bizarrely, holders did not just offer to give them away: they tried to pay other investors to take them.

This situation arose because all the shares were partly paid at four shillings in the pound — and when it looked likely that the Official Receiver would call up the other 16 shillings per share in due course as part of the bankruptcy settlement, some holders were offering as much as ten shillings per share to get rid of them, but found no takers.

The total of these unpaid calls was £300,000, and they brought some investors to ruin. Among those afflicted were six clerks at Ellis & Co. Some months after the crash — and long after they had lost their jobs — it was reported that this unlucky half-dozen faced between them a liability of £75,000 in unpaid calls on City Equitable shares. Their names had been used as nominee holders of the shares on behalf of Ellis & Co clients. But because the shares were registered to them, they carried the legal liability.

'The whole business is extraordinary,' one clerk told a reporter:

We held various amounts of shares at various times in our names. We had no option. We were simply told to do so. We never received any benefit at all. I think at one stage I was a nominee for nearly 50,000 shares. At the present moment my liability is more than £7,000. I am being asked by the Official Receiver to find the money, but of course I cannot do so. The other nominees are in exactly the same position... There can only be one end — that ultimately the money will have to be written off.

And so it would be — but that and much else in the clearing of the rubble of Bevan's fallen empire was yet to come. On 31 January, Van de Linde was appointed 'special manager' of the City Equitable and the City Equitable Associated group. On 3 February, the reinsurance company that had not long ago seemed such a roaring success, filed for bankruptcy.

The events that followed were not so much the story of a failed company rescue, but of what looked for several months like a remarkably successful personal escape.

CHAPTER SEVEN

Flight

'Edward Twisden, the solicitor: *You must decide quickly, to catch a boat train. Many a man has made good…*
Captain Dancy, the thief: *There are alternatives.*
Twisden: *Now, go straight from this office. You've a passport, I suppose; you won't need a visa for France, and from there you can find means to slip over. Have you got money on you?'*

John Galsworthy, *Loyalties* (1922 play)

Ordered Abroad

'My husband's health has entirely given way,' Sophie Bevan told a reporter from *The Times* on Friday, 10 February 1922. 'He has been ordered abroad for an indefinite period — to the South of France, I think.'

That 'I think' speaks volumes. Gerard Bevan had already brought humiliation upon his wife of almost 30 years by living openly with mistresses half her age at the Carlton Hotel in Haymarket. He had embarrassed Sophie, as we shall hear shortly, by sending an antique dealer to her house in Mayfair to take his pick of Chinese vases in settlement of a debt. He had brought the shame of newspaper headlines about a collapsed business empire.

Now, he was abandoning his wife and leaving her to care for their two daughters, the elder of whom, 20-year-old Christabel, was a particularly headstrong girl. Not only had he almost certainly asked Sophie to lie about his health as he fled the country, but he would tell an even bigger lie when he was finally apprehended: that he had only fled, against his own 'will and judgment' because Sophie had implored him to leave the country in order to spare her disgrace.

No direct evidence survives as to Bevan's real state of mind and health during his final days in London and his flight across Europe. Except, that is from the woman — not Jeanne, but the Belgian dancer Meddy Fabry — who would be referred to at his trial as having stayed in his suite at the Carlton in the weeks before he fled. She said that he had been sleeping badly and insisting that she play chess with him late into the night.

There was also the counter-evidence of a portrait photograph that would shortly be used on a 'Wanted' poster, distributed throughout Europe. The smoothness of face, the confident set of the mouth, the magisterial pose of the hand under the chin, index finger extended along the jowl, all suggested a man in full command of his circumstances. The picture was said to have been an excellent likeness when it was taken not long before — but it would have been little help in tracking him down, even if he had not been heavily disguised, because by the time he left for Paris those who knew him well said he was looking distinctly older and thinner.

If he also looked a little less smug, that would hardly be surprising. Having been the ringmaster for so long, he must have been gripped by a sense of the circus tent collapsing uncontrollably around him. His actions over the next few weeks nevertheless suggest coolness, cunning and forethought. So it seems likely that in the last hours before his departure Bevan asked Sophie and others to lay it on thick, if and when they were asked, about how distressed he had become.

Over the next few days, the London press quoted un-named 'friends' to the effect that he was in a 'highly strung nervous condition' as a result of business worries, and was intending to live quietly at an undisclosed location in France until 'his health improves or his presence is required by the authorities' in London — the suggestion being that he would return immediately when asked to do so. That was, of course, the very opposite of his true intention.

A week earlier a petition had been filed for the winding-up of the City Equitable, and the Official Receiver had been appointed as the company's provisional liquidator. What one paper described as 'the evil influence exerted by the liquidation of the City Equitable' spread within a few days to First National Reinsurance, the City Equitable Associated subsidiary. It too was heading for liquidation.

Bevan himself was last seen at the offices of Ellis & Co on Tuesday 7 February. Such conversation as he had with his four partners that day must have been pretty terse. Two days later, they issued a statement:

> We, the undersigned, being a majority of the partners of Ellis & Company of 1 Cornhill, E. C., hereby declare that we consider our partner, Mr. Gerard Lee Bevan, has been guilty of conduct detrimental to the partnership business, and we consequently in pursuance of the powers vested in us by Clause 26 of our Deed of Partnership, dated the 31st December, 1919, hereby as from today dissolve the partnership so far as regards the said Mr. Gerard Lee Bevan.

But Bevan had not waited around for this announcement. He had already fled the country, on Wednesday 8 February, by aeroplane from Croydon to Le Bourget near Paris.

Civil aviation was in its infancy in 1922, Croydon airport having been adapted from two adjacent military airfields less than two years earlier. So this was a bold, stylish and no doubt expensive way to flee the country: no *hoi polloi* Channel steamer for Gerry Bevan. And there was no established system for buying tickets — every booking was bespoke, making it all the more difficult to travel inconspicuously.

It is worth enquiring exactly how Gerard and Jeanne managed to do so. They had a choice of two British operators flying the London-Paris route, Instone Air Line and Handley Page Transport. There were also French and Belgian operators, though some flights carried mail and parcels only, rather than passengers, and there was no fixed timetable.

What can be said for certain is that Bevan flew in daylight, because the first night crossing was not achieved until a couple of months later. We may be fairly sure he arranged a morning departure, given the limited hours of daylight in February.

Activity was beginning to pick up at Croydon that week after the winter lull: records show that in the fortnight beginning Sunday 5 February 1922, there were usually three flights a day to Paris, making the journey in an average of just over three hours, excluding those that were forced to turn back because of bad weather or mechanical difficulties. Between them they carried 81 passengers in the fortnight, of whom Gerard and Jeanne were two.

Which air service did they use? By the time he arranged the flight, Bevan must have been very anxious that his creditors would try to have him arrested before he could flee the country — so the plan must have been secret. The booking was perhaps in Jeanne's name or a false one, possibly 'Lewis' which he used at some stage of his journey. He may have been helped to make the arrangements (so his family believed) by his younger brother Ivor — a philanderer to whom Gerard had been generous over the years, not only helping him financially but also finding a job at the City Equitable for Ivor's illegitimate son by his wife's maid.

Handley Page had one of its own aircraft flying the route that fortnight, most probably a Handley Page WE, which had an open cockpit but an enclosed passenger cabin big enough for a dozen passengers. Crucially for a man in Bevan's nervous condition, this was the first aircraft to be fitted with a rudimentary toilet cubicle. On the other hand, he would not have welcomed the company of inquisitive fellow passengers, and a little more detective work suggests that Handley Page probably was not his final choice.

Instone Air Line was part of the business empire of Sir Samuel Instone, a Jewish entrepreneur who made his name and wealth as the owner of ships carrying coal from south Wales. He was also chairman and principal owner of the Bedwas colliery, which supplied his fleet. In 1919, with his brother Alfred, he established an air passenger service from Cardiff to Paris via Croydon, flying the De Havilland 4 and the larger De Havilland 18.

Instone Air Line was the first civil carrier to introduce uniforms for its pilots and staff. It was also the first to transport a racehorse by air[1] and the first to achieve a telephone call from the ground — from Sir Samuel's London home — to a passenger in flight. Such details suggest a sophistication of service that would have appealed to Bevan, and he might well have used Instone aircraft before, given the regularity of his visits to Paris for business and pleasure.

Perhaps he had also had stockmarket dealings with Sir Samuel, a sometime lieutenant of the City of London whose principal office was at 52 Leadenhall Street, a short stroll from Bevan's in Cornhill. There must have been connections between Instone's shipping and coal interests and Consolidated Cambrian, the family business of Peter Haig-Thomas, who could have introduced Bevan and Instone to each other.

So let us picture Bevan and Jeanne making this journey together. The weather had been freezing in the first few days of the month — on Sunday the temperature in the city had barely risen above zero all day. By Wednesday it was beginning to turn milder, but it must still have been chilly and damp as the couple made their quiet getaway from the Carlton.

Reports said that they left at 8.30 in the morning, by taxi. A parting tip for the hotel doorman; petite Jeanne swathed in furs, Gerard in heavy tweeds, a rug over their knees, holding hands in silence as they are driven across Vauxhall Bridge; through Stockwell and Brixton as the grocers and ironmongers open their shops and the horse-drawn delivery carts go about their morning rounds; onwards to Norbury, Thornton Heath and Croydon.

For a man who would rarely have travelled without a valet, heavy monogrammed suitcases and a leather hatbox, the limited luggage permitted for flying must have added to Bevan's sense of escape. We

---

[1] A business which Sir Samuel's descendants still carry on today.

might wonder how much cash he was able to bring with him — and how many unpaid bills he had left behind. Whether he had settled his account at the Carlton, for example, or just given the doorman the impression that he was off for the day or for a long weekend and would be back on Monday.

The answer is that he told no one at the hotel he was leaving the country, and that he may well have had a small fortune on him — the fruit of a rather curious transaction in Chinese porcelain, of which more in a moment — and another stash waiting for him in Paris.

On recent trips to the French capital he had probably taken the precaution of putting something aside for a day such as this — perhaps in an account with Cox & Co, the Barclays affiliate which had branches in the major French cities and on the Riviera, or in a safe deposit box at Claridge's. He may even have diverted cash belonging to the City Equitable in France, over which he had made sure, a few months earlier, that he had personal control. His own later claim that he had only £250 to fund his escape, borrowed from a family member, seems one way or another to be highly unlikely.

We might wonder too what jewellery Jeanne was wearing, if necessary to be sold to fund their survival, and whether Bevan had slipped one or two valuable little *objets d'art* from the Carlton suite — Japanese *netsuke* perhaps — into his overcoat pockets.

Take-off at least meant a brief respite from the pressures of the previous weeks. The privacy of the enclosed two-seat passenger cabin of the Instone De Havilland 4 must have been comforting, even if the passage was turbulent.

Proofs of Debt

The news that Bevan had done a bunk — which did not become widely known until the weekend following Sophie's statement on Friday — provoked a variety of responses in London. *The Economist*, for example, permitted itself a literary reference, something of a rarity in the matter-of-fact business press of that era:

Once again, Mr H.G. Wells has proved his genius for antici-
pating history. In his novel *Tono-Bungay*, he made the great
financier whose schemes had fallen to ruin leave the country by
aircraft and come to rest in Spain. Mr Bevan, chairman of the
City Equitable, is now reported to be in France, now in Brazil,
now in Spain, but wherever he may be it is certain that, following the precedent of Mr Wells' Ponderevo, he left this country
unexpectedly and by aircraft...

The character of Ponderevo had in fact been modelled by Wells on
Whitaker Wright, the fraudulent company promoter whom we met
briefly in Chapter Two and who had fled first to France and then to
New York in 1903. Ponderevo's technique (similar to Hatry's) had
been to buy businesses 'at the vendor's estimate' and offer them to
the market at a substantially higher price — at the risk of being left
with many of the shares in his own hands. The comparison neatly
illuminated Bevan, who would still have been unfamiliar as a personality to most *Economist* readers, even if they had heard of some
the companies with which he had been associated.

Beyond the taverns of the City and the drawing rooms of Mayfair,
Bevan had never acquired a public profile. So his story was initially
confined to the financial pages of the daily press, making its way on
to the front pages (as far afield as the *Straits Times* in Singapore) as
the drama of his escape unfolded.

But in those first few days, more prominence was given to the situation in Ireland, where Sinn Fein gunman had been raiding Ulster
to kidnap prominent Unionists; to Tuesday's opening of parliament
by the King, and prime minister Lloyd George's subsequent debate
speech; to the report on national expenditure by Sir Eric Geddes,
published on Friday, which would lead to deep budget cuts; and
in foreign news, to the announcement in Rome of a new Pope, the
former Vatican librarian Cardinal Ratti who became Pius XI.

The Times nevertheless thundered about the contrast between
Bevan's speech at the City Equitable's annual meeting in June 1921
— in which he reminded shareholders how privileged they were to

participate in the business of insurance which was such a bastion of 'this great City' — and the collapse 'like a house of cards' of the ruined empire he left behind.

The Spectator's financial columnist, Arthur Kiddy, observed with some asperity that 'it is some time since the City has experienced so unpleasant and disturbing event as that disclosed in the affairs of the City Equitable... [and] the hasty departure of the Chairman at a moment when his presence would seem to be most required'.

Kiddy went on to raise a question that would be asked often in the following weeks as Bevan evaded his pursuers across Europe: 'The City really fails to understand why, in view of the rumours so freely circulated from the very moment that the troubles of the City Equitable were disclosed, these journeyings should ever have been possible.'

Elsewhere, companies and individuals who might have been connected to Bevan or the City Equitable made haste to point out that they were not, or at least not in a business sense. Among them was his cousin David Augustus Bevan, founder of the stockbroking firm of David A. Bevan & Co in Threadneedle Street, who also happened to be a long-serving director of the Equitable Life Assurance Society. Another City gent who was a more distant descendant of Silvanus Bevan, one Gerald Trevor Johnstone Bevan, put out a notice saying that he may have been confused with the fugitive but in fact had nothing to do with him whatsoever.

It was far too late for the remaining partners of Ellis & Co to dissociate themselves, however. O'Brien, Gordon, Tootal and Fellowes could count more than 80 years of service in the Exchange between them, and were never accused of anything other than failing to scrutinise their senior partner more closely. They would later argue in the bankruptcy court (where they were discharged in March 1923) that if the City Equitable had not gone down, Ellis & Co might have survived. But no mitigating factors could save them from their immediate fate.

Their firm had failed with gross liabilities of £2.6 million and a net deficiency of £1.2 million. Besides a huge debt to the City

Equitable (no precise amount was given for this at the time of the crash, but it is unlikely to have been smaller than the true figure hidden behind the 1921 balance sheet, of £911,000), some £240,000 was owed to banks and many smaller clients had been let down.

On the asset side, £259,000 of the deficit could be accounted for by losses on shares in the City Equitable and another £547,000 by depreciation of other investments. On Thursday 16 February the four partners filed a petition for the bankruptcy of Ellis & Co and notified the Stock Exchange committee that they had done so. Automatically, under Exchange rules, they ceased to be members.

But at least there was no public 'hammering' — the traditional three bangs of a gavel on the rostrum by the head waiter of the Exchange when announcing that partners of a defaulting firm 'cannot comply with their bargains'. Under Treasury regulations established during the war and still in operation, a notice was simply posted in the Exchange, and the news had little immediate effect on share prices as it was correctly assumed that most of the losses arising from the firm's liabilities would fall on banks and institutions such as the City Equitable (the connection between the two was well known) rather than other members of the Exchange.

Sophie, meanwhile, put out another statement:

> Mrs Bevan is deeply grateful for the many kind letters and for the very practical proofs of sympathy which have reached her from far and wide in her many misfortunes. She hopes to solve all the pressing problems shortly, and she will be in her own residence, 21 Upper Grosvenor Street, until matters have improved, when she hopes for a rest somewhere.

Even before Sophie had finished composing this poignant bulletin, her financial circumstances were made more complicated by a bankruptcy petition filed against her husband on 23 February by Eustacie Emma Millicent Hutton of Queen Anne Street, W1.

Mrs Hutton was the 75-year-old widow of a military man — a Crimean veteran, no less — with estates in Lincolnshire. There was a Hutton branch of the Kenrick family tree, but if this Mrs Hutton was related to them the connection must have been distant, and the detail of the business she had with Bevan is unknown.

It seems most likely that — like Colonel Grove in 1919 — she was simply a dissatisfied client of Ellis & Co. Had Bevan sold securities on her behalf and failed to send her the proceeds? Or put her money, at a late stage, into one or other of the shares in companies he controlled that had now collapsed? Was he holding securities on her behalf which she had been unable to reclaim because they had been pledged without her knowledge against Ellis & Co's debts elsewhere? What we do know is that the sum involved, when 'proof of debt' was tabled at a first meeting of creditors three weeks later, was £4,078.

As that meeting began, the presiding Official Receiver, W.P. Bowyer, remarked to general laughter that he supposed it was no use asking whether Bevan was present. That was the extent of the levity, however. The nub of the matter was that Bevan had left the country 'with intent to defeat or delay his creditors', and there were six more 'proofs of debt' to be taken into account, with more to come later.

The largest was on the part of Kleinwort, Sons & Co, which had made a personal loan of £168,000 to Bevan but held only £45,000 worth of securities against it; the precise shortfall was £123,472.[2] The smallest was for £31 to a Mr W. Wells Junior, who may have been a tradesman. Then came a Miss Colomb who seems to have been related to Mrs Hutton; the Hon. Mrs Evelyn Bethell, daughter of Mrs Hutton and wife of the heir to Lord Westbury; and the trustees of the Somerset Hospital in Cape Town. Finally, a Mr G. (though it may in fact have been Madame Gabrielle) Dejardin-Verkinder, a member of a French banking family, was on the hook for £5,844.

---

[2] The historian of Kleinwort Benson, Jehanne Wake, records, surprisingly, that in the end 'Kleinworts lost nothing on Mr Bevan', and that Sir Alexander Kleinwort, on learning of the failure of Ellis & Co and the City Equitable, was told by one of his managers that 'We have not got a penny owing to us on his account'; to which he exclaimed, 'Good Heavens! We should have done, he was a money maker.'

Also present at the meeting was a representative of the National Provincial Bank, who declared that his institution had 'a large personal claim' against Bevan but that proof of the debt was not yet to hand. Solicitors then argued as to whether these creditors should pursue their case against Bevan's personal estate, or ride two horses at once by pursuing Bevan personally and the former Ellis & Co partnership simultaneously. They decided to do the latter, with one trustee in bankruptcy and one 'committee of inspection' acting in both interests.

'Parle français couramment'

By the end of the second week of February, a warrant had been issued by direction of the Director of Public Prosecutions, Sir Archibald Bodkin, for Bevan's arrest. But where was he? Early reports followed Sophie's initial suggestion: 'To the South of France, I think.' Others thought he had remained in Paris, with or without Jeanne.

A version of the Bevan story published in the *Daily Express* almost 30 years later included this fanciful account:

> The couple parted in Paris but not before a dramatic scene outside an hotel that Bevan formerly owned [Claridge's, that is, though he had been a shareholder rather than the owner]. The fugitive, discredited and fallen, could not face the reproachful looks of the staff that had once fawned on him.
>
> Mademoiselle went in alone and left the financier hunched miserably in the taxi with his luggage and his thoughts. Inside she met, evidently by arrangement, two friends still loyal. Together they telephoned a King's Counsel in London to ask what the sentence would be if Bevan returned to face the law. "Five years," said the KC. The news was taken out to the taxi. "I can't take it," said Bevan, and drove off alone into the unknown.

This seems to be an elaboration of what the *World's Pictorial News* reporter claimed in December 1922 that Jeanne had actually said, which was: 'His pride forbade him to appear a worn, dishevelled and distraught figure on the glittering scene of his own triumphs. He refused to face the clerk and waiters who had for years bowed before him.'

Reconstruction of other fragments of information suggests that in fact he and Jeanne then lodged with a connection of hers, a Mademoiselle Germain at Avenue Fremiet in Passy, until Bevan left the French capital on Sunday 12 February, having first visited the British passport office to enlarge his potential choice of escape routes. His passport had been issued in London for travel only to France, Spain and Italy, but he was able to obtain a stamp in Paris rendering it also valid (with the appropriate visas) for Greece and Turkey.

He then took an overnight train to Marseilles, where he obtained Greek and Italian visas on the Monday and headed east along the Riviera, crossing into Italy at Ventimiglia on Tuesday. He was by now in a race against British bureaucracy-by-telegraph, because on Wednesday the British consul-general in Naples issued a request to other foreign consuls in the city to refuse visas to Bevan should he present himself to request them. Presumably all British embassies and consulates across western Europe did likewise, since there had been no specific intelligence to suggest that he was heading for Naples.

But that is where he went, and took rooms at the Hotel Royal on the sea front. And on Wednesday 22 February, he visited the Spanish consul in the city — who at that time also represented Turkey, pending Turkish ratification of the 1920 Treaty of Sevres between the Ottoman Empire and the victors of the first world war. Bevan asked for a visa for Constantinople but the consul refused, telling him he must first obtain an appropriate passport stamp from the British consul-general.

So, bold as brass, Bevan called at the historic British consular villa in the Via del Mille on the same day, only to have his passport confiscated — the passport he offered, that is, but not the second passport which the first one said was 'attached hereto' and which he was believed to be carrying. This was an older document (passports in that era consisted of a single sheet folded in eight, with a photograph attached, all held in a cardboard cover) that was already filled up with visa stamps but still valid for travel.

The consul had no power to detain him, however. By the time an arrest instruction reached Naples on the Saturday, Bevan had apparently left the city and the Italian police — despite keeping a special watch on ship passengers leaving the port — had lost his trail.

A report that he had been arrested in Naples on 1 March swiftly proved false. Theories abounded as to where he might be heading. One of the most speculative circulated, appropriately, on the floor of the Stock Exchange. It said that he was already mid-Atlantic, having secured a passage to South America — an ultimate destination which may well have been one of the choices in his mind from the start, since he knew both Argentina and Brazil well. He might even have thought of taking refuge on one of the Brazilian cattle ranches of which he was part-owner. There is, as we shall discover in Chapter Twelve, a poetic hint in that direction, and there were regular sailings from Naples for that part of the world.

More prosaically, some gossips said he had decided to return to Paris, with a view to returning to London to face the music. Others thought he might simply have holed up in an Italian resort more restful for a man living on his nerve-ends than the bustling port of Naples.

A special correspondent of *The Times* nailed that last one on 3 March. After 'a search lasting the whole night and all today' in the provinces of Naples and Salerno, 'the rumours of Mr Gerard Bevan's presence at Sorrento or Amalfi are as unjustified as the reports of his capture'. Naples' chief of police, meanwhile, embarrassed by his officers' failure to close the net, offered the more romantic theory that Bevan might have made his way across the peninsula to the Adriatic coast — to Termoli perhaps, or one of the little fishing villages of the Gargano peninsula — and escaped by sailing boat to Dalmatia or Albania.

Wherever he was, his flight was now gathering the momentum of a fictional chase. He had moved irrevocably away from the even-paced Galsworthian milieu of his previous life in London. Now he was caught in an action thriller — chronologically about midway between John Buchan's *Greenmantle* (1916) and Graham Greene's *Stamboul Train* (1932) — tinged with the psychological undercurrents of a Somerset Maugham short story.

The 'Wanted' poster issued by the commissioner of the City of London police, William Nott-Bower, published in the London press and dispatched in several languages across the continent on 7 March, added to the drama. In its French version (see Frontispiece), it described him as:

> *Age 52; taille 1m 77; corpulence moyenne, yeux noisettes ou bleus; cheveux blonds, tendant a boucler sur les côtes, clairsernés au sommet de la tête; front haut; d'habitude completement rasé. Parle français couramment.*[3]

Perhaps Bevan himself — hat pulled low over *front haut*, overcoat collar turned up, slipping through Innsbruck or Salzburg railway station — spotted the poster and decided to cease shaving from that day on. The thickness of his dye-darkened beard in a photograph after his arrest in mid June certainly suggests a couple of months' growth.

All is Squared

There were many adventures to come before the moment of capture. And in London, the unravelling of Bevan's financial affairs was proceeding apace.

A meeting of the City Equitable's creditors in the Holborn Restaurant on Monday 3 April saw the first revelations of the 'travesty of financial control' (as expressed by the Official Receiver, on this occasion represented by H.E. Burgess) over which Bevan had presided. The full detail of his mismanagement of the City

---

[3] 'Age 52, height 5' 9"; medium build, eyes brown or blue; fair hair tending to curl at the sides, thinning on top; high forehead; habitually clean shaven. Speaks fluent French.'

Equitable will emerge at his trial in Chapter Nine, but for now let us watch the rapid liquidation of his personal assets, then follow the financier himself as he makes his way across Europe.

In many instances, Bevan's personal, family and corporate interests were inextricably intertwined. There was, for example, a holding of 1,700 shares in Claridge's Hotel in Paris that Sophie believed had been put in the name of their 16-year-old daughter Sheila, but were in fact in the possession of Jeanne. In an attempt to reclaim them for Sheila, Sophie's lawyer brought a complaint in front of a Paris magistrate, Maître Pamart, on 23 June.

Jeanne appeared at the hearing to assert that the shares were legally hers — and the hotel's general secretary confirmed that Bevan had indeed transferred them to her. Jeanne went on to tell the magistrate that the holding was part of a nest-egg, managed by Bevan for her and largely invested in companies he controlled, which 'by speculation had attained to a sum of £80,000'. Equivalent to more than £3 million today, that was quite some fortune to shower on a mistress.

This sub-plot became more dramatic when Sophie herself arrived in Paris to attend a further hearing in the judge's chambers on 1 July. Jeanne was present too, and if it was not the first time they had ever set eyes on each other, it was certainly the first time they had been in the same room together for many months.

Jeanne showed the judge a document proving that the shares were hers, and threatened a libel action against Sophie if the latter persisted in making accusations of illegality. The judge confirmed that the law was on Jeanne's side, and Sophie's lawyer withdrew her claim.

The *Daily Mail*, rather cruelly, juxtaposed photographs of Sophie and Jeanne in its report: Sophie looked grim, the shape of her beige hat (over a black dress) rather heightening the mannishness of her jaw. Jeanne, with bobbed hair and dark, kohl-lined eyes, looked lovely, and fully thirty years the younger of the two.

The *Daily Express* took a more sympathetic line. Its reporter tracked Sophie to her room at the Hotel Bristol, where he found her

'pale, tired and upset, frequently on the verge of tears' and packing
to return to London. Her hatred of 'that woman' seems to have been
channeled into contempt for the entire French legal system.

> I came to Paris little knowing the laws of France regarding a
> wife's property. Their laws permit a man to give a pearl necklace
> to his wife one day and to take it back to give to another woman
> next day. These laws are mediaeval, shameful, degrading.
>
> The French have been kind to me, but can do nothing. The
> judge knew that my only reason for coming here was to try to
> redeem for my little daughter Sheila the [shares] given to her
> by my husband, but the judge is powerless to help me. I shall
> now have to work as best I can and try to get a living for myself
> and my little girl. People do not realise the terrible misfortune
> that has come over me since my husband went bankrupt.
>
> There is nothing more for me to do in Paris… I am so over-
> come by the whole business that I hardly know what to do.

At which point, according to the reporter, 'the bitterness and dis-
illusionment in the heart of Mrs Bevan surged up and broke all
restraint. In a voice broken by sobs she accused her husband of
having wrecked their home and destroyed their happiness, and
of having brought on them all physical, moral and financial ruin.'

'Four years ago we were the happiest family in the land,' Sophie
raged. 'Then he became acquainted with that woman. He left his
wife and family to run after her — or more possibly it was she who
ran after him.'

Then there was the matter of the Syndicate Inglez, the partnership set up by Bevan with Peter Haig-Thomas's enthusiastic participation, to invest in land in the state of São Paulo in Brazil. As we
have already seen, the City Equitable had been brought in on the
deal with a stake of some £150,000. The Greater Britain Insurance
Co turned out to be in there too, for £79,000.

The Duke of Sutherland, a pillar of the Scottish establishment
who would become air minister in the Conservative government

of Andrew Bonar Law later that year, was also in for £20,000 — though his lawyer claimed he was 'not a partner' before admitting a fortnight later that he was. The names of Clarence Hatry and Sir Alexander Kleinwort were mentioned as participants, but with no sums of money attached.

The syndicate's resident manager in São Paulo was Charles Fitzroy Ponsonby McNeill, whose wife was a Mosley aunt of the future British fascist leader Sir Oswald. McNeill was very much the junior partner in terms of his financial interest — which he said was £10,000, though Haig-Thomas later argued in court that it was only £5,000. When Brazilian banks heard the news of the City Equitable's demise and Bevan's disappearance, they refused McNeill funds to pay his workforce and carry on his trade in livestock.

So he rushed back to London, with his sub-manager by the name of Nairn, to seek relief in the courts. On 26 April, Mr Justice Lawrence appointed McNeill as receiver of the partnership, with the power to borrow up to £1,000 for the day-to-day needs of the enterprise and to employ Nairn to help him — but 'without prejudice to any questions arising' as the City Equitable saga continued to unfold.

Bevan had cattle interests on both sides of the Atlantic, as it happened. His Littlecote herd of 'pedigree Shorthorns, of the best Scottish breed' was sold at auction at the end of April for £2,294 and 15 shillings. As for his lease on Littlecote itself, he turned out to have deployed it in a last-minute swerve to try to hold one of Ellis & Co's creditors at bay.

In brief, a diplomat by the name of Herman Norman, who had been at school and college with Bevan but claimed not to know him socially or indeed to have seen him at all since 1914, had deposited £50,000 worth of securities with Ellis & Co, on the understanding that the firm would make use of them while paying any dividends received, plus one per cent, to Norman via his solicitor, a Mr Stanton.

Some time before the beginning of 1922, £30,000 had been returned to Norman, but the remaining £20,000 worth of securities turned out to have been pledged to Ellis & Co's bankers as security.

On 25 January, Stanton had asked for full repayment on Norman's behalf, but his demand coincided with a much larger one for the return of securities and cash to First National Reinsurance — the claim that effectively pushed Ellis & Co to the brink of insolvency.

Bevan visited the solicitor Stanton two days later to say that he hoped to return Norman's £20,000 by 1 March. Stanton got in touch with Norman, and the answer came back on Monday 30 January that they insisted on immediate repayment. But on the same day, a writ arrived at Ellis from First National, claiming £37,231 8s 4d, which was (or should have been) the cash balance on the insurance company's current account with the stockbroking firm.

It was not until the following Monday — when, as we know, Bevan was making final preparations to flee — that he attempted to get Norman off his back. He visited Stanton's office, taking the deeds of Littlecote with him. He claimed that the lease, which had a little over 20 years to run, was worth £25,000, and offered to execute a charge over it in Norman's favour, thus amply securing the £20,000 debt.

Stanton accepted the proposal and set about preparing the necessary documents — but before the charge could be formally executed, Bevan left the country. Nevertheless, the act of depositing the deeds with Stanton constituted 'equitable security', and the trustee in bankruptcy, Ernest Pegler,[4] in due course came to court to argue that it constituted a 'fraudulent preference' over Bevan's other creditors.

That matter was to be aired in court in July, in the same month that two adjacent properties to Littlecote — Froxfield Manor Farm and Eastridge, totalling a thousand acres and acquired by Bevan for their sporting rights — were sold on behalf of the trustee for a total of £15,500.

Of more immediate interest to followers of the Bevan saga in London during the spring was news of the forthcoming sale of his collections of Chinese porcelain, fine English furniture, antique

---

[4] Co-founder of the City accountancy firm of Spicer & Pegler, and co-author of standard texts on book-keeping and income tax.

tapestries and Persian carpets, which Ernest Pegler had caused to be collected from Littlecote and the Carlton suite (but not apparently from Upper Grosvenor Street, the contents of which were deemed to be Sophie's) and consigned to Mssrs Puttick & Simpson, auctioneers of 'literary property and works of art' at No 47 Leicester Square.

If Bevan was aware of the sale, he could take consolation from the grandeur of the venue in which his collections were about to go under the hammer. It had been the home of Sir Joshua Reynolds, and the octagonal, high-ceilinged auction room itself had once been the great 18th century portraitist's studio.

The first sale took place on 26 May, when 146 lots realised a total of £13,582. The porcelain was particularly fine (even though, as we shall learn in a moment, this can only have been a fraction of his collection) demonstrating not only that Bevan had a refined eye but that he had also taken the best advice. Some pieces came from well-known collections, and some had appeared in the bible of this esoteric field of connoisseurship, *Chinese Porcelain and Hard Stones* by Edgar Gorer and J.F. Blacker (1911).

London's leading dealers were in the thick of the bidding. Speelman Brothers paid the highest price, 1,000 guineas, for 'a Yung-cheng garniture with ruby ground, comprising three jars and a pair of beakers, brilliantly enamelled with birds'. Frank Partridge of New Bond Street bought a pair of fine eggshell lanterns, a pair of yellow Ming vases enameled with dragons, and an opium pipe formed as a lotus seedpod. Mallett of Davies Street bought a pair of ruby Chi'en-lung bowls, and a collection of standing and reclining figures.

As for the furniture from Littlecote, a set of five Queen Anne armchairs (originally from Wentworth Castle near Barnsley, seat of the Earls of Strafford) fetched 1,350 guineas from a dealer called Harris, who also picked up a William and Mary walnut marquetry cabinet. An entire room of oak panelling, newly made in the William and Mary style, which Bevan had not got around to installing in one or other of his homes or offices and had stored in the Pall Mall Safe Deposit, fetched 350 guineas. And the best of his rugs, a 16th-century sample ornamented with the floral pattern of Shah Habuz, reached 650 guineas.

Quite a hoard, but there was much more to come — a job lot of his antiquarian books came up at Puttick and Simpson's in August; some paintings, drawings and items of old and modern silver in October; some notable swords, a lacquered Chinese screen and a pair of early 18th-century bookcases early the following year. He had been a formidable collector, and his trustees in bankruptcy were determined to extract every penny out of his notoriety.

Even his £2,000 life insurance policy and a life interest in a trust fund yielding £250 a year came under the hammer (for £590 and £390 respectively) of a specialist in such matters, though they attracted only two cautious bidders — perhaps, as the auctioneer remarked, because Bevan had 'been rather in the limelight lately'.

And there were more stories to emerge about Bevan's *modus operandi* with the trade. The most intriguing of these concerned Alfred Samson de Pinna, a dealer in antique Chinese porcelain with premises in Devonshire Street W1. His tale also came out in the bankruptcy court in August.

It began in November 1920 when he had been introduced to Bevan by another dealer, called Hartley. De Pinna had visited Bevan in Upper Grosvenor Street and agreed to sell him a square black oriental vase for £5,500 — £1,000 of which was due the following January and was paid on time. But the balance, due in April, was not paid. After some to-ing and fro-ing, Bevan came up with another £2,000 in July 1921, but when the remaining £2,500 failed to appear, Hartley visited Bevan twice to negotiate on de Pinna's behalf. Bevan at first said he would pay up on 1 January 1922; then that he was waiting to sell a very valuable book and would settle out of the proceeds of the sale.

Finally, with his world crumbling around him, Bevan found time to call on de Pinna in Devonshire Street on 2 February — less than a week before his flight to Paris. By the dealer's own account, Bevan told him he had no cash to hand but still wanted to settle his debt and take possession of the black vase, so de Pinna would have to take other vases from Bevan's extensive collection instead of money in settlement.

De Pinna duly went round to Upper Grosvenor Street — taking with him, as arranged, the square black oriental vase — and rang the bell. Sophie, rather remarkably in the circumstances, had him ushered him and allowed him to choose three lesser vases. Then she telephoned her errant husband in his City office to confirm that it was in order to let de Pinna take them. De Pinna asked her to sign a receipt for the black vase, on which she wrote gaily: 'All is squared, like the vase.'

But de Pinna did not notice until he was back in his shop (so he said) that one of the three vases was damaged. That evening he went to the Carlton Hotel to confront Bevan again. Ever the persuader, Bevan agreed that he had not treated de Pinna well, and offered to assign to him a £500 debt that would be due to Bevan shortly from the dealer Frank Partridge — handing de Pinna a note addressed to Partridge to that effect, which was later produced in court.

That encounter at the Carlton was on the Thursday evening, and so far the de Pinna story, though colourful, sounds plausible enough. But over the weekend, a much larger and more surprising transaction took place: Bevan sold de Pinna no less than 63 pieces of oriental china, *including the square black vase* which had been in pride of place in Upper Grosvenor Street for barely 48 hours, for £15,000 in cash, in the form of 15 big white Bank of England notes of £1,000 each.[5]

Barristers on Ernest Pegler's behalf would argue before Mr Justice Lawrence that the transfer to de Pinna of the three vases and the £500 debt from Partridge constituted another fraudulent preference in relation to other Bevan creditors, and that de Pinna should give the vases or their money value to the trustee and re-assign the Partridge debt. There was plenty of proof, in the form of calls on Ellis & Co in late January from First National and others which had not been and could not have been met, that Bevan was

---

[5] £1,000 notes, printed on one side only, 8¼″ × 5¼″, were issued by the Bank until 1943, and ceased to be legal tender in 1945.

already insolvent by the time of these dealings with de Pinna. The judge concluded that Bevan's 'dominant motive' was indeed to prefer de Pinna over other creditors when he must have known that he had no chance of avoiding bankruptcy.

But what was not clear, to the judge then or to anyone enquiring into the case later, was whether Bevan was really motivated by a burning urge to own the square black vase. If he was, why did he sell it back to de Pinna two days later? The court does not seem to have concerned itself with the second, apparently more straightforward transaction — which did not involve a debt or a creditor, but simply the exchange of a large quantity of Chinese porcelain for a sum of cash equivalent to more than £600,000 today.

Had Bevan's assessment of his chance of financial survival changed dramatically on the single business day between the two transactions? Or had he gone through with the first transaction not so much to secure ownership of the coveted black vase as to secure the trust of de Pinna and encourage him to lay his hands on a huge wad of cash in readiness for the second transaction? And how had they settled on a price of £15,000 — more than the proceeds of that first auction sale in Leicester Square, almost as much as the sale price of a thousand acres of good Wiltshire farmland?

To catalogue and value 63 pieces of rare Chinese porcelain was a major undertaking — and de Pinna must surely have had access to Upper Grosvenor Street over a period of time, not just for one quick visit, which suggests that Sophie was in on the deal. She would have considered that the collection was by rights partly or wholly hers — her solicitors certainly made that argument to the bankruptcy trustee, as they did about some of the contents of Littlecote — and it seems highly likely that Bevan split the cash with her to cover her household expenses and look after the children after he had gone. Of all the loose ends of Bevan's story, the de Pinna sub-plot is one of the most intriguing; we shall return to it briefly in Chapter Nine.

If this cash injection had provided a partial solution to Sophie's 'pressing problems', as she put it in the February statement, she took a further step by leasing 21 Upper Grosvenor Street 'for the season' to a Major Francis, and removing herself to rural Berkshire to stay with her friend Lady St Helier, better known as Mary Jeune, a journalist, charity campaigner and society hostess whose claims to fame included a close friendship with Thomas Hardy and the fact that it was at her dinner table that Winston Churchill met his future wife Clementine Hozier.

Having written much on the subject of 'modern marriage', Mary Jeune no doubt had plenty of advice to offer Sophie.

The Farm Gate "Express": See Page 13.

The Daily Mirror

NET SALE NEARLY TWICE THAT OF ANY OTHER DAILY PICTURE NEWSPAPER

There is a laughable adventure—

—of Pin, Squeak and Wilfred on page 13.

WOMAN OF SIXTY-FIVE CITED IN DIVORCE SUIT: ALLEGATIONS OF A WIFE ONLY IN NAME.

GERARD LEE BEVAN'S BEARD: PHOTOGRAPH FROM VIENNA

Mrs. Roxburgh, aged sixty-five, intervener in the case.

Bevan as he used to appear in the City.

Mrs. T. G. Lowther and her husband, Mr. John Brabazon Lowther. An unusual divorce suit is that of Mrs. Tyra Gonborg Lowther, who seeks the dissolution of her marriage to Mr. John Brabazon Lowther, a professional singer, alleging misconduct between her husband and Mrs. Roxburgh, a woman of sixty-five.

Special photograph of Gerard Lee Bevan taken since his arrest. Documentary evidence to support the application for the extradition from Austria of Gerard Lee Bevan, the City financier, is stated to be on its way to Vienna. The charge is that of issuing a false balance-sheet.

QUIET WEDDING OF THE EARL OF DROGHEDA IN LONDON

BESSARABO TRIAL: RELEASE OF MLLE. JACQUES.

The Earl of Drogheda and his bride, Lady Victor Paget, after their marriage yesterday at the Kensington register office, Marloes-road. The ceremony, which was a quiet one attended mainly by relatives, was followed by a religious ceremony at St. Jude's Church, Hampstead.—(Daily Mirror photograph.)

Mlle. Paule Jacques (also right inset), daughter of Mme. Bessarabo (left inset), leaving yesterday the prison of St. Lazare and carrying her box of clothes. Her release followed her acquittal of the charge of aiding in the murder of her stepfather, while her mother was found guilty and sentenced to twenty years' penal servitude.

Printed and Published by The Daily Mirror Newspapers, Ltd., at 22-29, Bouverie-street, London, E. C. 4.—Friday, June 23, 1942.

Daily Mirror, 23 June 1922

CHAPTER EIGHT

Capture

'Great robbers always resemble honest folks. Fellows who have rascally faces have only one course to take and that is to remain honest; otherwise they would be arrested off-hand. The artistic thing is to unmask honest countenances.'

Inspector Fix on Phileas Fogg,
whom he suspects of robbing the Bank of England,
in Jules Verne, *Around the World in Eighty Days* (1873)

An Inspector Calls

What we can conclude from the de Pinna story is that Bevan's flight across Europe was not hampered by lack of funds. He had more than enough to pay for a succession of expensive hotels that suited his tastes — and for exceptional items such as the costs of obtaining a stolen French passport.

We have already noted that he briefly assumed the name of Lewis for his travels. But once he had the new passport, he became Léon Vernier — who was a real person, born at Tourncoing on 1 October 1892 (so almost 23 years younger than Bevan, and unlikely to have looked anything like him) and resident at rue des Processions in Lille, where the passport had been issued to him in May 1919 for a visit to Ireland.

When it was found in Bevan's possession, the issue date had been altered to 19 March 1922, suggesting perhaps that Bevan happened to have access to a handy date stamp on that day. A photograph of Bevan with his new beard had been stuck over the original picture of Vernier.

Newspaper reports differed as to when the passport had come into Bevan's possession. According to one, he already had it with him when he left London. According to another, Bevan himself said it came into his hands at Vicenza in northern Italy, where he must have paused in late February en route for the Austrian border. But from whom it came into his hands is unknown. It must have been stolen in France, because if Vernier had been travelling in Italy at the time, there would immediately have been a police hunt for someone passing himself off as Vernier, which would only have served to increase Bevan's risk of capture.

We might guess that during his four-day stopover at the apartment of Madamoiselle Germain in Paris, Bevan had paid someone with the right sort of connections to find him a stolen passport and arrange for it to reach him on his further travels. Perhaps that person was a low-life from the world of the dance halls familiar to Jeanne, or perhaps it was Maurice Langlais, the chief reception clerk at Claridge's who knew Bevan's habits extremely well and had no doubt received plenty of generous tips from him for services rendered in the past. Since Bevan's ultimate route was at that stage still uncertain, dependent on the availability of visas and the attentiveness of the police, he must have been in touch with the passport courier by letter or telegram to fix a rendezvous in Italy.

Whatever else we might say about Bevan, he was certainly a resourceful operator in his own interest. A reasonable guess is that Jeanne stayed behind in Paris until the passport was to hand, then caught him up at Vicenza and went on with him into Austria. It is also a possibility that his brother Ivor went along for part of the journey, or accompanied Jeanne (who might otherwise have looked conspicuous travelling alone) when she came from Paris to rejoin Gerard.

But there was no visa for Austria in the passport. Bevan told the court in Vienna that he had overcome that obstacle by crossing the well-guarded border on foot, and not through a frontier town

— which suggests that he hiked over the Brenner Pass on the road and rail route from Bolzano to Innsbruck, or via the remote mountain crossing point on the Otzalstrasse to the west.

That was the way the *World's Pictorial News* reporter seems to have imagined the crossing and described it as fact, though without place names. But could a 52-year-old with rheumatism really have stumbled, perhaps for two days or more, through thick snow on mountain paths?

More likely, he paid a driver to take Jeanne through the border by road (and to carry his luggage, which at this stage consisted of two small trunks) and pick him up on the other side, Gerard himself having walked across on a not too arduous path well known to locals who preferred to avoid the border checks. Alternatively, a geographically vague Bevan family anecdote has Gerard and Ivor jumping from a slow-moving train somewhere en route to Vienna, so perhaps that story refers to a train that was approaching the Brenner Pass border point.

Having achieved both the border crossing and the doctoring of the passport, Gerard remained invisible for a short while until Monsieur Vernier, who had apparently announced himself as an artist from Paris, for some reason began to attract attention in Salzburg.

Under the rule of the right-wing Christian Social Party, at a time of high political tension and economic turmoil, Austria was a country whose authorities kept a close eye on its small population, and on the comings and goings of foreigners. The Salzburg police took note of a Frenchman with a somewhat younger ('aged about 28') female companion who gave her name as Madeleine Vernier. Their colleagues at Innsbruck reported that the same man, or someone very like him, had stayed for three weeks at the Hotel Kreid — one of the Tyrolean town's most prominent hotels.

Some reports said he had a second companion. This might have been Ivor — who if challenged to show his own identity papers, could have pointed out that Bevan was a very common English or Welsh surname and that he did not look at all like the man in the poster. But in due course, word of this suspicious group reached the chief of the British passport office in Vienna, who alerted the Austrians that despite indications to the contrary, the other man in the group might be Gerard Bevan.

Salzburg and Innsbruck were favoured destinations for the kind of well-heeled English travellers who might have recognized Bevan, even behind his thickening facial growth. So he moved in late March to the greater anonymity of the capital city, where he put up at the Hotel Kranz — a late-19th-century palace (subsequently renamed the Ambassador) which somewhat resembled the Carlton in London and was much frequented by Austrian and German aristocracy, but less so by English tourists.

The couple lived at the Kranz in 'good but simple style' from 28 March until 1 June. Then Jeanne departed — Bevan having decided, no doubt, that the next leg of his journey, all the way across Russia in the hope of finally taking ship to South America across the Pacific, would be easier undertaken alone and that she should wait in Paris for news that it was safe for her to join him wherever and whenever he finally reached safety.

In any event, we know for certain that Jeanne was back in Paris by the latter part of June, to play her part in the magistrate's hearings over the matter of the Claridge's shares which had been transferred into her name from Sheila Bevan's.

Once Jeanne had gone, Bevan made for Reichenau, about 60 miles from Vienna — a fashionable watering hole where the Habsburg archdukes kept a hunting lodge — and from there a few miles further to the ski village of Semmering, where he stayed at the Grand Hotel Panhans, yet another Carlton lookalike.

By now, however, he was almost certainly aware that he was being watched: in a grand hotel in a small out-of-season resort, a pair of Viennese detectives would have had trouble making themselves inconspicuous in the dining room. They did manage to find out from a hotel servant — one who changed the towels in Bevan's room, presumably — that the man they had under observation was a frequent user of hair dye. But Bevan still succeeded in giving them the slip.

He was eventually tracked down again in suburban Vienna. He had asked a secretary at the Kranz to help him find a German teacher, and had been given an introduction to a Herr Wolfbauer, an artist and retired army officer who has once lived in London. Bevan and Wolfbauer got on well, and it was arranged that Bevan should lodge in a room in the Wolfbauer family apartment in Wiedner Gürtel, a wide street in the south of the city facing onto railway yards.

There he settled briefly into a quiet, domestic way of life that was not his style at all. He maintained the pretence of being French (Wolfbauer later claimed that he had not been fooled, having spotted the telltale signs of an English gentleman) and ingratiated himself with the family by bringing home cakes from a fine patissier in the neighbourhood when he went out for daily walks.

The Wolfbauers found him genial, and formed the view that he had ample means. Bevan and Herr Wolfbauer enjoyed regular pots of English tea together, and conversations about music; Bevan sometimes also spoke of South America.

The lodger ate in his room, or in plain local restaurants — and if all this sounds surprisingly relaxed, his inner tensions were perhaps evidenced by a glimpse of him later reported by a busybody neighbour. He had been spotted gesticulating wildly as he wrote at a table near the window — perhaps *billets doux* to Jeanne, or discreet instructions to Ivor, or letters that for fear of revealing himself he could not post to his daughters.

Or perhaps the gesticulation was Bevan's way of conducting the metre of his poetry. After his arrest, notebooks were found in his room containing what were described as 'comedies of his own authorship', but are more likely to have been drafts of new poems.

As we will discover in Chapter Twelve, it is not easy to relate Bevan's poems to the events of his life; most are set in a world of chivalric fantasy. But there is a sad one called *Exile* that might have been composed as he stared despairingly out across the Austrian railway tracks. It appears as the epitaph of this book.

Meanwhile, the net was inexorably closing. Having lost him at Semmering the police began to make new enquiries in hotels across

Vienna. The secretary at the Kranz warned his friend Wolfbauer that the search was on for a Monsieur Vernier, and Wolfbauer duly visited a police station to find out what the charges might be against his lodger — and laughed about chiding him for using so much hair dye. It was obvious that he had their prey in his house, and Wolfbauer agreed to make it easy for them to arrest Bevan, providing a plan of the rooms and a duplicate key.

None of this was being reported in the British press, of course — even though it later transpired that a 'special correspondent' of the *Continental Daily Mail*, which had been offering 25,000 French francs reward for information leading to Bevan's capture, had been living only a few doors away from the Wolfbauers' address. For a while, it was widely assumed in London that Bevan had made good his escape, and would never be seen again.

But the public appetite to see him brought to justice was whetted again during May by the trial of the journalist, publisher, serial bankrupt and swindler, Horatio Bottomley MP — the irrepressible scoundrel whose latest alleged offence had been to steal £150,000 of small investors' savings by means of a scam called Bottomley's Bond Clubs which he claimed to have conceived as an exercise in 'financially enlightened patriotism'.

Subscribers' money had supposedly been used to buy War Loan stock, thus supporting the nation's financial burden, while Bottomley offered cash prizes on a lottery basis akin to premium bonds. But this was really a form of Ponzi scheme: few War Bonds were actually bought with club subscriptions, most of which were diverted to fund his other schemes and his sybaritic lifestyle.

The trial was entertaining stuff. Bottomley had been granted a recess to allow him time to quaff his customary mid-morning pint of champagne, and had presented his own defence in the most tear-jerking terms:

> I who stood by the boys in the trenches... who held their hands
> in the great hospitals as they passed into eternity — scheming
> all the time to rob them and their families of their gold? If it be

so and I am he, when my turn comes to cross the barrier, may all the tortures of the damned be visited upon my soul. But the dear boys, whether they be sleeping or are still with us, know that I have not betrayed them!

In fact the weight of evidence against Bottomley was overwhelming, and the prosecution conducted by Travers Humphreys (who would defend Bevan a few months later) was hailed as a forensic triumph. It became apparent that during a period in which nearly a million pounds of other people's money had passed through Bottomley's hands, he kept no proper books of account, employed no auditor, and continually moved cash from one bank account to another, some in his own name and some in the name of the Bond Clubs. The receivers of the Clubs found only £23,000.

In his final speech to the jury on Friday 28 May, Bottomley pointed to the Sword of Justice hanging on the courtroom wall and declared: 'You will never convict me. The jury is not yet born who would convict me on these charges. It is unthinkable. That sword would drop from its scabbard if you gave a verdict of guilty against me.'

The Jury took that risk, returning to their task on the following Monday to deliver a guilty verdict within a matter of 28 minutes. The sword stayed in its place and Mr Justice Salter sentenced Bottomley to seven years' penal servitude for 'heartless frauds' committed with 'callous effrontery', in which he saw 'no mitigation whatever'.

Bottomley nevertheless stole the last word. Told by the judge that it was not customary for a convicted man in such a case to be asked if he had anything more to say, Bottomley let rip anyway: 'Had it been so, my Lord, I should have something rather offensive to say about your summing-up.'

The Spectator observed that Bottomley's irrepressible spirit won him some public sympathy, and that:

...the whole story is a tragedy of crookedness... amid all the contempt and anger which one must feel against a man like

Bottomley, one cannot help being deeply sorry that some different arrangement of the grey matter in his brain or some different mentorship in his youth did not launch Bottomley upon a great and noble career. For he had abilities, originality and powers of application which would have brought him to the fore anywhere.

The same might have been said of Bevan — if only his energies and financial skills had been correctly channelled, he might have built a great business empire. But his sins had less gaiety about them, and the public response at this stage was largely one of irritation that he had not been caught, and suspicion as to why that was so. Shortly after the Bottomley verdict, *The Times* took the opportunity to castigate the authorities for the failure to apprehend Bevan, or indeed to report any definite sighting of him since Naples in February.

Even though the City Equitable had been showing 'unmistakable signs of distress' for at least two weeks before he fled the country, the paper's editorial declared, the collection of evidence against Bevan has proceeded 'in a leisurely manner' and the police had utterly failed to keep track of the man himself. The reaction of the public in such a case was to 'question the impartiality of the law' and to 'mistake negligence for design… Even now there is a persistent suggestion, which does no credit to English methods of justice, that no adequate measures are being taken to execute the warrant which the Director of Public Prosecutions has issued.'

The insinuation of some kind of Establishment conspiracy to let Bevan flee (which found an echo in his trial, when he claimed that he had left the country only because 'someone' whose name was too sensitive to be revealed had urged him to go) was confounded by the news that on the morning of Tuesday 13 June, a man believed to be Gerard Lee Bevan had been arrested in Vienna and placed in a cell at the city's Central Criminal Court.

'My Poor Wife!'

Unlike the flat-footed constables of London and Naples, the Austrian police had been doing their job properly — declared the officer in charge, Inspector Wylbora, who either spoke remarkably fluent English or was rather freely translated by British reporters. Only the effectiveness of Bevan's disguise and the fluency of his French had made them hesitate, he said: 'Of course we had a close description of the person of the man sought, but his passport in the name Léon Vernier appeared unassailable; and his self-possession was disconcerting.'

At the very moment of his arrest, however, Bevan took temporary leave of his self-possession, or at least revealed a hitherto unseen side of it. When two detectives came to the Wolfbauer house and burst into the lodger's room, he reached into his waistcoat pocket, took out a small bottle containing a white tablet and put the tablet into his mouth. Assuming this to be a suicide pill (it was in fact an aspirin) the officers set about him and tried, to no avail, to extract it from his mouth or make him spit it out.

Bevan fought back wildly for several minutes — kicking, punching and even biting with such ferocity that reinforcements had to be called before he could finally be subdued and handcuffed. As they dragged him out, he reportedly muttered: 'My poor wife!'

In court, Bevan claimed that he had never intended to resist arrest when the moment came, which he knew it inevitably would, and that he had no recollection of having done so. If he had, he said, he must have been 'acting mechanically', as in a trance. His memory was blank from the moment the police burst into his room until he awoke in the courthouse cell some hours later.

Whether or not Bevan really knew what was happening — the court prosecutor poured scorn on the 'trance' story — the police assumed he had poisoned himself and took him straight to a first-aid station to have his stomach pumped. Not surprisingly, Bevan then fainted and was carried to the hospital cell of the Central Criminal

Court, where for two days he denied his true identity and gave every indication of having gone mad.

But by Friday he had regained his composure — and was showing three days' worth of light-coloured growth at the roots of his hair and beard, so asked for the prison barber to shave him clean. Inspector Wylbora visited his cell, held up a copy of the Wanted-poster photograph, and asked firmly, 'Who are you?' 'Gerard Lee Bevan,' came the reply.

Some 6,000 francs (worth about £120) and 100,000 Austrian crowns (worth very little at a time of runaway inflation) were found in Bevan's possession. If he had money or valuables stashed elsewhere to fund the next leg of his journey, none ever came to light. The only item at the Wolfbauers that immediately confirmed his true identity was a woollen collar marked with the initials 'GLB', though it was later said that 'Bevan' was chalked on the bottom of one of his trunks. He had destroyed most of his papers, except for a copy of an advertisement he had intended to place locally for someone to teach him Russian, and a railway ticket to Graz, 120 miles south of Vienna, dated for the following day, 14 July.

It came to light that he had struck a deal the previous week, with a hotel employee by the name of Panek in the second district of Vienna — the Jewish quarter also called Leopoldstadt, where such transactions were not unknown — to buy yet another passport. If he had been able to collect it, that document would have enabled him to travel via Graz through Austria's easternmost province of Burgenland into Hungary. From there his route, all by train, would have taken him via Kaschau (now Kosice) in eastern Slovakia, across Galicia in what is now Ukraine to Kiev, and from there to Moscow.

Given that Russia was still in the bloody throes of its post-revolutionary civil war — and that Leon Trotsky was busy ordering mass executions of Ukrainian peasants — this was a more than an exotic itinerary. It was a plan conceived in desperation by a fugitive with few options left.

It seems inconceivable that he intended to stay in Russia. Most likely, he hoped to take the Trans-Siberian Railway via Irkutsk on

Lake Baikal and onwards across the Soviet far east to Khabarovsk and the Pacific port of Vladivostok — a route through one of the world's emptiest and most hostile landscapes which had only been completed in 1916 and would have involved some ten days' continuous travel. Had all gone well, and assuming he could lay his hands on enough money to keep moving, he might have been at Vladivostok by early August.

Having found a berth on a sailing to Yokohama in Japan, he might then have crossed the Pacific, though he would have aimed to avoid landing at San Francisco for fear of extradition. Perhaps Panama would have served his purpose: from there he might have found his way around the coast to Brazil by late September or October.

It was a wildly improbable itinerary to equal that of Jules Verne's Phileas Fogg fifty years earlier. But Inspector Wylbora's satisfaction that, in the nick of time, his men had prevented Bevan from setting off on it was evident from his final remarks to British correspondents. Bevan 'would have had to be an exceptional man if once our suspicions were aroused, we had failed to corner him,' declared the Inspector. 'He was brought to bay and there is an end to the matter. We now await a demand for his extradition, with which we shall be happy to comply.'

Meanwhile, Bevan was moved to a special cell for what were described as 'prisoners of refinement', and one of the Austrian detectives who had arrested him — and apparently forgiven him for the punches he landed during their struggle — took the trouble to go back to the Wolfbauer house to collect Bevan's underclothes. The prisoner was even reported to have been provided with a supply of marmalade and to have received numerous letters from women in England offering him help and comfort. He declined to reply to them.

Extradition wasn't quite the simple matter that the Inspector had implied. It was initially expected that the Austrian authorities would drop the charges they might otherwise have brought against Bevan for living in Vienna under a false passport and assaulting the officers who arrested him, in order to allow the extradition to proceed as quickly as possible. That turned out not to be the case, however, and in any event an Austrian court would have to decide, after a preliminary hearing, whether there was a *prima facie* case for Bevan to answer in London.

The prisoner would then have a fortnight's grace in which to decide whether to fight the British application for his extradition. And the Austrian authorities would have to satisfy themselves that none of the charges against him were of a political nature.

The first informal hearing by an examining magistrate, Judge Remsauer, took place in a room adjacent to Bevan's cell on Monday 19 June. The press were not allowed to attend, and Bevan declined to offer them any statement. It took a further week before a senior British policeman — Detective Inspector Hubert Smith of the City of London Police — set off for Vienna. He arrived on 28 June, and was immediately allowed to speak to the prisoner, who he reported to be 'showing signs of irritability and nervousness' but who swiftly came round to the idea that it would be in his best interest to return to London as soon as possible, rather than trying to fight the extradition.

Indeed, Bevan went as far as to sign a document dated 30 June which said:

> I desire to waive all extradition formalities and return to England with Inspector Smith. I desire to meet all charges which may be preferred against me as soon as possible in the English courts, as if I had been in England, and I am prepared to surrender at once to Inspector Smith and proceed to England for that purpose.

But this piece of paper cut no ice with the Austrians. The usually taciturn Inspector Smith, who spoke no German himself, might also have shown signs of irritability when it was explained to him that Judge Remsauer required officially certified translations of all relevant documents to be laid before his court before he could rule that the charges against Bevan were not political.

For Smith, wrote one waggish reporter, 'a month's holiday in Vienna' was in prospect while the legal processes ground forward. Meanwhile pressure was mounting from London, where questions were already being asked in Parliament about the progress of the extradition.

On 3 July, Sir William Davison, Conservative MP for Kensington South, addressed a private notice question on the matter to the home secretary. An answer came from Sir John Baird, the Conservative member for Rugby who was under-secretary for home affairs in Lloyd George's coalition.

Applications for Bevan's arrest with a view to extradition had been made in several countries, said Baird. 'When Bevan was arrested in Vienna, steps were at once taken to obtain his surrender, as soon as all the charges against him have been formulated and the necessary documents relating to each prepared and submitted.'

'Can the Honourable Member say when these proceedings will be completed, and when it is likely that Bevan will be put on his trial in this country?' Davison pressed. 'It is impossible to say that', was all Baird could offer.

Two days later, Sir Frederick Hall had a go, addressing himself to the Home Secretary, Edward Shortt, a close Liberal ally of Lloyd George. The Conservative MP for Dulwich, Hall was very much a City man — a member of the committee of Lloyd's, a long-standing member of the Baltic Exchange, director of a number of electricity companies — who would almost certainly have crossed paths with Bevan. He had a reputation for genial tenacity in his questioning of ministers.

In view of the widespread distress resulting from Bevan's dealings, Hall asked, could the House be assured that all possible measures will be followed to secure his return to this country?

'The usual procedure has been followed and every effort is being made to secure Mr Bevan's return at the earliest possible date,' said Shortt, before embarking on a rather ponderous legal explanation as to why the delay might be important to the process of finally bringing Bevan to book in an English court.

'Some delay is inevitable,' the home secretary offered, 'because the Act of 1870 precludes any prisoner extradited from a foreign country from being tried in this country for any offence committed before his surrender except such as may be proved by the facts on which his surrender was granted. It is therefore obviously undesirable that Bevan's extradition from Austria should be effected till the Austrian Government has been put in possession of evidence relating to all the charges on which it is desired to try him in this country. Care is necessary in selecting and formulating such charges, but it is hoped that the evidence will be completed in the course of this week.'

'But may we assume that there will be no extraordinary difficulty placed in the way by the Austrian authorities?' Hall followed up. Shortt said he had no reason to suppose that would happen — and indeed a few days later the head of the legal section of the Austrian foreign ministry issued a statement emphasising his government's eagerness to be co-operative within the constraints of the law.

As of 6 July, this official pointed out, no formal request for extradition had been received by his ministry, and the Bevan file consisted of little more than the details of his arrest. One sworn deposition from London had been delivered, but other supporting documents were still to come (they were in fact delivered about a week later). So long as all this was in good order, Austrian officialdom stood ready to 'expedite Bevan's departure as much as possible'.

Two days after that, Bevan himself issued a statement to the British press, via Reuters. Given everything we now know about his situation, it makes fascinating reading. It began with what we can assume to be a pack of lies, enhanced with a touch of pathos:

> I left England on February 8th, at the request of my wife who had information to the effect that a warrant would be issued for my arrest on the following day and begged and implored me to spare her the disgrace. In her interests, therefore, I consented to go away, though very much against my own will and judgment.
>
> To begin with, I foresaw that such a step would inevitably prejudice me in the eyes of public opinion; secondly, it was

against the principles and practice of my whole life to run away from trouble, as anyone who knows me well would testify, but above all to exile myself from my children was to impose upon myself pain infinitely greater than any world could inflict. I may add that I had about £250 in my possession.

We might imagine Bevan pacing his small cell, polishing carefully weighted phrases over several days as he had once paced his Cornhill office or the Long Gallery at Littlecote while perfecting the text of his addresses to City Equitable shareholders. He must have irritated his gaolers with calls for more paper and ink — but he was determined to set out concisely what at that stage he clearly intended to be the outline of his defence when he arrived back in London.

The nub of it was largely to put the blame on to Edmund Mansell for the mismanagement of the City Equitable:

For my own part, since grave charges have been brought against me, it is my desire to come to grips with them at the earliest opportunity and to confront them with the facts. Knowing absolutely nothing of law, I am unable to form any idea as to what decision may be reached upon technical grounds, but this I do know — nothing dishonourable can be proved against me, for the simpler reason that I have never committed a dishonourable action.

As regards the so-called falsification of the balance sheet of the City Equitable Fire Insurance, a certain block of securities was sold on my instructions and through the agency of my firm [Ellis & Co], and Treasury bills were bought in their place for the purpose of the balance sheet and re-exchanged soon afterwards. This operation, I contend, was well within the limits of what is ordinarily known as window-dressing, more especially as the prospects of the company at the time, so far as I or any of the directors knew, were literally without a cloud.

With regard to the relations between the company and my firm, these were of a close and cordial nature during the six years I was Chairman. The company was in the habit of lending considerable sums to my firm and received a high return on its money. They were perfectly normal and legitimate transactions.

Further, my firm was concerned in the handling of various deals during the said period and usually offered the company participation. These transactions were naturally intended to be mutually profitable, but while I can recall no instance in which my firm set out with the objective of getting the better of the deal, I could quote a number of cases where either my firm or myself made gratuitous sacrifices in the interest of the City Equitable Fire Insurance.

It is true that eventually, when called upon to pay their loans, my firm was unable to do so, but this arose from the fact that the securities against which my firm had obtained advances from their various bankers consisted so largely of City Equitable shares themselves, and our fortunes were thus inextricably bound up with those of the company.

If then I must say so, though our manager [Mansell] was a brilliant business-getter, the real weakness lay in the internal organisation of the company itself. Had this been more thorough, and had the directors been better advised as to the outlook and possible requirements of the company, a different investment policy would have been pursued, funds would have been kept more liquid, and the present catastrophe would never have occurred.

Homeward Bound

The Austrians had by now brought charges against Bevan for false registration, holding a false passport and resisting arrest. When these came to trial on 12 July, counsel for the defence accused the arresting officers of excessive zeal in the way they had jumped on Bevan, and pointed out that they carried no lasting or obvious bruises from their tussle with him. This seems to have persuaded the judge, who set aside the assault charge and found Bevan guilty of the false registration charge only. Bevan was sentenced to a token three days' imprisonment, but deemed to have served the time already, having been held on remand for almost a month.

Still the extradition process seemed to be progressing at a glacial pace, and complications also loomed for Bevan's journey home. Although Inspector Smith would accompany him at all times, formality required that he be guarded by Austrian officers as far as the border, and by officers of whichever countries he set foot in after that, with all necessary permits in good order. And if the route were to pass through France, the French might intercept him in order to deal with complaints lodged against Bevan in their own courts — extradition rules between Britain and France having been established by a series of 19th century treaties which had overlooked the issue of transit of an accused person across French territory.

While Inspector Smith pored over the railway map of Europe to find the least troublesome route home, the Austrian Foreign Office acknowledged on the day after the trial that it had now received all necessary documents via the British Legation, and that the magistrate was treating the case with urgency. A 19-page statement by the Official Receiver in London had already been translated into German, and a further eight pages of typescript, detailing a single charge against Bevan sufficient for the purpose of extradition, was in hand.

How long would it all take? Bevan 'should be well on his way home three weeks from now,' an Austrian official told a British reporter, 'assuming that the British authorities will have arranged by that time for the prisoner's unhindered journey through the territory of other states.'

By 18 July, the Austrian Supreme Court had sent a report to the Ministry of Justice, and a formal decision to extradite was expected imminently. But then a fresh bundle of charge documents arrived from London, and had to be sent for translation. So the extradition request was not formally granted until 2 August — by which time an appeal court had decided to reverse the decision to drop the assault charge against Bevan. He was convicted and given two months' hard labour to run from the date of his arrest. On completion of this sentence, he was to be permanently ejected from Austria.

On hearing this, Bevan leaned indolently against the judge's table and smiled, according to one report, earning himself a sharp reprimand from the judge. Asked how he was feeling by one of the British press crew, his reply was laconic: 'As well as can be expected in the circumstances. It's not how I'd prefer to spend the summer.'

So at last on Monday 14 August, sentence served, looking quite well considering his incarceration, Bevan was driven to Vienna's main railway station, where he took the trouble to thank a prison official for the considerate treatment he had received and was presented with a copy of a London newspaper by one of the British reporters on hand. He made some attempt to conceal from the press that he was in handcuffs, and was said to be irritated that he had left without a final visit from the prison barber to remove a couple of days' stubble from his chin.

With his Austrian guards — plus Detective Inspector Smith and a second City of London officer, Sergeant Hipsley, who had been sent out to join the party — Bevan took his place in a reserved second-class carriage (he ought to have been in third, one reporter noted, but the train had only two classes) on the 7.15am Eastern Express via Passau on the Austrian-Bavarian border to the port of Hamburg in northern Germany. Once aboard, he was released from the handcuffs, and gave a perfunctory wave as the train pulled out.

As they travelled, Smith read Bevan the full set of charges which had been prepared against him. Bevan allowed himself some unguarded remarks in reply which Smith must have promptly leaked to the gentlemen of the press who had also boarded the train. One of these concerned the other directors of the City Equitable, the most sensible of whom, the late Theodore Barclay, had resigned in October 1920 at a crucial juncture — leaving Bevan even more at liberty to dip into company coffers for his speculations. 'He was the oldest and best friend I had in the world,' Bevan said, laying it on with a trowel, 'and there was not a straighter man in the City.'

The train was due into Hamburg at 7.15 the following morning, leaving a narrow margin of time for the two policemen and their prisoner to embark on the Cunard liner *Caronia*, which was due to sail at eight for New York via Southampton, and on which three second-class berths had been booked. The train did indeed run late — but a fall-back arrangement had been made for them to board at Cuxhaven, where the ship would drop her pilot before passing from the Elbe estuary into the North Sea.

On reaching Cuxhaven, however, they were told *Caronia* had developed a problem with her propeller, and returned to the dock-side at Hamburg. A repair was swiftly completed. Bevan and his escort boarded as planned and *Caronia* sailed for Southampton, where she arrived on the morning of Thursday 17 August.

And Whose the Fault?

Bevan was back in England. Waiting for him on the quay was his daughter Christabel, who had travelled down from London the previous day — which happened to be her 21st birthday, but must have been a subdued celebration. At Southampton West railway station she was permitted a brief reunion with her father, but on the train to Waterloo she had to travel in a separate compartment from the one reserved for the escort party, with its blinds drawn down.

They would hardly have had time to discuss Christabel's chief preoccupation, which was her own wedding plans. She had recently met and fallen in love with a middle-aged French Canadian of somewhat mysterious background, who announced himself as Major Maurice Gervais, and she intended to marry him as soon as possible.

She may well have come into money or shares or jewellery that her father, in better times, had placed in trust for her — and not reclaimed for other purposes, as he had done with her younger sister Sheila's allocation of shares in Claridge's — or that had come from the Kenrick side of the family. Now that Christabel had attained the age of majority she was free to marry whomsoever she chose, and that prospect must have been another cause of considerable stress for Sophie Bevan, waiting in London for her own reunion with her errant husband.

Arriving at Waterloo at 1pm, Bevan was marched smartly across the platform by his two escorts to a waiting taxicab which took them to Moor Lane police station, close to Moorgate in the City, where a large crowd was waiting to catch a glimpse of him. He was formally charged and put in a cell, his long-awaited appearance before City magistrates having been deferred to the following day — because it would be too late in the day to convene the court, and to allow him a night to recover from the journey. His response to the charges was, 'I prefer to say nothing now'.

And so finally Bevan appeared in the Justice Room of the Guildhall (the medieval 'town hall' of the City of London) before Charles Batho, Alderman of Aldgate ward and future Lord Mayor, on Friday 18 August, six months and ten days after he fled the country. He faced charges of publishing false balance sheets and a false prospectus, and of 'fraudulent conversion', which means dishonest acts in relation to the ownership rights of others.

After brief evidence from Inspector Smith about the extradition process and the homeward journey, Bevan was remanded for a week — with an indication from Vincent Evans, counsel for the prosecution, that a further remand would be requested until early September.

Bevan's defence brief, E.B. Knight, then asked if his client might be taken to Brixton prison in a taxi cab at his own expense — a touch of the old Bevan style, you might think — rather than in a Black Maria, because he was not feeling well. Alderman Batho assented to the request.

Sophie was in court, and before Bevan's taxi left she was allowed to speak to him in his cell. There is no record of what was said between them.

They might have discussed Sophie's household finances, or whether anything could or should be done to put a stop to Christabel's wedding. Or it might have been an opportunity for Sophie to hiss bitter recrimination across the bare table between them, to lament her husband's total failure to live up to the ideal of the English gentleman she had so often written about, and to let him know that he would be hearing from her divorce lawyer as soon as he had a permanent address at Her Majesty's pleasure.

Or it might just have been a quiet moment of mutual regret — in which case, it found a later echo in one of Bevan's poems, a lachrymose sonnet called *Parting*:

> *Is this the end then? Must we say good-bye?*
> *I'd give you back your roses if I could,*
> *You'd give me back my smiles. Yet, it seems odd;*
> *We, who've so often watched the firelight die*
> *As we sat talking, we who used to try*
> *Each to be first to catch the other's mood,*
> *And thought we knew — did know, and understood —*
> *We're going to part, just touch hands, presently.*
> *And whose the fault? Forbear! We've both been mad*
> *To float so far down the star-haunted streams;*
> *It's not for either of us to upbraid;*
> *And in the coming darkness, when it seems*
> *The void's past bearing, sometimes we'll be glad*
> *Of smiles and roses — though they're now but dreams!*

G. L. BEVAN BROUGHT BACK TO LONDON

Gerard Lee Bevan (centre) leaving Waterloo between detectives yesterday.

One of Bevan's daughters watches her father board the train for London.

Bevan (left) walking down the gangway from the Caronia at Southampton.

The arrival of Gerard Lee Bevan, ex-chairman of the City Equitable Insurance Company, at Waterloo, yesterday, was watched by a large crowd. He was charged at Moor-lane Police Station with issuing a false balance-sheet, and will be brought up at the Guildhall to-day. One of his daughters awaited him at Southampton.

Daily Mirror, 18 August 1922

PETS BEGIN THEIR SEASIDE TOUR TO-DAY.

The Daily Mirror

NET SALE MUCH THE LARGEST OF ● ANY DAILY PICTURE NEWSPAPER

No. 5,865.   Registered at the G.P.O. as a Newspaper.   SATURDAY, AUGUST 19, 1922   One Penny.

BEVAN CHARGED AT GUILDHALL | ACTRESS DEAD

By the death of Miss Genevieve Ward, at the age of eighty-five, one of the most distinguished figures of the dramatic profession is lost to us. She received royal recognition in becoming Dame Commander of the Order of the British Empire in 1921.

ENVER DEAD? | TEN WICKETS!

Enver Pasha, the famous Young Turk leader, is reported to have been killed while fighting against Bolshevist forces in Turkestan.

Collins, of Kent, the first bowler this season to take all ten wickets in an innings. This he did against Notts for 65 runs.

Gerard Lee Bevan, the City financier, standing in the dock at the Guildhall yesterday charged with fraud.

Bevan leaving the Guildhall to go to Brixton prison.

Some of the big crowd at the Guildhall going in to the court.

Mrs. Bevan leaving the court after her husband had been remanded.

Mr. Gerard Lee Bevan, ex-chairman of the City Equitable Fire Insurance Company, who was arrested in Vienna in June, appeared at the Guildhall yesterday on six charges of publishing false balance-sheets and alleged fraudulent conversion. He was pale and nervous as he stood in the dock and his solicitor said that he was ill.

Daily Mirror, 19 August 1922

CHAPTER NINE

Trial

Edward Graviter, solicitor: 'The public wants its money's worth, always does in these Society cases; they brew so long beforehand, you see.'
John Galsworthy, *Loyalties* (1922 play)

At the Guildhall

'Is that all?' Bevan was heard to ask as he was taken back to the cells after a further remand hearing on 25 August.

That was followed, a week later, by the first of 15 days of committal hearings at the Guildhall in front of Alderman Sir George Truscott, a printer and stationer by trade who had served as Lord Mayor in 1908–9. Sitting as the examining magistrate, it was Sir George's role to decide, on the basis of prosecution evidence, whether there was a *prima facie* case against Bevan for which he should be committed to stand trial.

Bevan arrived in a Black Maria from Brixton looking well groomed in a navy blue suit and black tie. An upright chair upholstered in green leather was provided for him on a small dais, because carpenters had not yet finished constructing a suitable dock. He listened attentively and made copious notes as the charges against him were recited. One reporter noted a slight nervous tic which made him blink excessively behind his spectacles as he concentrated. Sophie was there to watch, at least for part of the time.

In truth it cannot have been very scintillating for any of the participants or attendees. The case was set out in laborious detail, day after day, by the prosecuting counsel, Sir Richard Muir QC, a specialist in murder (he had prosecuted the wife-murderer Hawley Harvey Crippen in 1910) as well as in fraud, but an advocate with a reputation for a formidable tediousness of style.

Armed with the accent of his native Renfrewshire and a notoriously dour manner, Muir was famous for leaving no stone unturned, whether in prosecution or defence. He was said to be the only advocate who had ever sent a Bow Street clerk to sleep in court. Competent though he clearly was, he was not much loved by his brothers in the law. The young Norman Birkett, later a judge at the Nuremberg trials, did not hold back when he described Muir after defending against him in another fraud case as 'a silly, pompous, self-opinionated, vain, hard, emotionless, despicable ass'.

Leading Bevan's defence was a more popular and sociable member of the bar, and later a very distinguished judge, Travers Humphreys, whose name had been one to conjure with in the profession ever since he had appeared as a junior in the cases linked with the downfall of Oscar Wilde in 1895. Dry in manner, he brought 'cool good sense and knowledge of the world' to all his cases, according to one biographer; most recently it had been the calm skill of his cross-examination which secured the conviction of Horatio Bottomley. Yet he barely got a word in edgeways for several days as Muir presented a comprehensive case against Bevan.

Three kinds of offences were involved, Muir began. One group of charges were brought under the Larceny Act, which made it an offence for a director of a public company to issue any statement in writing which was false in any material particular with intent to deceive or defraud shareholders or creditors. Bevan stood accused of making such false statements in the balance sheets of the City Equitable for 1919, 1920 and 1921, and in the prospectus for City Equitable Associated.

The second class of offence alleged fraudulent conversion of assets of companies of which Bevan was a director. And the third class of offence was to do with obtaining money and securities by false pretences.

Muir went on to paint a picture of Bevan's position in Ellis & Co and the City Equitable, with a view to establishing his prime responsibility for the things that had gone wrong or astray. At Ellis & Co:

> his partners said he dominated the concern; that he conducted all its financial operations to the exclusion of the other partners, and entered into share and [company] promotion transactions without even consulting them... Bevan was not communicative to his partners concerning the business which was theirs as well as his, and they were obliged to apply to Pirie [the managing clerk who carried out Bevan's instructions from day to day] for information which ought to have been in their possession to begin with.

'In a phrase, Bevan was Ellis & Co and Ellis & Co was Bevan.' Likewise at the City Equitable, where he held sway over the three-man finance committee which took all the crucial decisions, 'in fact, Bevan was the Fire Company'. Multiple witnesses from both companies would attest to this unhealthy situation.

Muir gradually warmed to his task. The concept of reinsurance depended fundamentally, he said, on the ability of insurance companies to place faith in the balance sheets of companies such as the City Equitable from which they sought reinsurance.

> The man who tampers with the accuracy of balance sheets is tampering with the currency of commerce. The man who puts a false colour on his balance sheets in order that his company may appear to be in a position of greater stability and solvency than the facts warrant... is gilding silver to make it pass as gold. That is the class of charge which is made against the prisoner.

As to the precise nature of that deception, the first thing that the manager of an insurance company looked for in a reinsurer's balance sheet was 'British government securities, which could be most fully relied upon as the equivalent of money... The man who by trick or artifice passed off... industrial securities as British government securities was passing false coin.' And the only possible reason for doing so was to defraud.

Comparisons would show, said Muir, that in the City Equitable's balance sheet of 1916, before Bevan got his hands on the company, British government stocks made up 45 per cent of the investments — whereas in 1921 they made up only 14 per cent. Likewise, cash in the bank and in hand in 1916 made up 22 per cent of the company's assets, but less than 5 per cent in 1921.

The bulk of the difference was made up by the City Equitable's holdings of shares in companies promoted by Bevan, Hatry and Haig-Thomas, in which 'large profits were made but large risks were also run'. Shares of that class, the court would hear from experts in due course, 'could never be spoken of, much less held, by an insurance company'.

Furthermore, 'Ellis & Co owed enormous sums of money to the Fire Company [but] when the balance sheet time came around [at the end of February 1919] that debt was concealed under the temporary guise of British government securities'. Ellis's debt was shown as £51,423 when in fact the true figure was £319,523, while an investment was shown in British Treasury Bills of £198,576. But no such investment existed.

The deceit had been achieved by a set of transactions with Kleinwort, Sons & Co, a firm 'of high standing in the City', whereby Ellis & Co contracted to buy the £198,576 worth of Treasury Bills on 27 February and to sell them back again on 3 March. The bills never left Kleinworts' custody, but a certificate was issued by Ellis & Co that the bills were held by Ellis & Co for the account of the City Equitable.

In fact, Muir pointed out:

Ellis & Co never held them, were never entitled to hold them, and never intended to hold them... To call that either a purchase or an investment was to give the thing a name which it did not deserve…[It was] a mere trick and device to give a debt due from Ellis & Co the appearance in the balance sheet of the Fire Company of an investment in Treasury Bills.

As for stocks and shares held as security against Ellis & Co's real debt to the City Equitable, there was only £133,000 worth of them, meaning that the best part of £200,000 was unsecured. Some stocks and shares supposedly held by the City Equitable against Ellis & Co's debt had in fact been pledged by Ellis & Co elsewhere, while such British government stocks as the City Equitable did actually hold were largely pledged with other insurance companies — the only freely held British government paper amounted to a mere £41,000 worth.

One way or another, Muir argued, if the balance sheet had shown the true position, 'the Fire Company would have stopped business the next day'. Yet this was almost three years before its final crash.

The great clanking steamroller that was Sir Richard Muir's exposition of the case against Bevan rumbled forward. In the City Equitable's 1920 balance sheet, the debt due from Ellis & Co was shown as £11,000, when the true figure was £473,180. Once again, a short-term sale-and-repurchase of government stock had taken place, and a false certificate had been issued by Ellis & Co. In reality, the City Equitable had no free assets in the form of government stock at all, though it showed more than half a million pounds worth of holdings.

Likewise in February 1921, Ellis & Co's debt was shown at a more credible figure of £350,000 but was in fact £910,961, against which security was held covering barely a third of the total. And the balance sheet deception had been even more blatant than in the previous two years.

A holding of £200,000 in National War Bonds as at 28 February was certified in a letter from Ellis & Co, signed by Bevan himself and dated 1 March. But in fact the simultaneous sale and repurchase of bonds which supposedly gave substance to this balance sheet item had taken place with a jobber — Harry Creswick of Hopkins Blake & Co — on 4 March, four days *after* the balance sheet date. Creswick would later give evidence that he had called at Ellis & Co to effect the sale and repurchase in a matter of no more than five minutes, earning his firm a 'one thirty-second' turn, amounting to £62 and ten shillings, received by cheque from Ellis & Co on 8 March.

'To call this transaction ephemeral was to flatter it; it had not even the day's existence of a butterfly,' Muir waxed briefly poetical. More to the point, it had not existed at all at the moment the balance sheet was struck, but Bevan's letter and its carbon copy had been back-dated to create the impression that it had. 'A more patent and palpable fraud than that transaction it would be impossible to conceive'. Only someone who knew that the company was on the brink of ruin might risk tampering with documents in this way to save himself. '…And that person is before you.'

Meanwhile, there was another glaring irregularity at the City Equitable. It appeared to have been making loans to Edmund Mansell, its general manager, which had risen from some £15,000 in 1919 — extended to him to buy Buckhurst Lodge, a country house and estate near Wadhurst in Sussex — to around £50,000 in 1920 at the time of Bevan's return from his long trip to South America.

Mansell greeted him with: 'There's one thing Lepine [the auditor] wants to see you about before he signs off the balance sheet. It's my loan.' Presented with the facts, Bevan had, so he said, discussed them with Lord Ribblesdale and retrospectively signed off the loan, against which Mansell had deposited some property deeds.

But by February 1921, the loan had somehow risen to £96,233, the equivalent of £3.7 million in 2010. This was an enormous multiple of Mansell's pay packet, which consisted of £2,000 of base salary plus commission, at two and a half per cent on new business gained, which rose from £1,000 in 1916 to £7,194 in 1921.

The loan also exceeded the finance committee's limit of authority many times over. But one director, Sir Douglas Dawson, would testify that the rest of the board had no knowledge of it at all until January 1922.

Was this permitted and 'cloaked' by Bevan merely to retain Mansell's good services, or for more nefarious reasons? This was a mystery yet to be unravelled — and it was Henry Grenside, the solicitor and third member of the finance committee, who threw light on it from the witness box at the beginning of October. The explanation seemed — at least in the first instance — to reveal a quite startling laxity of financial control and corporate governance, rather than anything approaching criminal conspiracy.

In February 1921, the company's accountant had asked Bevan whether he was aware that Mansell had continued making large drawings — that is, helping himself to large sums from company funds which were then recorded in its books as loans. Mansell did not have the power simply to write company cheques to himself in order to achieve this. But it turned out that various directors, including Grenside, had helpfully signed cheques under they impression that they were 'on account of salary and commission'.

Grenside said that in his own case it was entirely possible, since he signed 'a great many cheques', that some had been signed 'without noticing what they were'. The company's routine procedures would not have helped him, since cheques were often placed on the boardroom table before meetings, or sent for signature to directors, without any sort of explanatory note attached. It turned out that nine cheques to Mansell had been signed by Bevan, and 43 by other directors. Other cheques may have been made payable direct to third parties to whom Mansell owed money.

Bevan claimed he had not been aware what all this amounted to, and was 'thunderstruck... very much upset about it' when it was pointed out to him by the company accountant. He registered a 'very strong protest' with Mansell and discussed the matter with Haig-Thomas, who claimed to have advised him to sack Mansell and take legal advice. But Bevan had argued that 'a great part of the business of the company was retained in the goodwill of Mr Mansell', and they could not afford to lose him.

So Bevan and Haig-Thomas agreed that the loans would eventually have to be repaid by Mansell out of future commission income, and could meanwhile be secured by an insurance policy on Mansell's life in addition to charges over his house and farm.

They also agreed that for the time being he could carry on borrowing more, up to a limit of £110,000 — and that if the debt had not been fully amortised out of commission earned by 1932, at the rate of £11,200 per year, the balance would be written off. More remarkable still, there was a clause which said that the balance would also be cancelled if the company failed or was wound up before the loan was fully repaid.

The agreement was dated 4 March 1921, bore Bevan's signature, and was referred to by Bevan at a board meeting on that day, though in court he claimed only to have been vaguely aware of the repayment terms, which he said had been approved by Grenside in his capacity as a solicitor — 'and when you have a colleague who is a solicitor, and who says that the agreement is all right, it is not unreasonable to think that it is all right'.

Haig-Thomas thought he might have signed it too — though if so, he had signed without reading it, 'being in a hurry at the time'. As for Grenside, he said he was only told about this agreement after it had been decided, but at least he was told about it in full. The rest of the board was told only that a salary increase from £2,000 to £5,000 and an increase in commission to four per cent had been offered to Mansell, who might otherwise have left to take up 'a bigger position and higher remuneration' elsewhere in the City.

The board meeting heard no mention at all of loans to the general manager, large or small. As we shall see in a moment, the finance committee's minutes were fudged to cover up the whole matter and Mansell continued helping himself until he had broken through the £110,000 ceiling. The grand total of his drawing from 1918 to the end of 1921 was £123, 865.

It was all a very odd way to run a public company. And there was some very suspicious shuffling of cash going on. The court would hear that in September 1921, Bevan and Grenside had signed a City Equitable cheque to Mansell for £5,000, and on the following day Mansell had written a cheque for £5,000 to Bevan. A month later,

£3,000 had passed from City Equitable Associated via Mansell to Bevan in the same way. No consideration was shown in the companies' books against these payments. When the onward path of the £3,000 payment was traced, £1,000 of it was found to have gone to a builder who had been doing work for Bevan and £2,000 to his bank account at Hungerford, from which he paid the running costs of Littlecote.

And when it was discovered in due course that Mansell had overdrawn even beyond the increased limit of £110,000, Bevan was still not prepared to sack him — because, apart from the fact that the loan would inevitably have had to be written off, 'no one else in the office was capable of conducting the business'.

While Bevan's committal hearing was continuing, more light was thrown on the matter of the Mansell loan when Mansell himself appeared in the Bankruptcy Court — where it swiftly became apparent that he had been enjoying a way of life very far from the conventional picture of a City insurance manager.

It must be said that Mansell did not look like a voluptuary or a playboy. He had a thin face and sharp features, and a large photograph of him that appeared in *The Daily Mirror*, in three-piece tweed suit, watch chain and rimless spectacles, made him look more like a country doctor. But he had been living far beyond his legitimate means, and the real truth was that he had been personally insolvent since at least March 1919.

Yet one report had it that 'for the past three years Mr Mansell had been considered one of the wealthiest men in Sussex, where he lived in a magnificent country house.' He also farmed many acres of surrounding countryside — an enterprise into which he had sunk more than £50,000.

As well as living the life of a country squire above his station, Mansell was quite the man about town. He was separated from his wife, though he had made payments to her of £8,000, plus another £1,000 for his daughter. He had in fact been living with another woman, who seems to have been an actress, in whose divorce proceedings he was cited as co-respondent. This other woman had consumed another £8,000 of his money, £3,000 of which had been ventured unsuccessfully to finance a play at the Scala Theatre in Charlotte Street.

He had spent had many thousands of pounds of his own money on business entertainment. This was in fact money he had diverted to himself from the company, but only on the basis — so he claimed — that Bevan had agreed he could make drawings and call them commission when no commission was actually due but might be due in the near future. He repudiated the suggestion that this amounted to an arrangement to defraud the company — a question that would in due course be tested at his own criminal trial.

For the time being, the key facts established were that Edmund Mansell's personal liabilities amounted to £157,862, his net assets amounted to very little, and he was by no means the pillar of quiet rectitude that a general manager of an insurance company might have been expected to be.

Proceedings resumed in earnest at the Guildhall in mid September, after a lighter moment when Sir George Truscott said it had been reported to him that someone had brought a camera into court that morning and that if he found out who it was, the miscreant would be removed at once — though presumably by then the photograph of Bevan in the dock, reproduced on page 215, had already been snatched.

The spotlight then fell on Frederick Van de Linde, the accountant who had been appointed to investigate the City Equitable's affairs just before its fall. Much of Van de Linde's evidence confirmed the initial analysis of the balance sheet by Sir Richard Muir a fortnight earlier. But the accountant added context by setting out the timetable of his discussions with Bevan and others between mid January and Bevan's departure.

He also did his best to illuminate one of the mysteries of the case, which was the matter of whether, after rumours had become rife about the City Equitable's true position, a large bundle of unmarketable industrial securities held by the company had been sold for cash to what came to be known as the 'CB Syndicate', and if so, whether that cash had ever been received. It was part of the prosecution case that 'no such transaction ever took place and no such syndicate ever existed'.

Van de Linde explained that, having been appointed special manager of the City Equitable, Greater Britain Insurance and City of London Insurance after they filed petitions for bankruptcy, he met Bevan at the Official Receiver's office on 7 February. Here Bevan had referred, not for the first time, to the CB Syndicate as having bought the shares in question, though he did not give any detail as to how or when payment had been received. But Van de Linde had been unable to identify any members of the syndicate. 'There is no trace of the syndicate in the Fire Company's books [nor] any record of a money payment in respect of the shares.'

After a week's adjournment, Muir cross-questioned Van de Linde more broadly about the City Equitable's investments and balance sheets. Were the miscellaneous securities held by the City Equitable in 1920 'of a class usually held by insurance companies'? 'In my opinion they are not, to a large extent... I refer especially to such securities as the Brazilian Ranch, Claridge's Hotel (Paris), Amalgamated Industrials, and Southern Brazilian Electric.' In round figures, these holdings were valued in the balance sheet for that year at around £400,000.

Van de Linde was also asked about the relationships between the City Equitable, Ellis & Co and the companies in the City Equitable Associated group. The accounts of the Greater Britain Insurance Corporation, City of London Insurance and City Equitable Associated itself were in various respects 'misleading' or 'inaccurate', he said. On the matter of City of London's balance sheet, Muir repeatedly pressed him to use the word 'false' — and at last Travers Humphreys intervened:

Humphreys: *Six times the witness has given his own views, and now he is being almost bullied in an effort to try and make him say something he has refused to say.*

Muir: *I am entitled to ask him whether it is true or false.*

Humphreys: *You have asked him that several times, and the witness's answer is that it is misleading.*

Sir George Truscott, from the bench: *I think we ought to have something more definite than "misleading". Why is it misleading?*

Van de Linde, from the witness box: *Because certain assets are not accurately described. To that extent it is false.*

And so the arguments proceeded. Humphreys' task was to try to pinpoint areas in which Van de Linde had been less than clear in his analysis, or seemed to have changed his mind, or might have overlooked some circumstance that might have been marginally favourable to Bevan — the fact, for example, that Bevan had been abroad from 2 February to 1 June 1920, so could not have directed in any detail the manipulation of the City Equitable's balance sheet for the 28 February year-end, which must instead have been the handiwork of Mansell.

Other witnesses came and went, largely to confirm the pattern of sale and repurchase of government stocks that Muir had high-lighted as the central deception in the City Equitable's accounts. Underlining the interconnectedness of the 1920s City, one of the brokers called to testify to these transactions was Christopher Gurney Barclay of Sheppards & Co, whose late uncle Theodore had been a City Equitable director as well as Sheppards' senior partner.

And alongside the revelations about the management of the City Equitable, Ailwyn Fellowes was the first of Bevan's Ellis & Co partners to offer an insight into the idiosyncratic workings of the stockbroking firm. Fellowes himself had served in the war, had been captured by the Germans, and had been in poor health when he came home, to the extent that he had been unable to take much part in the business until the end of 1919 or thereabouts.

Bevan's dominance of the firm reflected the fact that in their partnership agreement redrawn in December 1919, Bevan held £108,000 of Ellis & Co's £200,000 capital, Fellowes told the court. While he and the other three partners (O'Brien, Gordon and Tootal) dealt for their own clients, Bevan chiefly attended to buying and selling on the firm's account, as well as his complex portfolio of personal interests.

In earlier days, the other partners had a say in the firm's own-account dealings, but after Donald Pirie had been made up to salaried partner in September 1921 — at Bevan's instigation, of course — Bevan and Pirie handled matters without consulting the others. And if Bevan was absent, Pirie operated alone, raising questions as to how complicit Pirie might have been in Bevan's misdeeds.

Bevan and Pirie also managed the firm's finances, including its loans from banks. On the finance side, Fellowes was at least occasionally consulted, but he did not make much scrutiny of the firm's accounts himself, relying on monthly reports from a small firm of accountants called Bartrop & Co, who kept the books. He had no knowledge of the year-end sale and repurchase deals done with the City Equitable.

'I take it you had every confidence in Bevan,' Muir asked Fellowes. *Yes.*

'Did any of the other partners ever object to anything that was done?' *Not as far as I know.*

Gordon and O'Brien echoed Fellowes. Both seemed to have known little of what Bevan and Pirie were up to, though when O'Brien dined with Bevan in May 1921, Bevan told him that 'they had lost about half their capital'. By November, the position was considerably worse: over another dinner, Bevan revealed that 'as they had lost all their capital, he intended to devote himself to insurance, but he would put the capital right before he left'. With this his partners were apparently satisfied: 'We thought he was quite capable of doing it.'

And could O'Brien throw any light on the CB Syndicate? Bevan had told him in January that a syndicate had indeed been formed to acquire the City Equitable's industrial share portfolio — and to save the face of 'a certain person' on the City Equitable board, who also happened to be a director of 'a certain concern in the City which was identified with these industrials'.

'I appreciate your delicacy in not bringing in other people's names,' Muir told O'Brien — but pressed him nevertheless to reveal who and what he was talking about. It was of course Peter Haig-Thomas, and Hatry's Commercial Bank, though we should not forget that Grenside was also on the Commercial Bank board, as was the Earl of March, though he had by this time resigned from the City Equitable's.

> Did anybody ask who the CB Syndicate were? *That was my orig-inal question [to Bevan].*
> And what was Bevan's answer? *His answer was 'you may well ask'.* (At which the court report records 'laughter, in which Bevan joined'.)
> Did he ever explain who the CB Syndicate were? *No.*
> To this day, have you learned who they were? *I have not.*

And indeed during the rest of the committal hearings no further light was thrown on this curious question, except that an account-ant called William Cash, who had been working alongside Van de Linde, offered the opinion that the CB Syndicate was in fact identi-cal with Ellis & Co.

Next into the box was Sir Douglas Dawson, the courtier and mil-itary man who had been a director of the City Equitable since 1915 but seemed to know remarkably little about its business beyond what was presented to him in its annual accounts. Yet still his answer to the question 'Had you the greatest confidence in [Bevan]?' was 'Certainly I had.'

> As to the balance sheets for 1921 [which Dawson actually signed], did you believe that they disclosed the true finan-cial position of the company? *I certainly did; I was very proud of it.*

Such was his confidence, indeed, that in June 1921 he con-sented to become a director of two of the connected companies, the

Greater British and the City of London. A month later, he found his name listed as a director in the draft prospectus for City Equitable Associated, and not only consented to take up that position but subscribed £500 for shares in the new company.

His evidence was calmly presented, but his real feelings were expressed five years later in his memoir, *A Soldier Diplomat* (1927), in which he wrote of 'a loathsome episode' which left him 'broken in both health and pocket':

> It was only at a great sacrifice that I provided the funds necessary, and when I afterwards found that at the time I handed over my cheque for £500 (as qualification for a directorship) the shares were not worth the paper the cheque was written on, I realized in what a callous, brutal manner I had been swindled.

Dawson was every inch the upright military gentleman, a persona that is well highlighted in a portrait of him in Garter robes painted at about this time by the Belgian artist Nestor Cambier — which would have made a good pair with 'The Ancestor', Sargent's famous portrait of Ribblesdale. The 'soldier diplomat' does indeed seem to have been ruthlessly taken advantage of by Bevan, yet we must ask what motivated Dawson to acquire a portfolio of half a dozen directorships as he did. The cynical answer must be that it offered a useful stream of fees for little effort or intellectual engagement or understanding of the markets in which the companies operated. So we should not feel excessively sorry for him.

If Dawson was semi-detached as a director of the City Equitable, it was more surprising to find that the shipbuilder Sir Henry Grayson, a serious businessman of whom better might have been expected, was if anything even less well informed about the company's affairs.

Grayson had benefited from the reorganisation of his own family business by Hatry, with Haig-Thomas's assistance, in 1917–18, and was one of their trusted circle of associates. Haig-Thomas and Bevan evidently felt Grayson's marine expertise would be valuable to the City Equitable, but it had been rarely called upon.

He never became a regular attender at board meetings and in fact — because of the demands of his Admiralty role — had not attended at all between September 1918 and May 1920. He 'knew nothing about the details' of the 1919 balance sheet, or about the various controversial Treasury bill and War Loan transactions. And he had sufficient faith in Bevan to lend £100,000 worth of War Loan bonds to the City Equitable to ease its position late in 1921.

Likewise Grenside showed remarkable ignorance of what had been happening, even when it was done in the name of the finance committee whose £5,000 limit per security had so often been breached. Muir pointed out to him that the minutes of the committee for various dates in 1919 and 1920 all said exactly the same thing, in identical handwriting:

> The various alterations and re-investments authorized to be effected at the Chairman's discretion at the previous meeting were approved. The general list was discussed. The Chairman indicated several further changes as desirable in the early future, and he was authorized to execute them as opportunity offered.

Grenside had to agree that not only did these minutes record nothing at all about the actual securities dealt in, but that he had no recollection of the minutes of each meeting being read and approved at the next meeting, as would have been routine in any well-run company, or of the committee's proceedings then being reported to the board. In fact, he said, he had never seen these minutes before, was not aware that anyone had been taking notes during the meetings, and did not know who wrote them afterwards. The handwriting did not look like that of a clerk, he observed helpfully.

It was established in due course that Mansell, the general manager, had written the minutes himself. This was an unusual arrangement, and it seems doubly odd that Grenside was not familiar with Mansell's script. We might guess that in order to satisfy the auditors by giving an impression of orderly administration, Mansell had scribbled in the minute book long after the actual meeting dates.

One minute, for 22 February 1921, was a little more specific than most of the others: it recorded that all three members had agreed revisions to Mansell's salary and commission arrangements. But Grenside's recollection was that the matter had not been discussed at all in committee — he had simply been told about it by Bevan afterwards, just ahead of the 4 March board meeting.

Another minute, in November 1921, said it had been 'unanimously resolved' (between Bevan and Grenside, that is, Haig-Thomas being absent) that Bevan should have sole authority over the company's investments and cash balances in France.

> Was there any reason given why Bevan should have this sole authority? *I do not recall the reasons that were given.*

Grenside also admitted that he took no direct part in actual dealings in the company's investment portfolio — in effect, admitting that his membership of its innermost committee gave him no knowledge of what Bevan was up to beyond what Bevan chose to tell him. Later he would be asked about a holding of £45,000 worth of shares in an obscure company called Willoughby Sumner.

> What was this company? *I think it is a company in Canada.*
> Did it ever pay a dividend? *I do not know.*
> Did not you ever take an interest in the question whether the investments which were being made were producing dividends or not? *I made no enquiries about this company.*
> What check had the finance committee on the Chairman's operation? *In a way we had no check.*
> When you turn to the minutes of the previous meeting, you do not find any record of what was authorized. How did you know that you had authorized what the chairman had done? *We ratified what he reported he had done.*
> Did the chairman consult you at all about investments and changes in them? *We used to have discussions at some of the meetings as to what was desirable.*

But Grenside could not recall any instance in which they refused to authorise an investment that Bevan had proposed. At best, 'sometimes suggestions were dropped by general agreement after discussion'.

Had you every confidence in Bevan? *Absolutely.*

Bevan's defence, as we shall see in a moment, was always likely to lack plausibility, but at least he stuck fluently to his line. It was Grenside, at the committal hearing, Bevan's trial and the subsequent 'misfeasance' case against the directors, who gave the least impressive account of himself under cross-examination. His feebleness as a witness produced one particularly memorable exchange:

> Henry Maddocks KC, defending: *Did not you think that the questions yesterday were directed to show you were an absolute fool?*
> Grenside: *Perhaps the answers were not particularly bright.*
> Mr Justice Avory: *Do you want the witness to say whether he is an absolute fool?*
> Maddocks: *I thought your lordship might ask him that question when I had finished.*

Who was 'Someone?'

At last, on 24 October, Sir George Truscott committed Bevan for trial at the Central Criminal Court, familiarly known as the Old Bailey. When asked whether he had anything to say, Bevan replied 'I only wish to say I have a complete answer to all the charges that have been brought against me, and I will reserve it for the judge and jury at the proper moment.' He duly pleaded 'Not Guilty' when the charges were put to him in court on 20 November.

For the trial itself, there was an even weightier line-up of lawyers than for the committal. The judge was 72-year-old Sir Horace Avory, a veteran of major fraud cases from his days as a leading counsel, including the prosecution of Whitaker Wright in 1904. Austere in manner and precise in language, he discouraged levity or prolixity in his court. It was once said of him that he was 'spare of flesh and sparing of compliments, but never spared criminals'.

Leading for the prosecution was Sir Ernest Pollock KC, the MP for Warwick and Leamington who had recently become attorney general. The defence was to be led by Henry Maddocks KC, originally a solicitor in Coventry and latterly MP for Nuneaton.

In his opening statement, Pollock told the jury that Bevan was entitled to a fair hearing because 'a man who has stood as an outstanding figure in the City of London is entitled to rely on the position he has earned by merit.' But Pollock would have to ask the jury:

> whether a man who has been a captain of industry, a leader of finance, who has secured the confidence of many, when he was found to have resorted to fraudulent devices, to tortuous stratagems, should go unpunished, or should have to answer for his serious conduct, which has involved so many in disaster and ruin.
>
> The defendant is entitled to every consideration, but the contrast between the actual position of the companies and the represented position will, I believe, lead the jury to the conclusion that this could not be the result of a mistake. This mastermind, this forceful personality, has misused his opportunities for a sinister purpose.

In his answers to Pollock's later cross-questioning, Bevan smiled amiably as he strove to replace this picture of a sinister mastermind with that of an honourable man of business driven by circumstances to behave in an extraordinary way:

> Did you think on 30 January last that the position might be brought round? *It might easily have been brought round.*
> You had no misgivings as to your conduct? *I had no misgivings as to my conduct at any stage.*

Then why did you flee the country on 8 February? *Because I was asked.*

And why did you adopt the identity of Leon Vernier? *Because I was asked to go.*

Why did you disguise yourself by dyeing your hair black and having a black beard? *I went away in response to a strong request.*

And remained concealed for six months in response to that request? *Certainly, I intended to do so.*

And yet you had no misgivings as to your own conduct? *None.*

And were not the least afraid to meet any question put to you? *Not the least.*

It was Travers Humphreys, concluding five and a half hours of defence cross-examination, who asked the question that must have given the jury special pause for thought about the nature of Bevan's motives:

Have you, as a result of these transactions, put away one farthing of money? *Not one farthing.*

The jurors must also have been very intrigued by 'Because I was asked to go'. In his statement issued via Reuters in Vienna, Bevan had said only that it was Sophie who asked him to go abroad to spare her reputation. But in court he declined to say where the 'strong request' had come from. 'He was urged, by whom I am not permitted to tell you, to go away,' Maddocks would reiterate on his behalf.

There is a distant echo in all this of Oscar Wilde after his arrest for gross indecency in 1895: 'Everyone wants me to go abroad.' But did Bevan's mystery adviser really exist, and if so who was he, or she? Let us make some educated guesses.

Could it have been Sophie's cousin Austen Chamberlain, who was Lord Privy Seal and leader of the Conservative Party within Lloyd George's coalition government at the time, and certainly would not have wanted his name bandied about in court? Given her strident political views, Sophie is unlikely to have been Austen's favourite relation — but might she nevertheless have sought his advice and then associated his name with her own request to Gerard that he should disappear?

Or was it Cosmo Bevan, the stuffed-shirt head of the Bevan clan? He would certainly have been concerned for the family name, and for any stain on his own career that might result from association with scandal — but as a stickler for correct form, might not the eldest brother have preferred to see Gerard brought to justice rather than remain at large as a headline-making fugitive?

Let us construct a hypothesis, which takes us back to the de Pinna sub-plot in Chapter Seven. During the weekend before he fled the country in February, Gerard Bevan had received £15,000 in £1,000 notes from de Pinna, the Chinese porcelain dealer. Suppose Gerard had given ten or twelve of those notes to Sophie, to keep hearth and home together and provide for Christabel and Sheila. What would Sophie have done with them? After all, each big white note was worth, in modern terms, more than £40,000. She needed to bank them immediately. She could not otherwise change them or make payments with them.

Might she have gone round to call on Cosmo at his townhouse in nearby Tilney Street, Mayfair (inherited from his father Frank) and asked him to take the notes to Lombard Street on Monday and credit them to an account in her name? Might Cosmo have told Sophie that Gerard was — according to the talk in the City — in much deeper trouble than she already knew, and that the best thing his errant brother could do for all of them was to flee before the police felt his collar? Might Cosmo even have telephoned his younger brother Ivor to urge him to help Gerard get away?

All that is possible — but not wholly persuasive. It seems just as likely that if Bevan had indeed asked for (or received unsolicited) advice from a person or persons whose identity was too sensitive to be revealed in court, he would have been given a different message altogether, one which urged him to make amend in the most dramatic and final way for bringing shame on himself and his family. The example of Whitaker Wright's end might have been quoted.

Put simply, a chap who had let the side down in matters of money or women or both was expected, in rarified social circles and literary models of the era, to 'do the decent thing'. That is, to take a revolver — usually a standard-issue first world war officer's Webley Mk IV, of which many were in circulation in the post-war years — and shoot himself.

Galsworthy, once again, is our guide to this arcane ritual. A classic example occurs in his play *Loyalties*, written in the year of Bevan's fall. In it, the down-on-his-luck Captain Dancy has been identified as the thief who stole a wad of cash from a wealthy Jewish guest, De Levis, at a country house party — money which Dancy needs to pay off a woman who is not his wife. Dancy's solicitor, Edward Twisden, advises him to escape to Morocco. But Dancy stays in England, hoping to find a way out of his troubles — and when the inevitable Inspector calls to arrest him, he knows what he has to do to save the honour of his wife, Mabel.

'A sudden change comes over Dancy's face; from being stony it grows almost maniacal,' says Galworthy's stage direction. Shortly afterwards, a pistol shot is heard offstage.

'Neatly, through the heart,' reports Major Colford, a brother officer who is at the scene, before reading out the suicide note:

'Dear Colford, this is the only decent thing I can do. It's too damned unfair to her. It's only another jump. A pistol keeps faith. Look after her, Colford; my love to her, and you.'[1]

Did 'someone', or anyone, suggest to Bevan that he ought to do the decent thing, rather than running away? For that matter, did Bevan ever consider suicide of his own accord, if not in London then in Vienna when he knew his luck was running out? What was

---

[1] Another fine example occurs in *The Unpleasantness at the Bellona Club*, a Dorothy L. Sayers 'Lord Peter Wimsey' detective novel of 1928. Dr Pemberthy is discovered to have administered a fatal poison to General Fentiman, in the hope of getting his hands on the general's fortune. Wimsey confronts the doctor at his club, and offers him a last chance to behave like a gentleman — which includes writing a confession that will exonerate Ann Dorland, the doctor's former lover and the general's heiress. Pemberthy takes the proffered revolver, prompting the immortal line from a fellow clubman: 'I say, you fellows, here's another unpleasantness. Pemberthy's shot himself in the library. People ought to have more consideration for the members.'

the real intent behind the swallowing of the white pill when the Austrian police arrived to arrest him? We can but surmise.

Window-dressing

A more persuasive element of Bevan's defence was the proposition that the balance sheet manipulation was nothing out of the ordinary: a matter of 'window-dressing', commonly practiced in the City. In his experience 'six out of ten balance sheets published in the United Kingdom showed more cash at the date of the balance sheet than the company was in the habit of holding during the rest of the year. Every big man knew perfectly well what was done.'

This was almost certainly true, though the 'big men', if asked, would have said (as with many forms of financial misbehaviour) that it was all a matter of degree. Window-dressing the balance sheet of a fundamentally sound business to give it a more conventional ratio of cash to other assets was not in the same category of sin as concealing huge blocks of unmarketable investments held by a company that was expected to hold only the sort of highly liquid, low-risk invest-ments that would support its day-to-day insurance activity.

Bevan made a version of the same point. If the assets of the City Equitable had been declining, he agreed with Pollock, then it would have been 'immoral and indefensible' to show bogus holdings of Treasury bills. But in fact there had been an enormous accretion of assets during the period concerned which made it 'perfectly proper'. In any case, said Bevan, he did not think the company's reinsurance clients much cared whether it held government stock or industrial shares (he was surely wrong in that assertion) though he realized that Mansell may have thought otherwise and may therefore have been concerned to boost the apparent proportion of gilts held.

As for the sale and purchase of War Bonds on 4 March 1921 for which the contract had been altered so that the bonds could be shown on the 28 February balance sheet, Bevan agreed that he had signed an 'untrue document', but described it as having recorded a transaction that was 'finished at a later time' rather than 'faked'.

This mishap was apparently the fault of Pirie at Ellis & Co, who had forgotten to get the transaction done when asked. But 'when a contract was brought to me to sign I never dreamed of looking at it. I do not pretend I ever read our contracts… I relied on our officials to present me true documents.'

> Did that mean he didn't care whether the company's adminis-
> tration was orderly or not? *Of course I cared; had I known the date*
> *was inaccurate, I should not have authorized it.*

And as for what had ultimately caused the City Equitable's downfall, Bevan contended that it was all to do with the state of the insurance market, not his concealed use of the company as a high-risk invest-ment piggy-bank and source of funds for Ellis & Co. 'The principal cause was the disastrous marine experience of four companies in 1921… People in Lloyd's told me it was the worst year in the history of marine insurance.'

'I submit that the truth is not to be found in the mouth of Bevan,' said Pollock in a two-hour closing speech to the jury that was described by one reporter as 'a model of terseness, lucidity and power'. At one point he introduced the phrase 'malevolent genius'. Bevan listened intently, head resting on his left hand, occasionally passing notes to his solicitor, as Pollock dissected every element of the defence case.

Window-dressing might, within limits, be a common practice in the City, he argued. But it was certainly not common practice for the chairman of a great insurance company and a great stockbroking firm to pass documents under his signature which were 'false in date and false in the meaning they intend to convey'.

And if Bevan had really been thunderstruck at the discovery of Mansell's unauthorised drawings, why had he agreed to let him draw even more, on such easy terms of repayment? 'With reluc-tance', Pollock invited the jury to put 'the most sinister construction upon these dealings. Have you got the truth about the loan to Mansell?'

Pollock concluded:

> It is an unhappy story. But it is a story which, on the facts, which
> are largely admitted, carries but one impress, the impress of a
> man who has been working through falsehood and fraud to
> try and right the position, but who has failed; a man of great
> personality working for his own ends, master alike of the Fire
> Company and the other companies, and who was responsible,
> if man ever was responsible.
>
> You cannot attribute all these matters merely to misfortune
> or coincidence. They all converge to the one point — that
> Bevan is responsible... I am going to ask you, after consider-
> ing the evidence with great care, to find him guilty — guilty in
> the interests of justice, much as you may regret that you have
> to contemplate the chequered spectacle of a man who com-
> manded so much respect and in whom was centred so great
> responsibility, but who dealt with that responsibility and that
> respect in disgrace, dishonour — and disaster to so many.

Maddocks, concluding for the defence, did his best to paint Bevan
as the victim of circumstance, a man who had made mistakes under
pressure and had perhaps been negligent, but had not sunk into outright dishonesty. It was notable, for example, that in the evidence
of his Ellis & Co partners, 'we do not find one trace of bitterness
against Bevan. Not one word of reproach has escaped those men.
That is a tribute to Bevan's character.'

As to Bevan's claim that he had not looked closely (or at all)
at many of the City Equitable papers that bore his signature, well,
'many of us sign deeds prepared by a solicitor without reading them'.
And as for the inadequate state of the finance committee minutes:

> No one can throw a stone at Bevan for not seeing that the min-
> utes were properly kept. There is no distinction to be made
> between the chairman and the other directors in the question of
> neglect. It is a joint liability on all the directors of the company
> to see that the business is properly conducted.

There seems to be an anxiety in this case to try and place the whole responsibility on Bevan. It occurs to me that if there are to be any civil proceedings regarding the management of the Fire Company, it may be the defence of other directors to say that the loss was entirely due to the crime of Bevan, in conspiracy with Mansell... If that is so, it explains why they are not so free and frank in accepting joint responsibility with Bevan as they might be.

Perhaps, he implied, that was why Mansell had not been called as a witness for the prosecution. And as for the loan agreement with Mansell, which certainly contained 'most extraordinary, even ridiculous provisions', the draft had been submitted to Grenside, who was a solicitor, and if any man was to be attacked for allowing it to pass, it was Grenside rather than Bevan. 'For a lawyer to read it and not have a fit is the greatest wonder I can imagine.'

Nor was the balance sheet window-dressing a clear-cut misdemeanour, Maddocks argued. Had not an authority on company law, Palmer, written: 'A balance sheet need not disclose the true position of a company'?

That gambit was too much for Mr Justice Avory, who called it 'misleading'. 'Would your Lordship like to see the passage?' Maddocks asked. 'No, it would offend my eyesight... I say it is wrong.'

Despite this rebuke, Maddocks ploughed on towards his histrionic peroration. If the jury were to treat Bevan's flight as simple evidence of his guilt, he declared, they might be doing a gross injustice:

Just imagine for one moment. Ruin on all hands! Ruin among his friends, his partners. The various companies he had to do with in the industrial world all brought into the same category of ruin. People looking at the man who had made this intolerable failure because he banked on industrials and was wrong. He was urged to go away. He was overworked, his nerve was largely gone, and when he was urged — by whom I am not permitted to tell you — to go away, can you wonder that he went?

Is that without parallel? Have you ever heard of men so stirred with the idea of being charged with a criminal offence that they have attempted to take their own lives, although they were perfectly innocent? I am alive to the fact that it is the strongest evidence that the Crown has against Bevan, but can you regard it as an admission of guilt?… He may be liable in another court for negligence, but in this court I ask you to say that he has preserved the honesty of an English commercial man and that he is not guilty of the charges against him.

Muddled Away

It was a bravura performance by Maddocks, but it cannot have offered Bevan much or any hope of acquittal. On Tuesday 5 December, the defendant smiled to friends in the courtroom and calmly took his seat in the dock to await the judge's summing up and the jury's verdict. 'Many well known City men were present,' reported *The Times*, 'and a number of women occupied reserved seats behind counsel.'

One of Bevan's brothers was identified in the crowd — perhaps Raymond the clergyman, or Owen the fellow stockbroker, or Ivor who had allegedly tried to help him get away; but not Cosmo or Bertie, the two who had made such respectable careers in Barclays. Christabel was there too, but was too upset to stay in court to hear the verdict.

The jury took an hour and 35 minutes to deliberate, returning to the courtroom at twenty minutes to three in the afternoon. They found Bevan guilty of 15 of the 16 charges that had eventually been brought against him; the sixteenth, a charge of obtaining money under false pretences from an individual, having been withdrawn. After intoning the word 'Guilty' 15 times, the young man who was the foreman added a hugely important sting in the tail:

We should like to add a rider that the offences were rendered possible owing to other directors not properly carrying out their duties.

The ramifications of that statement would in due course set a hugely important legal precedent. But the judge did not address it until after Bevan had been taken down, when he told the jury that he had no power to act upon it. First, to the convicted man, he pronounced:

> Gerard Lee Bevan, I am indulging in no mere commonplace when I say that the duty which now falls upon me of passing sentence upon a man of your education and extraordinary ability is a most painful one. In determining the sentence appropriate to your offence, I have to consider not only the financial ruin that you have brought upon individuals but also the effect of your conduct in destroying the confidence of the public in insurance business and the injury you have done to the commercial reputation of this city.
>
> Your offence is further aggravated by your flight from this country, leaving your partners and your co-directors to bear the burden of the disgrace which you had brought upon the firm and upon the company...

He proceeded to sentence Bevan to be detained in penal servitude for seven years in respect of the charges relating to making false statements and fraudulent conversion, and five years — to run concurrently — in respect of the 'false pretences' charges. Bevan listened calmly, merely raising his eyebrows and giving a slight shake of the head as he heard the sentence. 'The little redness that he has in complexion paled,' wrote one reporter. 'The lines on his face were graven deep, and his mouth was a rigid line of suppressed emotion.'

A warder tapped him on the shoulder and he turned and walked quickly down the stairs from the dock — without bowing to the court, 'like a final act in disdain of the decencies,' said the *Daily Sketch*. Travers Humphreys then asked whether Christabel could visit her father in his cell before he was taken off to prison. The judge granted the request.

Was it a fair judgment and a fair sentence? *The Economist*'s comment on the verdict was perhaps the most quoted passage ever written about Bevan:

The extraordinary feature of the whole affair — that which distinguishes it from the Jabez Balfour and Whitaker Wright prosecutions — is that nobody seems to have got anything for himself out of the irregularities which have sent Mr Bevan into penal servitude. Mr Bevan contrived in the course of a year or two, by mismanagement quite incredible in its fatuity, to destroy a reinsurance company which was in fairly good repute, and to bring to bankruptcy one of the oldest firms in the Stock Exchange. Why he did it is a mystery. It was not for personal gain, seeing that he was himself destroyed in the general ruin, and fled the country practically penniless. A common rogue would have bolted with a sackful of plunder.

We have pointed out more than once that the City Equitable failure had nothing to do with insurance. The company and its associates failed because the assets had been muddled away. Yet it cannot be denied that the repute of insurance has suffered. Here was a London reinsurance company issuing fraudulent balance sheets and prospectuses, and so little suspected of wrong-doing that many of the big [insurance] offices had accounts with it, and went on doing business with it until just before the crash came. If the experts could be deceived in this fashion, of what avail, the public may ask, are accounts and balance sheets and auditors' certificates?

The reply must be that against fraud there is no sure remedy and no sure protection. Sooner or later detection comes, and with it punishment, but no external precautions or deterrents can wholly restrain those who are not restrained by their own consciences. The City Equitable case stands fortunately by itself as a warning that even in so reputable a market as that for insurance there may for a while exist unsuspected fraudulent chairmen and what Mr Justice Avory bluntly calls "dishonest" managers.

The *Manchester Guardian*, however, took a kindlier view of Bevan:

> One may believe without being suspected of casuistry that he is not of the truly criminal type. He did not set out like Bottomley with the almost avowed object of swindling the public.
>
> He followed a path which circumstances made easy for him. His own dominating personality, the easy manner in which his partners and his co-directors accepted their responsibilities, and, finally, the gross inadequacy of the legal regulation of balance sheet drafting and auditing made the descent to Avernus easier than it would have been... That is the true lesson of the Bevan case. Legal regulations will not prevent the true criminal from following his bent, but they can remove some of the temptations to which those who set out with no criminal intent not infrequently succumb.

The seven-year sentence was generally recognized in the City to be just, wrote Hubert Meredith, the author of *The Drama of Making Money* (1931), who had opened his account of the case by revealing that he disliked Bevan personally when he knew him in business.

> At the same time, while I agree with the City's opinion, I feel that Bevan's actions were not based on any criminal intent and, reprehensible as they undoubtedly were, had markets boomed instead of slumped, the result would have been advantageous to the City Equitable. Of all the Money Making Dramas with which I have dealt in this book, I have found the Bevan case most perplexing. A careful scrutiny of every word of evidence uttered, while emphasising the seriousness of Bevan's offence, indicates clearly how the downward path was taken and convinces me, taken unwittingly.

Another contemporary, the veteran company promoter H. Osborne O'Hagan, in *Leaves From My Life* (1929), encapsulated Bevan thus:

> He deliberately, when past middle age, did everything he could to forfeit his position and to ruin the fortunes of himself, his partners, his friends and his clients, and what for? I don't see how he could possibly have benefited from any of his criminal acts. I ask, "What was his kink?" The only answer which comes to me is, "Vanity — pure vanity."

'Trouble with a man like that was that if he once admitted to having made a mistake he destroyed the legend of his infallibility,' wrote Galsworthy of his own thinly disguised fictional version of Bevan, whom we shall meet in Chapter Twelve. But, Aylmer Vallance wrote in *Very Private Enterprise* (1955), 'there remains the enigma — fool or knave?' Clarence Hatry, whose crash a few years later was to outdo that of the City Equitable, 'had a constructive vision, in whose pursuit he broke the law'. Had Bevan?

> There is no evidence in support of such a view... His Counsel argued, on his behalf, that it is easy to be wise after the event. True; but the folly of Gerard Lee Bevan began before the onset of the 1921 slump, which wiser men than he had failed to foresee, and which finally swept away his shaky financial edifice.
>
> Character is fate: men are betrayed by what is false within. Bevan, I suggest, was throughout the gilded Etonian — civilized, politely arrogant, and certain the world owed much to him. He never grew up to a sense of responsibility, and was never as astute as he believed himself to be. If he got a bad press from the Conservative newspapers which he had been in the habit of buying, it was because the Etonian had let down his side.

To which R.P.T. Davenport-Hines, in a concise but perceptive entry for Bevan in the *Dictionary of Business Biography* (1984–6) adds:

> Bevan was an elegant, plausible man who traded on his family connections and whose hereditary privileges left him arrogant, vain and irresponsible... [but he] could not have sustained his frauds without the naiveté and ignorance of his aristocratic guinea-pig directors or the laxity of his accountant.

At a distance of 90 years, and with the benefit of all these commentators' judgements in addition to Mr Justice Avory's, we can attempt a final summing-up.

There was indeed something 'false within' Bevan — a streak which for the first 25 years of his business career manifested itself only in a tendency to exercise a certain liberty with the truth and a certain slipperiness in his dealings, the sort of thing that caused his brother Cosmo to label him a 'blackguard' long before there was any sign of trouble at the City Equitable.

But such behaviour was by no means unusual in the stockbroking milieu, and there was also within Bevan a genuine entrepreneur-financier, a man who wanted to build successful businesses and become another 'mighty Rockefeller', who believed in his own ability to do so — and whose powerful personality made others want to follow him.

His talent was limited, however, by a critical lack of discernment about risk. This did not matter in relation to the way he invested his own money — that was entirely his own affair, and for many years his luck was good — but it mattered greatly when he began investing the City Equitable's liquidity in unsuitable and unmarketable shares. Most of those investments were not strictly *ultra vires* for the company, but they were wildly imprudent and the concealment of them from fellow directors, shareholders and clients, thereby giving a false impression of the company's solvency, was rightly judged to be a crime.

And there was evidence of a more profound character fault in Bevan's response to the deteriorating situation of his businesses in 1921 and early 1922. Too conceited to admit his misdealings when there might still have been time to save the City Equitable, he multiplied the deceits and the promises that could never be kept, and scammed a new set of investors with the City Equitable Associated prospectus. Lacking the moral courage that might have made him face the consequences of his actions, he simply ran away — and when apprehended, refused to admit that anything he had done was wrong.

In short, using those other writers' most telling phrases: a dominating personality, not of the truly criminal type but never as smart as he believed himself to be, he unwittingly muddled away his own and other people's fortunes by mismanagement so full of lies that it earned him a seven-year sentence. Having come to know so much about Bevan's life, it is possible, with the *Manchester Guardian*'s editorial writer, 'to have some sympathy with Bevan'. But perhaps only a modicum.

CHAPTER TEN

Misfeasance

*'They were all so honourable that they dared not scrutinize each other,
or even their own collective policy. Worse than their dread of mistake or
fraud was their dread of seeming to distrust each other.'*

Soames Forsyte on his fellow directors of the
Providential Premium Reassurance Society,
in John Galsworthy, *The White Monkey* (1924)

Mansell in the Dock

If ever a criminal trial could be said to have been a foregone conclusion, it was Bevan's. He really didn't have a leg to stand on. But there
was another trial to come, of Edmund Mansell, the high-living general manager of the City Equitable, in which culpability was much
less clear-cut but the whiff of conspiracy with Bevan was pungent.

And beyond that was another court case, in which the liquidators
of the City Equitable sought to establish that Bevan's fellow directors had been wilfully negligent. That case would become much
more famous than the original trial, because it created a hugely
important legal precedent.

But first, the mystery of Edmund Mansell. On a Saturday evening
in February 1923 he was approached in East Street, Marylebone, by
Detective Inspector Frederick Wagstaffe. Detective Sergeant Hipsley,
who had accompanied Bevan from Vienna with Inspector Smith, was
also at the scene. Wagstaffe told Mansell he had a warrant for his arrest.

'What for?' replied Mansell, as anyone might. The answer was for conspiring with Bevan between December 1918 and February 1922 to obtain by false pretences sums of money amounting to more than £110,000 from the City Equitable.

'Very well,' said Mansell. Taken to Moor Lane police station and formally charged, he gave his address as Portman Mansions, Baker Street, though there was some question as to whether this constituted his 'fixed abode' — it was probably the home of his theatrical mistress. He said he no longer had any occupation. He was refused bail.

When Mansell came up in front of Sir George Truscott, the Guildhall magistrate, a few days later, it was once again the humourless Sir Richard Muir who appeared for the director of public prosecutions. Having rehearsed the facts of the case, Muir pointed out that no director other than Bevan knew anything about Mansell's enormous unsecured overdraft with the company, and submitted that Mansell and Bevan must have been 'acting in guilty conspiracy'.

For his side of the bargain, Muir proposed, Mansell must have agreed in March 1921 not to disclose to the City Equitable board or anyone else the true scale of Ellis & Co's debts to the company — nearly £1 million, it will be recalled, at the February 1921 balance sheet date — while Bevan in return had agreed to conceal the fact that Mansell had already misappropriated nearly £100,000 for himself.

Mansell's defence brief, G.W.H. Jones, told the hearing that Mansell strongly denied the charges and would offer a 'perfect answer' to them. Since he had not 'bolted or concealed himself', bail was again asked for on Mansell's behalf — but was again denied. So he stayed in his cell until early March, when Truscott relented and set bail at £3,000.

As the hearings continued, several of the former City Equitable directors trooped into the box to give evidence that they had known nothing of the general manager's borrowings, but that he had otherwise been held in high esteem: the near-tenfold increase in premium income between 1915 and 1921 was, by general consensus, very largely down to his efforts.

Grenside in particular pointed out that 'reinsurance business is to a considerable extent personal', and that the directors knew Mansell had secured most of the City Equitable's treaties himself, with the help of a lavish entertainment budget. With hindsight, Grenside admitted that the repayment terms set down in the March 1921 agreement looked far too favourable to Mansell. But the only alternative would have been to ask Mansell to leave, and 'the directors shrank from taking that risk'.

As for the rather casual signing of personal cheques to Mansell which turned out to be unauthorised drawings, Moir Milligan — the least compromised member of the board — offered the opinion that 'directors were entitled to assume that cheques placed before them by their responsible officers were in order'.

Finally, the company's auditor, Cecil Lepine, testified that the reinsurance portfolio Mansell had built up was 'good, solid, cash business, and the books were kept properly from year to year' — though he was not prepared to stick his neck out a bit further and say categorically that it was Bevan's speculations in industrial stocks and Brazilian land that had brought the company down, rather than the routine and above-board insurance commitments for which Mansell was responsible.

Mansell came to trial before Mr Justice Acton at the Old Bailey in late April, and pleaded 'Not Guilty'. Henry Grenside again gave evidence about the March 1921 agreement with Mansell — and, as he invariably did, cut a pretty unimpressive figure. Though he had been 'shocked and scandalised' when Bevan told him about Mansell's loan, it had not occurred to him that he ought to tell fellow directors such as Lords Ribblesdale and March about it, because 'I thought Bevan would have told them'.

'And if you were shocked and scandalised at hearing of the overdraft of £96,000, how came you to agree to its increase to £110,000?' asked Jones for the defence. 'Bevan said that was the amount required to arrange the matter.' Grenside had, after all, heard from Mansell himself that he had received 'attractive' job offers from elsewhere at a time when aggressive new competitors were entering the London reinsurance market.

Finally, the judge asked: 'What was your point of view, that Mansell — however reprehensible or improper his conduct might have been, was an honest man?' 'Certainly,' said Grenside, who, if he was as guileless as his evidence in all the hearings and trials related to the City Equitable suggests, must go down as one of the least effective company directors in the history of the City of London.

But then again, as Mr Justice Avory had observed in his summing up at Bevan's trial: 'It may have suited the purpose of Mr Grenside to appear in the witness box less wise, or shall I say more foolish, than he really is.'

In his own evidence, Mansell said that 'from first to last' at the City Equitable, no one but himself had negotiated reinsurance treaties, and that these represented some 95 per cent of all the company's business. He had achieved that feat by making himself 'a very popular person in the insurance world', entertaining clients and connections at Buckhurst Lodge at the weekends as well as in London.

This lavish way of bringing in business had been established by the dominant German reinsurers before the war, when they had typically allowed their managers entertainment expense accounts of £50,000 or £60,000 a year.

Given all the business he was drumming up — in an increasingly competitive market after the end of the war — he felt he was entitled to 'drawings on contingent commission'; that is, helping himself to advances against the commission he might earn when new treaties were formalised and premium income flowed from them. He had been very proud of the company and of his own career, and felt he was entitled to 'generous treatment'.

What's more, he claimed, he had received a clutch of other job offers promising as much as £75,000 in cash up front plus £10,000 a year salary and five per cent commission, compared to two and a half per cent at the City Equitable throughout the years of its spectacular rise.

'In view of your work for the company,' Jones asked him, 'would you have regarded a grant of £110,000, let alone a loan, as excessive remuneration?' 'No, and I could have got it elsewhere.'

Adjusted for nine decades of inflation, £110,000 in 1921 would have been worth £4.2 million in 2010, offering an interesting reflection on modern arguments about excessive remuneration in the financial sector. Though seven-figure sums are regularly offered as performance-related bonuses when top performers are poached from one City firm to another, not even the most aggressive investment banker of today, and no executive in the rather lower-profile reinsurance sector, would demand or expect as much as £4.2 million as an unconditional 'golden hello'.

And the truth of the matter was that Mansell had been living wildly beyond his means, as well as treating the company's money as his own in a way which was highly irregular if not downright dishonest — so he would have been a dangerous man for any other employer to poach. 'Do you think [Mansell could have secured a highly paid job elsewhere] if they had known his habits?' Mr Justice Avory had asked Bevan at the earlier trial, to which the answer was 'No, I do not think he could.'

The denouement of the Mansell trial, on its seventh day, came as a surprise. Jones argued that Muir had suggested the defendant had a hold over Bevan because he knew Bevan was falsifying the City Equitable balance sheet — but the Crown had not actually brought a charge of being party to that falsification. If they wished to bring such a charge they would have to do so 'on a subsequent occasion'.

The judge expressed sympathy with the argument, and put Muir on the spot. 'The Crown, in justice, ought to say that they made no point about the balance sheet as against Mansell.' Muir seemed to flounder in his attempt to stand up the case for a conspiracy between Bevan and Mansell without this additional charge. His elaborate circumlocutions contain a hint of Renfrewshire testiness behind the expected courtesies: 'Your Lordship having expressed that opinion, I of course give way to it... If his Lordship expresses a view, then whatever my own view might be, I should bow to his Lordship's...'

Thus chastened, Muir ploughed on with his cross-examination of Mansell. But he had clearly come to the conclusion the case was lost. He suddenly halted his questioning — at which point Jones immediately rose to ask for a 'Not Guilty' verdict. The judge said he did not know why Muir had stopped. 'I am breaking off because I think it is useless to continue,' said Muir, perhaps a little too sharply for the judge's liking. 'That does not help me,' Acton shot back. 'My Lord, I do not think I can be more explicit... I cannot withdraw the case unless your Lordship thinks I ought to do so.'

Judge and advocate then both declared themselves in positions of difficulty and embarrassment. But Acton untied the legal knot by asking the jury whether they wished to hear more. If they did not it would signify that the prosecution had not satisfied them Mansell had committed a crime. The jury agreed that they had heard enough, and found him 'Not Guilty'.

It can be argued with hindsight that Mansell was lucky to have got off on the basis of this lacuna in the way the charges against him had been framed. In truth, the only convincing explanation of why Bevan allowed Mansell to help himself so lavishly to the City Equitable's money, at a time when both men knew that the City Equitable's accounts concealed serious financial problems, was that Mansell was the only person who could have exposed Bevan's irresponsibility and deceit.

Was that threat of exposure ever made, or merely left implicit? We can only guess. But Mansell was surely more than greedy. The pattern of his behavior suggests he was as deceitful and cunning as Bevan himself.

He appeared again three months later when he applied to have his bankruptcy discharged — his creditors being promised a dividend of a shilling in the pound. But the judge on this occasion told him that while he had been absolved of anything fraudulent, the way in which he had expended his money was 'extravagance in itself', and suspended the discharge for two years.

As a footnote to Mansell's story, we might wonder what happened to Donald Pirie, Bevan's loyal managing clerk at Ellis & Co. He had been accused during the bankruptcy proceedings of receiving sums of money privately from Bevan — and a question mark hung over the fact that Bevan had made him a 'salaried partner' in

September 1921, when his co-operation was surely needed to help Bevan hide the true state of Ellis & Co's finances.

Pirie denied such accusations, pointing out that he had always lived modestly, had 'no expensive tastes' and had made only one big mistake, which was to place too much trust in Bevan. The Stock Exchange committee took a sympathetic view, and in May 1923 granted him partial rehabilitation by acceding to his request that another member firm should henceforth be allowed to deal on his behalf.

Wilful Neglect?

The most important of all the courtroom dramas provoked by Gerard Bevan was still to come. It was, in effect, the legal system's delayed response to the 'rider' added by the jury foreman at Bevan's Old Bailey trial, that the offences were rendered possible by the board of the City Equitable 'not properly carrying out' its duties.

The Official Receiver, as liquidator of the City Equitable, took this as his cue to pursue an order in the Chancery Court that all the active directors of the company, and not just Bevan alone, were guilty of 'misfeasance and breach of trust'. If a Chancery judge found for the Official Receiver, this would have had important implications for the directors' liabilities to the bankrupt company's creditors — thus increasing the chances of the creditors getting a decent portion of their money back.

Not all the directors of the Bevan era were drawn into the case, however. Proceedings were 'stayed' against Lord Clanmorris, who had resigned from the board to concentrate on his military duties in 1918, before the company's hidden troubles began. The shipbuilding magnate Sir Henry Grayson, who had lent £100,000 of War Loan bonds to the City Equitable in November 1921 and was therefore a substantial creditor as well as a former director, 'made his own arrangements' with the Receiver. And the position of Theodore Barclay, who had resigned in October 1920 and died in March 1921, did not have to be considered by the court.

So the respondents in the case were Dawson, Grenside, Haig-Thomas, Lord March and Milligan — plus poor old Lord Ribblesdale, who had been too ill to take any part in City Equitable affairs since the summer of 1921 and was now in such a reduced state of mind and health that he probably did not even know he was being sued through a *guardian ad litem*, a representative appointed by the court to act for him in the case. The action was also brought against the auditors, Langton and Lepine, and it came to court on 4 February 1924 before Mr Justice Romer.

Sir Mark (later Lord) Romer was a Cambridge mathematician before he became a lawyer. He built a solid, unexciting reputation during a long career at the Chancery bar before being appointed to the bench in 1922. Courteous but decisive, he was well liked in the legal profession. His judgment in the City Equitable misfeasance case was to be a milestone in his judicial career and a benchmark text in English company law.

Arrayed in front of him was a very expensive line-up of London's best legal brains. Each director had his own team of two, and in some cases three, defence barristers. Including two King's Counsels who represented the Official Receiver, there were a dozen silks in court.

Sir John Simon, the Liberal politician who was said to be the highest paid barrister of his generation, appeared for Sir Douglas Dawson. So did Sir Malcolm Macnaghten, the Unionist MP for Londonderry and a near contemporary of Bevan's at Eton and Cambridge.

Peter Haig-Thomas was represented by the up-and-coming Frederick Barrington-Ward, who was also a fellow of All Souls College, Oxford. Sir Walter Schwabe, recently returned from a three-year posting as chief justice of the High Court in Madras, took on the challenge of speaking for Henry Grenside. Wilfred Greene, a future Lord Justice of Appeal and Master of the Rolls, spoke for Moir Milligan.

Arguably the most distinguished name in the list was Frederic Maugham. This monocled future Lord Chancellor was an older brother of the novelist and short-story writer W. Somerset Maugham, and the model for at least two of his characters, Dr Garstin in

The Painted Veil (1925) and the disagreeable judge Sir Edward Landon in the 1947 version of *The Happy Couple*, a revision of a story originally written in 1908.

The Times once described Maugham's courtroom manner as 'slightly supercilious and never very genial'. He happened to be Sir Mark Romer's brother-in-law, but that was no obstacle to his representing Lord March. The silken roll-call concluded with Stuart Bevan, no relation, who appeared for the auditors.

But no defence was to be offered on Gerard Bevan's behalf. Since he had already been convicted of fraud, it would have been pointless to claim that his own default was anything other than wilful. His liability thus already established — for what little it was worth to the creditors — the former chairman of the City Equitable was not in court, and no one appeared for him. Everyone else was thereby at liberty to heap as much blame and opprobrium on him as suited their arguments.

It was Alfred Topham KC — a name known to generations of law students as the author of standard textbooks on company law — who set out the Official Receiver's case. The City Equitable finance committee made up of Bevan, Haig-Thomas and Grenside had made 'grossly improper investments for a company of this kind', notably in such entities as Southern Brazil Electric and Claridge's Hotel in Paris.

> …But it is inconceivable that with a large board of distinguished men as directors, this procedure by Bevan could have been concealed. If their account is to be believed, they knew nothing… The Official Receiver is actuated by no ill-feeling or animosity [towards the directors] in commencing these proceedings, but feels that is a duty to the creditors to do so… Are the shareholders to bear the whole loss?

He asked the court to reaffirm what he described as an old common law principle in relation to negligence, that where a person undertakes an operation which requires skill, he is responsible if damage is done through not exercising a reasonable degree of such skill. In the case of the City Equitable's directors, that would have meant three things:

> That a director should ascertain from time to time what were the investments in which the funds under his control were invested. That there should be a system provided for the care and custody of those investments. And that the investments were reasonably proper for the class of company of which they were directors.

In the simplest terms, 'the cause of the loss was the leaving of everything to Bevan'. So the question underlying the whole case was: 'Could a director of the City Equitable escape liability by saying "I know nothing of insurance matters and I left everything to Bevan", and then when the crash came say "I trusted in Bevan implicitly"?'

After all, Topham argued, shareholders invested in companies largely on the faith of the names that they saw listed on the board. They believed they could rely on these people as men of integrity, who would look after their business. 'And a man of integrity is no use if he is incompetent or idle.'

Much of the evidence that followed revisited ground already well covered in the criminal trial. At one stage, Romer admonished Topham and his fellow counsel for the Receiver, Mr Bennett KC, that 'you do not have a series of millionaires to attack here'. He urged them to concentrate on a representative sample of allegedly irresponsible investments rather than the whole list, lest the case should 'last until Easter'.

Thus it was that much of the case focused on the investments in Claridge's, Southern Brazil Electric and a third name which had not featured largely in the 1922 trial because it did not crystalise as a significant loss until 1923: United Brass Founders & Engineers Ltd.

This business was not one that had been assembled by Hatry with Bevan's assistance during the post-Armistice boom. It was a combination of four 'brass, steam and water fittings makers' in the north of England that had amalgamated in 1910. But it was under the guidance of Hatry and the Commercial Bank, with Ellis & Co as brokers, that the group had attempted to refinance itself by floating a new company with the same name as the old one in 1920.

The issue had been under-subscribed — hence we may assume that the City Equitable was left with an unmarketable bundle of its shares — and a large loan had to be raised, secured by debentures, to keep the new company going, at least for a while. In 1923 the new United Brass Founders went into voluntary liquidation, blaming government disposals of large quantities of scrap brass which had undermined the market.[1]

A few other nuggets were unearthed as the hearing proceeded and, perhaps surprisingly, a few things were said in mitigation of Bevan's conduct, albeit in phrases that were carefully double-edged. Cross-examined by Barrington-Ward on behalf of Haig-Thomas, the investigating accountant Frederick Van de Linde agreed that 'put bluntly', Ellis & Co had 'stolen hundreds of thousands of pounds' from the City Equitable, but even so he would describe Bevan as 'an extraordinarily shrewd man... the things he dared do amazed me'.

He had never doubted Bevan's integrity until, 'to be perfectly fair, Bevan himself put me on the track' by telling him in January 1922 that he should ask for a more up-to-date list of the City Equitable's miscellaneous investments, rather than rely on the uncontroversial but out-of-date list from the previous October that first came to hand. Other directors repeated, in self-justification, their oft-stated position that they had regarded Bevan as a man of high ability and undoubted integrity, until he had finally revealed himself otherwise.

But if they were unanimous on that point, counsel for the four directors who had not been part of the finance committee (Dawson, March, Milligan, Ribblesdale) were at pains to differentiate their position from that of Haig-Thomas and Grenside, who had been

---

[1] The business was bought from the liquidators by an entrepreneur called Richard Hattersley, whose original firm in Ormskirk was one of the four that had combined in 1910. Hattersley valves are still manufactured today.

members of it and had therefore, at least in theory, been privy to Bevan's decisions.

Milligan's brief, Wilfred Greene KC, was particularly eager to establish that his client — who arrived from Aberdeen for the hearing suffering from a heavy bout of influenza, and had to be questioned in his hotel room — occupied a separate niche from all the others. It was Milligan, after all, who had rushed to London to 'tackle' Bevan in December 1921, the first director to do so: 'It must have been a dramatic moment... when Bevan realised that at last the game was up. It was probably Mr Milligan who stopped Bevan's career at a time when another week or two might have brought further disastrous losses.'

And Greene must have been gratified to see the *Daily Express*'s report of his speech headlined 'Bevan's Waterloo'.

Henry Grenside also helped to highlight the differences between the directors' positions by putting up yet another notably weak performance in the witness box, claiming that he 'very soon forgot' the board minute in 1916 authorising the finance committee to invest only up to a maximum of £5,000 per security, but declining to admit that this could be called careless.

With regard to the loan to Claridge's in Paris, Grenside said, they had all agreed it was 'a good use for money of the company that was lying idle in France', Mansell having confirmed this money was available. Thereafter, 'at every finance committee Bevan produced papers showing how well the hotel was doing'.

Haig-Thomas was more persuasive on the same point, reminding the court he had backed his view that Claridge's was a good bet by buying 25,000 of its debentures and 5,000 of its ordinary shares, an outlay of some £30,000 for his own account alongside the company's £228,000; just as he had invested £104,000 of his own alongside the company's £150,000 in the Brazilian ranch.

Finally, it was Lord Ribblesdale's barrister, Mr Gover KC, who made the crucial argument that 'a complete answer to every claim' made against the four non-members of the finance committee was to be found in Article 150 of the company's founding document, its articles of association. This 210-word sentence is an indigestible lump of legal language, but one which demands to be quoted in full (with italics to highlight the crucial point) if we are to understand how Romer came to his historic judgment:

> The directors, auditors, secretary and other officers for the time being of the company shall be indemnified and secured harmless out of the assets and profits of the company from and against all actions, costs, charges, losses, damages, and expenses which they or any of them… shall or may incur or sustain by reason of any act done, concurred in, or omitted, in or about the execution of their duty, or supposed duty, in their respective offices or trusts, *except such (if any) as they shall incur or sustain by or through their own wilful neglect or default* respectively, and none of them shall be answerable for the acts, receipts, neglects or defaults of the other or others of them… or for any bankers or other persons with whom any moneys or effects belonging to the company shall or may be lodged or deposited for safe custody, or for insufficiency, or deficiency, of any security upon which any moneys of or belonging to the company shall be placed out or invested, or for any other loss, misfortune, or damage which may happen in the execution of their respective offices or trusts, or in relation thereto, *unless the same shall happen by or through their own wilful neglect or default* respectively.

For clarity, Gover added, 'If it did not occur to a person to do anything at all, that could not be called wilful default.' For default to be wilful, alternative courses of action must have been presented to the mind of the person so accused, and a choice made. If it never crossed the mind of a director to take a certain course, 'how could he be said to be guilty of wilful default in respect of it?' And that was the position of his ailing client, who had done his duty 'conscientiously and honourably' and was not only free from blame but from 'any imputation of negligence'.

An Historic Judgment

The 24-day hearing came to an end on 5 March with Topham's closing arguments, but the court did not reconvene until 22 May to hear Romer's judgment. It ran to 40,000 words, and took half a day to deliver.

Having rehearsed the facts of the case, the judge began by addressing the issue of Article 150 and 'wilful default'. He cited the case of *Re Brazilian Rubber Plantations and Estates Limited* (1911), in which directors had been acquitted of negligence because the company's articles had contained a clause exonerating them from liability for loss or damage unless it happened through their own dishonesty. The judge, Mr Justice Neville, had concluded:

> I do not see how to escape from the conclusion that this immunity was one of the terms on which the directors held office... I do not think that it is illegal for a company to engage its directors on such terms. I do not think therefore that an action by this company against its directors for negligence, where no dishonesty was alleged, could have succeeded.

Romer said he proposed to follow Neville 'without expressing any opinion of my own'. But in fact he proceeded to lay out, with great clarity, a set of general propositions which stood for many years as a working definition of the duties of company directors under English law. He began by making the point that not all companies are by any means the same, so that there can be no hard and fast rules as to divisions of responsibility between directors and managers:

> It has sometimes been said that directors are trustees. If this means no more than that directors in the performance of their duties stand in a fiduciary relationship to the company, the statement is true enough. But if the statement is meant to be an indication by way of analogy of what those duties are, it appears to me to be wholly misleading. I can see but little resemblance

between the duties of a director and the duties of a trustee of a will or of a marriage settlement. It is indeed impossible to describe the duty of directors in general terms, whether by way of analogy or otherwise.

The position of a director of a company carrying on a small retail business is very different from that of a director of a railway company. The duties of a bank director may differ widely from those of an insurance director, and the duties of a director of one insurance company may differ from those of a director of another.

In one company, for instance, matters may normally be attended to by the manager or other members of the staff that in another company are attended to by the directors themselves. The larger the business carried on by the company the more numerous, and the more important, the matters that must of necessity be left to the managers, the accountants and the rest of the staff.

The manner in which the work of the company is to be distributed between the board of directors and the staff is in truth a business matter to be decided on business lines. To use the words of Lord Macnaghten in *Dovey v. Cory* (1901): "I do not think it desirable for any tribunal to do that which Parliament has abstained from doing — that is, to formulate precise rules for the guidance or embarrassment of business men in the conduct of business affairs."

Romer then set out his three abiding principles:

1. A director need not exhibit in the performance of his duties a greater degree of skill than may reasonably be expected from a person of his knowledge and experience. A director of a life insurance company, for instance, does not guarantee that he has the skill of an actuary or of a physician.

In support of this point he cited Sir Nathaniel Lindley, Master of the Rolls from 1897 to 1900, in the case of *Lagunas Nitrate Co. v. Lagunas Syndicate* (1899):

> If directors act within their powers, if they act with such care as is reasonably to be expected from them, having regard to their knowledge and experience, and if they act honestly for the benefit of the company they represent, they discharge both their equitable as well as their legal duty to the company.

In short, said Romer, directors cannot be held liable for mere errors of judgement.

> 2. A director is not bound to give continuous attention to the affairs of his company. His duties are of an intermittent nature to be performed at periodical board meetings, and at meetings of any committee of the board upon which he happens to be placed. He is not, however, bound to attend all such meetings, though he ought to attend whenever, in the circumstances, he is reasonably able to do so.

> 3. In respect of all duties that… may properly be left to some other official, a director is, in the absence of grounds for suspicion, justified in trusting that official to perform such duties honestly… Business cannot be carried on upon principles of distrust. Men in responsible positions must be trusted by those above them, as well as by those below them, until there is reason to distrust them.

To support his third principle, Romer cited a House of Lords judgment *In re National Bank of Wales Limited* (1899) in relation to a director who had been deceived by the manager and managing director of the bank:

Was it his duty to test the accuracy or completeness of what he was told by the general manager and the managing director? This is a question on which opinions may differ, but we are not prepared to say that he failed in his legal duty. Business cannot be carried on upon principles of distrust. Men in responsible positions must be trusted by those above them, as well as by those below them, until there is reason to distrust them. We agree that care and prudence do not involve distrust; but for a director acting honestly himself to be held legally liable for negligence, in trusting the officers under him not to conceal from him what they ought to report to him, appears to us to be laying too heavy a burden on honest business men.

'These,' said Romer, 'are the general principles that I shall endeavour to apply in considering the question whether the directors of [the City Equitable] have been guilty of negligence.'

He began by ruling out plain idleness or lack of interest as a factor. He was satisfied that none of the directors had merely lent their names to the company in a passive way. Each respondent had taken as active a part in the work of the board as their circumstances had permitted, and had been 'willing and anxious to give of his best'. But had they, individually or collectively, erred?

To start with, they had not been wrong in appointing the three-man finance committee. It was within the board's powers to do so, and it was 'a most reasonable thing to do' — even though the £5,000 limit seemed swiftly to have been forgotten by the board as well as the committee itself.

As for investing in Claridge's Hotel, and even lending it money to stock the wine cellar, the finance committee had been 'most unwise' but it had not exceeded the powers of the company and he was satisfied that — whatever Bevan's motives might have been — Haig-Thomas and Grenside has acted 'with complete good faith'. It was, he thought, impossible to charge this duo with anything worse than an error of judgement and for that, 'a director cannot be made responsible'.

Likewise, he was not prepared to find Haig-Thomas or Grenside liable to make good the loss to the company on its investment in United Brass Founders, and nor could he therefore find the other directors liable.

It was 'at first sight, somewhat surprising' that the others were so ignorant even of the existence of these two investments. It was surely their duty as directors, at a time when the balance sheet was being considered and a dividend was about to be declared, to know *something* about the company's holdings. But it was not their duty to supervise the work of the investment committee in any detail, and the investments were not in themselves *ultra vires* or otherwise obviously improper. The other directors were 'entitled to assume, in the absence of evidence to the contrary, that the committee had good and sufficient reasons for what they had done'.

Next Romer dealt with the Brazilian ranch investment — which Topham had argued certainly was *ultra vires*, and which the directors other than Grenside and Haig-Thomas had known nothing about until shortly before the liquidation. But Romer was not prepared to agree that it was *ultra vires*, and thought that if proper care had been taken in 'defining and guarding the company's interest', it might not necessarily have been imprudent.

As it was, the terms on which money went into the ranch were left to Bevan, who increased the sum involved until it reached £150,000 without ever securing 'a proper partnership deed'.

In not ensuring that such a deed was in place, and not satisfying themselves that the matter had been brought before the board as it should have been, Grenside and Haig-Thomas were guilty of negligence — but their negligence was not wilful, and the loss to the company on the investment might not in fact have been obviated by the existence of more adequate documentation. So he could not make any of the respondents liable for that loss.

Next, the loans to Mansell. Here again, only Haig-Thomas's and Grenside's specific actions were in question, as well as the more general weaknesses of the company's procedures for authorising and issuing cheques. Haig-Thomas did not see the March 1921 agreement until 'after the trouble had arisen' and could not be held responsible for the subsequent loss resulting from Mansell's inability to repay.

As for Grenside, it was impossible to acquit him of carelessness in the matter, 'and carelessness of such a degree as might well constitute negligence' — but Romer did not doubt his 'complete good faith' and was not prepared to make him liable.

The loans to Ellis & Co 'give rise to difficult questions', Romer continued. The directors other than Haig-Thomas and Grenside were under the impression that the finance committee had oversight of all the funds not immediately required for the company's reinsurance business. But Haig-Thomas and Grenside thought the finance committee's role was to deal with long-term investment, rather than the placement of funds 'on loan or in short-dated securities', which was how the Ellis loans were categorized and which turned out to have been left wholly in the hands of Bevan and Mansell.

The directors had failed 'to come up to the strict standard of their duty' in not making enquiries into this item when the balance sheet was presented to them. But given Bevan's high reputation, it was not difficult to understand why they had allowed themselves to be satisfied by assurances from him as to the nature and value of these items, 'fortified by the certificate of the auditors'.

In fact, both the directors and the auditors had been tricked and defrauded by Bevan, 'a daring and unprincipled scoundrel', and neither had received the protection and assistance they were entitled to expect from officials of the company (chiefly Mansell) 'whom events had shown to be unreliable'.

Nevertheless, Romer said, the directors did less than the law required of them. They should not have been satisfied as to the value of their company's assets merely by the assurance of a chairman as distinguished and honourable as Bevan appeared to be at the time, nor by the reassurance of an auditor as competent and trustworthy as Lepine 'was and still is'. (No evidence had been brought forward as to how boards of other insurance companies conducted themselves, but we might interject here that it is hard to imagine the sharp-pencilled professional directors of the Pru or the North British & Mercantile taking such a superficial interest in an issue so fundamental to the health of their business.)

The City Equitable directors should have asked for an accurate list of the company's assets, Romer said, and but for the get-out clause that was Article 150, he would have been obliged to find them (all except Lord March, who had been absent from all three of the relevant board meetings) liable for the losses that might have been prevented if such lists had been called for by the board before it had approved the balance sheets for 1919, 1920 and 1921.

But he was satisfied that they had erred in good faith and in ignorance of their duty, and they were therefore protected by Article 150 and could not be found liable for losses suffered as a result of the connection with Ellis & Co. Likewise, they were exonerated in respect of a £6,952 loan to Bevan himself, and the two dividends paid to City Equitable shareholders in 1921 that the company could not in truth afford to pay.

So the Official Receiver's case against the directors failed even though the directors had made errors of judgement and had in some specific respects fallen below their duty.

Similarly, the auditor Lepine should not have accepted the certificate of Ellis & Co that they held large blocks of securities on behalf of the City Equitable, should have insisted that those securities be put in proper custody, and should have alluded to the matter in their annual report to the company's shareholders.

That constituted negligence, against which Lepine too was protected by Article 150 — but the finding of negligence did not alter the fact that Lepine had conducted his work with 'great skill, care and industry', and had 'honestly and carefully discharged what he conceived to be the whole of his duty to the company... If in certain matters he fell short of his real duty, it was because, in good faith, he held a mistaken belief as to what that duty was'. The application against Lepine was also dismissed.

The only person against whom the Official Reciever was entitled to relief, said Romer, was Bevan — though even he could not be held liable for every transaction that had been put before the court. On the Claridge's investment, there was not sufficient evidence to make Bevan responsible for the loss.

But Bevan had clearly acted fraudulently in relation to the stakes in United Brass Founders and the Brazilian ranch, Mansell's loan arrangement, the excess of the unsecured loans to Ellis & Co over what had been authorized by the finance committee, and some smaller items.

Romer duly entered judgment against the penniless convict for the sum of £247,783, and we can imagine the thin smile with which Bevan received that news at Maidstone in a letter from his solicitor.

The Official Receiver was not prepared to throw in the towel. The extent to which the City Equitable and City Equitable Associated creditors could expect to get their money back still depended on the final outcome of the case — and they had, after all, been left short of well over £3 million between them.

As yet, there was no useful indication as to the level of compensation they could expect. In August 1925, three and a half years after the collapse, it was announced that distributions could finally be expected of up to 14 shillings in the pound for creditors of the Greater Britain and 12 shillings and sixpence for City of London Insurance, but that the position in the case of the City Equitable — by far the bigger problem — was 'still very obscure. So far as can be estimated at present, it is probable that the ultimate dividend will be between one shilling and one shilling and sixpence in the pound.'

A reversal of Romer's decision by the House of Lords might therefore have made a considerable difference to the creditors. The appeal was heard in the autumn of 1925 by Sir Ernest Pollock, who had prosecuted Bevan as attorney general in 1922, but had by now been given (by Prime Minister Stanley Baldwin) promotion to Master of the Rolls, the presiding officer of the civil division of the Court of Appeal — a job for which many of his legal brethren did not feel he was especially well qualified.

He was sitting on this occasion with Lord Justice Warrington, of whom it was said 'the higher he went the better he got'; and Lord

Justice Sargant, an amiable figure known for being neither ambitious nor industrious but for relying on common sense: 'looking at the matter broadly' was a phrase he often used. To the Receiver and the creditors' disappointment, they upheld and commended Romer's judgment.

But the Old Bailey jury's rider about the feebleness of the board had stuck in the public mind, and there was widespread disquiet that the 'other directors' got off scot-free. This was one of the factors that led to the appointment of the Company Law Amendment Committee, under the chairmanship of the recently knighted Sir Wilfred Greene KC. It reported in 1926, making wide-ranging recommendations which led to a new Companies Act three years later.

On the matter of directors' liability, it pronounced:

The decision in the City Equitable case has directed public attention to the common article which exempts directors from liability for loss except when it is due to their "wilful neglect or default". Another form of article which has become common in recent years goes even farther and exempts directors in every case except that of actual dishonesty (see *Brazilian Rubber Plantations and Estates Limited*, 1911). We consider that this type of article gives a quite unjustifiable protection to directors. Under it a director may with impunity be guilty of the grossest negligence provided that he does not consciously do anything which he recognises to be improper.

The evidence satisfies us that in the great majority of companies in this country, directors conscientiously endeavour to do their duty. The public interest excited when exceptions are brought to light is perhaps the best proof of their rarity. But the position is one which in our opinion calls for an alteration of the law. To attempt by statute to define the duties of directors would be a hopeless task and the proper course in our view is to prohibit articles and contracts directed to relieving directors and other officers of a company from their liability under the general law for negligence and breach of duty or breach of trust.

We are satisfied that such an enactment would not cause any hardship to a conscientious director or make his position more onerous and, in our view, there is no foundation whatever for the suggestion that it would discourage many otherwise desirable persons from accepting office. A director who accepts office does not consciously do so upon the footing that he may be as negligent as he pleases without incurring liability. It is only when he has been negligent and the company has suffered a loss, that he is content to take shelter behind the article.

It is, moreover, in our opinion fallacious to say that the shareholders must be taken to have agreed that their directors should be placed in this remarkable position. The articles are drafted on the instructions of those concerned in the formation of the company, and it is obviously a matter of great difficulty and delicacy for shareholders to attempt to alter such an article as that under consideration.

On the other hand, it has been forcibly brought to our notice that under the modern conditions of company administration it is in many cases quite impossible for every director to have an intimate knowledge of or to exercise more than a quite general supervision over the company's business…

A first step towards fulfilling the recommendations that followed from this analysis was taken in the Companies Act 1929, and a more definitive step in section 205 of the Companies Act 1948, which declared that:

> …any provision, whether contained in the articles of a company or in any contract with a company or otherwise, for exempting any officer of the company or any person (whether an officer of the company or not) employed by the company as auditor from, or indemnifying him against, any liability which by virtue of any rule of law would otherwise attach to him in respect of any negligence, default, breach of duty or breach of trust of which he may be guilty in relation to the company shall be void…

There have been several further attempts to tighten and codify the duties and responsibilities of non-executive directors since then, and it is not the purpose of this book to chronicle all of them. Suffice to say that the same syndrome recurs, time after time and however the rules are written.

After every major financial disaster or scandal — whether it be the colossal exercise in false accounting that was the energy trading giant Enron Corporation in the United States before its bankruptcy in 2001, or the catastrophic expansion strategy of the Royal Bank of Scotland that led to its emergency government rescue in 2008 — exactly the same point is made about supine board members in the thrall of over-powerful chief executives as was made so eloquently by Bevan's jury foreman in 1922:

> *The offences were rendered possible owing to other directors not properly carrying out their duties.*

Stung by a Tart

We might pause here to wonder what happened to Bevan's City Equitable colleagues in later life.

Edmund Mansell disappeared from public view but lived to the ripe age of 87, dying in Greenwich, south-east London, in 1959. Lord Ribblesdale, by contrast, had only a few months to live. He passed away in October 1925, aged 70, and his barony died with him. His physical decline had been exacerbated by the stress of the City Equitable affair, which received no mention in a clutch of obituaries that focused principally on his love of hunting.

As a small boy, *The Times* recalled, he had 'hunted the stag in the forest of Fontainebleau and was blooded by Baron Lambert, the *sous-veneur*...

> ...Throughout his active life he hunted hounds, and hunted with other people's hounds, whenever and wherever he could, combining the hard rider with the good sportsman in a way

which is by no means universal. At a comparatively advanced age he broke his leg in four places in the Badminton country, and, though unable thereafter to wear a boot, he continued to hunt as hard as ever in a garb which did nothing to diminish the picturesqueness inseparable from his figure... He loved stag-hunting for more than the mere sport. He loved it for its medieval associations and for all the ancient lore, which he had at his fingers' ends, as readers of his book *The Queen's Hounds and Stag-Hunting Recollections* will not need to be told.

It had not all been hunting, however. Another tribute said he was 'earnest in his views of the responsibilities of the peers, and once astonished the House [of Lords] by suggesting that only those who put in a certain number of attendances should be allowed to vote.'

Ribblesdale's widow Ava never remarried. In 1929 she returned to live in the United States, where she announced that she wished to be known as 'Mrs Ribblesdale'. She died in New York in 1958, aged 89.

Sir Douglas Dawson also suffered poor health after the strains of the City Equitable collapse, but his reputation in royal circles remained sufficiently intact to bring him the consolation of a knighthood of the Order of the Bath in 1925, to add to the knighthood of the Royal Victorian Order he already held. He died at his home near Henley, aged 78, in January 1933.

The Earl of March succeeded his father as the 8th Duke of Richmond in 1928, inheriting not only a full set of aristocratic titles but 280,000 acres of Sussex and Scotland — 45,000 of which, in Banffshire, had to be sold to pay death duties. He died seven years later at the age of 64. Again, *The Times* made no mention of his role at the City Equitable or the Commercial Bank of London, preferring to talk about his regimental loyalty and love of the Turf.

The *Daily Express* did remember the connection, but gave a suitably bland account of it: 'When he was still the Earl of March, he had made a name for himself in the City and in spite of his great responsibilities as a landed proprietor and his war wounds he continued his interest in big business and high finance. He was one of the directors of the City Equitable...'

The shipbuilder Sir Henry Grayson's reputation was untainted by his City Equitable connection. He remained prominent both in the Merseyside business community and on the isle of Anglesey where he lived. He died in 1951, aged 86.

No more was heard of Henry Grenside, who we may assume retreated with some relief to the obscurity of his solicitor's practice and his suburban family life; he died in Surrey in 1956.

As for Peter Haig-Thomas, the most exciting passages of his life — both good and bad — were yet to come. He was known in later years not as a corporate financier but for his deeply embarrassing part in yet another high-profile court case, for his prowess as a rowing coach, and for his rather unlikely achievements as a lepidopterist: his extensive butterfly collection was eventually bequeathed to the Natural History Museum in London.

His family business, Consolidated Cambrian, suffered a slump in profits in the depressed conditions of the early 1920s and was taken over in 1924 by Guest, Keen and Nettlefolds, the metalworking conglomerate associated with the Chamberlain family, which had foundries in South Wales in need of steady supplies of coal. Since Haig-Thomas was a substantial shareholder in Consolidated Cambrian, the takeover (even if it took place at a 'distress' price) must have yielded a welcome infusion of cash to replace some of the hundreds of thousands he had lost investing with Bevan and Hatry.

But it was not a winning gambit for GKN. The disruption of the 1926 General Strike caused many industrial users of coal to turn to imported supplies, while the eventual settlement with the miners raised coal-owners' operating costs; by the end of the decade the major Cambrian operating companies were in liquidation, and GKN had written off the whole of its investment.

Peter Haig-Thomas, meanwhile, seems to have abandoned a hands-on business career to become a sporting celebrity through his association with the annual Oxford-Cambridge Boat Race, which was broadcast live on BBC radio for the first time in 1927. It became a national sporting event, the rival teams cheered on by millions of listeners who had no connection to either of the ancient universities. Haig-Thomas was one of the race's most enduring names, not least because Peter's son David was also a Cambridge blue in the early 1930s.

From 1924 to 1934 Peter coached 11 successive winning Cambridge crews, the last of which broke the course record and was considered a particularly fine example of the traditional English style of oarsmanship which he advocated with some force. That style was passing out of fashion, however, and we may infer some falling out between Haig-Thomas and the powers-that-be of Cambridge rowing from the fact that he then changed sides to coach Oxford — intermittently and with less success, but with a win in 1946.

In 1948 he achieved the rare distinction of having some part in training both Boat Race crews as well as the British Olympic team, and he could claim to have coached more winners in top competition than any other Englishman of his generation. A photograph from that year shows him larger than life, wearing a battered trilby and a huge bearskin coat — naturally, he had shot the bear himself — as he bellowed at his crew from a motor launch through an oversized megaphone.

But his private life was by then in disarray, and his finances were heading in the same direction. To the irritation of his cousins, he had sold off much of the family's land holding in South Wales; a 100,000-acre sporting estate in Sutherland — where he spent part of the second world war serving in the Home Guard — had to go too. He was perpetually trying to drum up cash, but equally open-handed in lending or giving it to any acquaintance who pitched a good story to him.

An inveterate skirt-chaser, he had lived apart from his second wife Lady Alexandra since some time in the early 1930s, not long after the birth of their seventh child. One evening in Soho in November 1947 he was propositioned by a Mrs Evelyn Holder, a veteran prostitute known as 'the Queen of Lisle Street', and was persuaded to part with £2 10s (plus five shillings for her maid) for her favours.

He began to visit her regularly, apparently fell in love, conceived an urge to help her change her life, and for a time even moved into her rooms in Lisle Street. His first romantic plan was to take her with him to Kenya, but the occupational hazards of the oldest profession made it impossible for her to obtain the necessary papers.

It turned out that she had a string of convictions to her name, and the added complication of a husband who was in prison. Later Haig-Thomas decided they should go to South Africa together and booked two single berths on a ship from Glasgow, but they never sailed.

In the meantime he started giving her sums of money, at first small and then in amounts of £3,000 and more at a time, supposedly to buy leases on Soho clubs that she was either going to run or sell on at a profit. But she actually bought only one, the New Cabinet Club in Gerrard Street, and no sales ever transpired despite repeated promises and her elaborate invention of a buyer who was always about to sign.

Haig-Thomas continued writing cheques nevertheless, to cover everything from bogus tax demands (she had never been assessed for tax in her life) to non-existent drain repairs for her non-existent clubs. Over a two-year period at least £30,000 of Haig-Thomas's money disappeared in this way, leaving him more or less penniless, or so he claimed. When he started to demand some of it back, Holder paid a visit to the startled Lady Alexandra at her Hampshire manor house, to threaten her with unpleasant exposure if the police became involved.

The case came to trial at the Old Bailey in June 1950. Though it was very clear from the evidence that Haig-Thomas had been well and truly fleeced by Holder and her accomplice-lover, a club doorman some years her junior by the name of Victor Cooney, they pleaded 'Not Guilty'. Holder stuck to her story that Haig-Thomas was just a sad old punter who had insisted on giving her a stream of cash presents.

On the proceeds, Holder and Cooney had taken holidays in Cannes, gambled in casinos, and had frequently been seen in

Brighton armed with wads of fivers and riding about in a 'large blue American car'. They were found guilty of conspiring to defraud Haig-Thomas and each sentenced to two years in prison.

When Holder came before the Bankruptcy Court after her release, it was revealed that she had also taken £10,000 off another man during the same period — but very little of the £40,000-plus that had passed through her hands could be traced.

Though the embarrassing publicity obliged him to resign his remaining business involvements, Haig-Thomas himself was robustly philosophical about the whole episode. He certainly wasn't the first man to be stung by a tart, he said, but at least he'd had the courage to go to the police and do something about it: 'I'm not worried about what people like to say about me. I have that sort of nature... I wouldn't warn anyone against going into Soho. I'm no spoilsport. After all, it's human nature... But you've got to be careful.'

A year later, having been divorced by Lady Alexandra, he proved his resilience by getting married for a third time — 'blue eyes twinkling beneath a bowler hat at a jaunty angle' according to the *Daily Express* — to a Mrs Joyce Holloway Leach, who had written to him during the Old Bailey trial to offer sympathy.

This time, the honeymoon was spent fishing in Norway, and at the end of the trip (according to family legend) Peter put Joyce on a ship for home and announced that he was staying for a few more days with his rod. In fact, he fancied his chances with a pretty girl in the hotel.

But Joyce was by all accounts quite an operator herself — a serial pursuer of gentlemen in need of sympathy who looked as if they might be generous with their chequebooks. Haig-Thomas obliged as best he could, provoking suspicions among some of his offspring that what was left of their inheritance had been diverted. Several years after Haig-Thomas's death in 1959 aged 76, Joyce found herself another husband — by the name of Tetley — but not a happy ending. She eventually took her own life.

Haig-Thomas's obituaries made no mention of his business career in Wales and the City, nor of his Soho entanglement. Instead he was remembered — even on the BBC radio news — as a grand old man of the river.

His legacy to his sport was *The English Style of Rowing; a New Light on an Old Method* (1958), co-authored with Matthew Nicholson — a slim volume which combined a thinly disguised encomium to Haig-Thomas's own best years as Cambridge coach with a forthright dismissal of almost everything that had come afterwards:

> Probably at no time in the history of English rowing have more people rowed worse than today. The numbers are impressive, the amount of enjoyment derived from all this endeavour admirable, but it is sad to see so much wasted effort... At Henley each year the Grand Challenge Cup goes abroad to the best foreign crew that happens to have entered... In the Thames Cup ever-increasing numbers of indifferent crews contend for the honour of being beaten by the American School... No one in England today can be happy about our present technique.

In an attempt to rectify this deficiency, he coached the Trinity 1st & 3rd boat club at Cambridge until the last summer of his life. One young oarsman of that era, the Scottish novelist Allan Massie, recalled 'an old boy who was regarded with some awe'. Haig-Thomas was, concluded *The Times*, 'dogmatic in his beliefs, as he could well afford to be. But he was always ready to help any crew, however humble, providing they were prepared to accept his teaching.'

Having been worth a couple of million at his financial zenith 40 years earlier, Haig-Thomas's estate on his death was valued at £150.

CHAPTER ELEVEN

Family Matters

'Do you know who I am? Do you know that before my misfortune I was the greatest power in English finance? Let me tell you that there are only three men living who fully comprehended the events that brought about the holocaust of '29 and '30, and I am one of them. If I had not put my trust in titled imbeciles, if I had not been betrayed by a skulking moron...'

Convicted embezzler Montague Thringle alias Legge,
in Ngaio Marsh, *Death at the Bar* (1939)

The Prison Librarian

After his sentencing, Bevan was taken immediately to Maidstone prison in Kent.

Opened in 1819, this grim edifice was an archetype of the kind of penal institution familiar to Charles Dickens and his readers. It crops up in *David Copperfield*; and shortly before Dickens's death in 1870, when he was working on his last and unfinished novel *The Mystery of Edwin Drood*, the author is said to have asked his illustrator Luke Fildes to use Maidstone as the setting for a drawing of the murderer Jasper in his condemned cell.

In the early 20th century, unmodernised in any significant way, Maidstone was a favoured place of incarceration for out-of-the-ordinary convicts, including Irish republican leaders such as Eamon de Valera and murderers such as 'Brides-in-the-Bath' Smith (who we met briefly in Chapter Four) as well as middle-class fraudsters. The prison's stone exterior was to become familiar to television viewers of the 1970s in the guise of 'HMP Slade' in Ronnie Barker's much-loved situation comedy *Porridge*.

Bevan's first consolation on arrival was the discovery that the prison's governor was wearing an instantly recognisable black tie with a thin blue diagonal stripe. Forgetting that he was expected to stand silently to attention in the governor's presence, Bevan reportedly stepped forward to offer his hand as a fellow Old Etonian.[1]

It was probably age and unfitness for hard labour, rather than this old school connection, that secured Bevan a first job in the prison print-shop, setting type. But even that proved physically demanding for him. Having complained that he was not used to being on his feet for so many hours in a day, suffering as he did from rheumatism in his legs, he was allowed a perch to sit on as he worked.

Later he was put in charge of the library, which must have suited him much better and which he reorganized with great efficiency, and part of the garden, where he created a pleasant rockery.

He never accepted his guilt. 'If people will regard my actions as crimes, then of course I have to suffer for it,' he told a visitor, 'but far worse things are done in the City every day.' Nevertheless he seems to have taken his punishment without complaint. As best he could, for a fastidious man in such a dehumanising institution — with its drab regimentation and slopping-out routines — he retained his personal dignity.

His moderate habits of eating and drinking stood him in good stead — although he missed the cakes and pastries to which he was occasionally partial. A prison visitor reported to his family that he looked 'spick and span' and that the warders addressed him as 'Sir'.

He may or may not have found consolation in the fact that Horatio Bottomley, the populist politician, journalist and swindler, was a fellow prisoner. Denied his habitual and colossal daily intake of champagne, Bottomley went to pieces in prison. His egotistical

---

[1] Lest this anecdote should be suspected of being anachronistic, it should be pointed out that the OE colour was first introduced in 1902.

ramblings, larded with patriotic bombast and self-pity, must have been tiresome to fellow prisoners in a confined space.

Bottomley seems to have been less favoured than Bevan: he was put to work on the traditional, mindlessly repetitive prisoners' task of stitching mail-bags. A visitor who came across him one day said 'Ah Bottomley, sewing?' — to which he is supposed to have replied, 'No, reaping.' It's hard to picture Bottomley and Bevan discussing books or playing chess.

But we can guess that the tedium was relieved for Gerard by visitors, though less frequently so than is allowed to modern prisoners. Even his solicitor, bringing legal papers for him to sign from time to time, would have been a welcome face. He must have been in continuous — and from his side, poetic — correspondence with Jeanne but would have seen her rarely: she had presumably returned to the music hall stage in Paris to earn her living, her nest-egg having been diminished by the collapse of Gerard's companies.

She still had her shares in Claridge's, however, and she also had such *bijoux* as Bevan had not reclaimed to turn into cash before his fall. And she evidently had enough money to buy works of art that caught her eye: one such was a 1914 painting called 'The Sunblind' by the Spanish Cubist Juan Gris, which she bought from the Galerie Simon in Paris in 1926.[2]

Christabel was probably Bevan's most regular visitor and provider of books for the library. But he would have seen much less of Sheila, who did not reach her 21st birthday until April 1926 and was still very much in her mother's ambit; that must have been a sadness to him.

The only Bevan sibling to visit was his half-sister Evie, who had married a genial, pipe-smoking engineer called Warren. The Bevan brothers, even Ivor to whom Gerard had been so generous and who had allegedly helped him to get away, refused to have anything more to do with him, such was the shame they felt he had brought on them.

---

[2] Jeanne sold this painting at Christie's in London in 1937 for 23 guineas; it is now in the Tate collection — and vastly more valuable. The record price for a Gris work at auction is $28.6 million for 'Violon et Guitare' at Christie's in New York in 2010.

The women of the family had even felt obliged to offer the bank-ruptcy trustee the jewellery they had received from Gerard as gifts. But it was his brother Owen who took the scandal worst. Even though some of his broking clients at Pember & Boyle increased their orders as a gesture of solidarity and trust during Gerard's trial, Owen was never quite the same again: 'It was as if he had been hit on the head, he became so quiet,' wrote his daughter-in-law Pleasance, 'It really did knock him for six.'

Owen's son and Pleasance's husband-to-be Hugh was another who suffered. After a tough war — as a 19-year-old he had been cap-tured during the retreat from Mons in 1914 — he worked at the City Equitable in a junior capacity, and smelled a rat some months before the collapse when there did not appear to be enough cash left in the company to pay routine claims. He told his father of his suspicions, and Owen put them to Gerard — who characteristically dismissed the suggestion that anything was wrong, a deceit for which Owen never forgave him.

After the collapse, Hugh Bevan 'wore through the soles of a pair of shoes walking round London trying to get jobs for all the City Equitable's employees, and didn't try to look for a job for himself until he had found jobs for them all', Pleasance recalled. But Owen 'behaved very badly and made no effort to help', including refusing to take Hugh into Pember & Boyle on the grounds that there was 'no future in the Stock Exchange'.

Hugh, 'quite pea-green and exhausted' and unable to marry his fiancée for lack of means, found work at the Commercial Union but was by now 'fed up of insurance' altogether. After a stint as a manager of a coal merchants, and despite his father's reluctance, he eventually became a partner of Pembers.

Decree Absolute

As for Sophie, she had wasted no time in bringing divorce proceedings against Gerard and embarking on a new life for herself — to the dis-gust of those in the Bevan family who retained sufficient affection for the black sheep to feel that she had been hypocritical. Their accusation was that she maintained a façade of marriage long after Gerard left her for Jeanne but while he was still stinking rich — then dumped him abruptly at the nadir of his fortunes.

A more sympathetic view might be that having suffered more humiliation from him than any wife, however disagreeable, could possibly deserve, she was well entitled to get shot of him as soon as the law allowed.

Having rented out 21 Upper Grosvenor Street for the summer of 1922, she sold the leasehold to Lord Invernairn, a shipbuilder and arms manufacturer who had made his fortune during the war. And in November, in the midst of Bevan's trial, she bought herself a new home, Wickhurst Manor near Sevenoaks. It happened to be just a few miles from Maidstone — though proximity to the prison to which her husband was likely to be confined was surely not her reason for moving there.

The house was described in estate agents' language as 'cosy and alluringly picturesque'. Parts of it dated from the 15th century, and its large fireplaces and grand oak staircase must have offered reminders of happier days at Littlecote — all the more so because she had brought with her a fine set of furniture from the Long Gallery, which she had persuaded the bankruptcy trustee was hers rather than Gerard's.

Though the new house itself was relatively compact, it came with 70 acres of 'exceedingly pleasant' ornamental gardens and parkland. And Sophie increased her new estate to 112 acres by buying a neighbouring small farm, where she no doubt intended to take up where she had left off at Littlecote, growing her own food and keeping a menagerie of livestock.

Press coverage of the purchase prompted an exchange between Travers Humphreys and Gerard Bevan at the Old Bailey:

> Are you absolutely ruined and penniless? *Absolutely.*
> I ask that question because of something that has been adver-
> tised in every newspaper today, with pictures, that your

wife has bought a house. *My wife has private means of her own. The house is a very small one. She has told me that she bought it on a mortgage of £1,000.*

Bevan had not lost his skill for disguising the truth. In fact, whatever the balance between the sale of the lease in Upper Grosvenor Street and the purchase of Wickhurst Manor, the running costs of Sophie's new home are unlikely to have been much smaller than those of the townhouse she had left behind. However devoted to self-sufficiency she had become, she would still have needed a cook, a housemaid and a couple of gardeners, and presumably her butler Alfred Thompson moved with her.

All this suggests that for the time being, and despite her rather hysterical protestation of poverty during the row over the Claridge's shares a few months earlier, Sophie's finances were on a steady enough footing to enable her to move on towards the complete removal of Gerard from her life.

The divorce case, heard by Mr Justice Hill in June 1923, was reported by the press in some detail. Though reference to sexual matters was largely suppressed or left oblique in 1920s literature,[3] and even more so under the Lord Chamberlain's censorship regime in the theatre, divorce evidence was often carried by newspapers in a matter-of-fact tone that left little to the imagination.

It was King George V himself who complained, after seeing the coverage of another celebrated case during the winter of 1922–23, that 'the pages of the most extravagant French novel would hesitate to describe what has now been placed at the disposal of every girl or boy reader of the daily newspapers'.

This was a reference to *Russell vs Russell* — which included, among other titillating material, speculation as to whether the then Christabel Russell, whose marriage had according to medical evidence never been fully consummated, could have become pregnant

---

[3] D. H. Lawrence's *Lady Chatterley's Lover*, for example, was first published in Italy in 1928 but not in England until 1960, and even then the publisher, Penguin, was prosecuted (unsuccessfully) for obscenity.

by using a sponge in a bath which her sexually incompetent husband, the future Lord Ampthill, had recently vacated.

Another theory was that he might have achieved coition, or some partial version of it, while sleepwalking. The paternity of Christabel's son Geoffrey was the matter at issue and despite the naming in court of several possible co-respondents it was eventually upheld, so that Geoffrey was able to succeed to the Ampthill peerage.[4]

Partly in response to the king's intervention, reporting of divorce evidence was subsequently restrained by the Judicial Proceedings (Regulation of Reports) Act of 1926. But that was too late for Sophie, who was not spared the embarrassment of intimate accounts of her own troubled marital life on the news-stands.

The marriage had been 'fairly happy' until around the end of the war, she told the examining counsel, R.C. Bayford KC — who had also played a courtroom role in the Russell case. But in late 1918 Gerard told her he had had 'four hard years' and would in future be away a good deal. He left home in January 1919, and from that time he never lived with her as her husband — though we might suspect that their sex life had petered out some years earlier.

Gerard came to Upper Grosvenor Street to visit the children from time to time, she explained, but never stayed the night. Thompson the butler confirmed her account. Mr Bevan, he said, 'had very little to do with Mrs Bevan.' Bayford pressed her for confirmation.

Had he anything to do with you on these visits? *He used to quarrel with me nearly all the time.*
Did you see anything of him? *Only at meal times. Otherwise he was with his daughters.*

They occasionally spent the night under the same roof at Littlecote (and perhaps, on rare occasions, in other people's grand houses in the country) but always in separate rooms. Given the vast scale of Littlecote, and Bevan's preoccupations with his collections, his garden and his pheasant shoot, the couple hardly needed to meet while

---

[4] He became a respected deputy speaker of the House of Lords, and died in April 2011.

they were in residence other than at lunch or dinner. Even then, having no interest in food, Bevan was notorious for arriving late to the table and leaving it before the last course had been served.

'Did you see him in 1920?' Bayford continued. *Yes. He went to South America for five months in 1920, and on his return in June I asked him why he was staying away. He said that he had finished with me and that he was going to remain away. He said that he thought he had made a great mistake marrying me, and my answer was "It's rather late in the day".*

Evidence was then presented, having been 'taken on commission' from Maurice Langlais, the chief reception clerk of Claridge's in Paris, confirming Gerard's adultery with Jeanne on frequent occasions between June 1919 and January 1922. In the barest pretence of respectability, she had occupied the room next to his, Langlais attested, but the interconnecting door had always been left unlocked and Gerard had always paid her bill.

It was reported to the court that he admitted adultery with Jeanne, but denied it with another woman named in the petition — and the judge noted that there was 'really no evidence' against this other woman, whose identity was unreported but who must have been Meddy Fabry, the Belgian dancer who was staying in his Carlton suite and playing chess with him during his sleepless nights before he departed with Jeanne.

It seems odd that Bevan bothered to deny a sexual relationship with Meddy and that no evidence was brought forward in the conventional way, from a member of the Carlton's staff, to prove that they had shared a bedroom. Perhaps she really was just a platonic companion at a time of stress, but it seems highly unlikely. It is more likely that she was a friend of Jeanne's, and that they maintained — in shifts, as it were — some kind of *ménage a trois*. Perhaps he denied adultery with Meddy in order to protect Jeanne's feelings, having already asked her to marry him whenever he was released both from Sophie and from prison.

Again, an element of doubt hovers over accounts of Bevan as a relentless womaniser. 'At the age of 50 he collected mistresses with the abandoned vigour of a libertine,' wrote Bernard Wicksteed in 1951 in a *Daily Express* piece that also claimed the middle-aged Bevan had abandoned lifelong sobriety and taken enthusiastically to drink when his business empire began to crumble. For that, there is no evidence at all.

On the accusation of desertion, matters were more straightforward however. Bevan had said simply that he had not lived with his wife for a long time, so that was that. The judge accepted that this did indeed constitute desertion — 'at any rate since June 1920, when he told his wife he had finished with her, and we know that before that he had formed a liaison with [Mademoiselle Pertuisot].'

Sophie was duly granted a *decree nisi* by Mr Justice Hill, and the decree became absolute six months later. She was also granted custody of 18-year-old Sheila, and the Bevan's younger daughter seems to have come through these traumas to find a happier and more settled life than her mother and her elder sister — who was meanwhile facing the consequences of her own marital disaster.

The Bogus Major

The wedding of Christabel Bevan and Major Maurice Gervais had taken place on 20 September 1922, in the midst of her father's committal hearings, at St George's Register Office in Prince's Road, Kensington. The venue suggested that this was not the groom's first wedding (the Bevan family believed that he had been married twice before) and that it had been arranged at short notice without the support or co-operation of the bride's mother. Her father, commuting from his Brixton cell to the Guildhall dock, could not have done much to help even if he had wished to.

Christabel was quite a pretty girl with a broad face and a good figure, to judge from the picture of her — in a smock dress with a single string of pearls — published with the engagement announcement. She had been a debutante in the 1920 season and, with Sophie in attendance, she had been presented to King George V at court not long after her father's return from his long trip to South America.

On that occasion, Christabel had worn soft ivory satin with an overdress of silver lace, while Sophie was got up in 'a Princess gown of "coat of mail" jet with an embroidered design in shades of claire de lune'. Both outfits came from the exclusive fashion house of Callot Soeurs on Avenue Matignon in Paris, much favoured by wealthy American ladies. The gowns must have been fabulously expensive, no doubt involving trips to Paris for fittings, but Gerard could afford conspicuous extravagance in those days, and whatever the tensions in the marriage, mother and daughter must have been on closer terms. We can picture Sophie among a gaggle of nervous mothers and dowager grandmothers, scrutinising their girls' carefully tutored curtseys to the grumpy monarch.

Now, a couple of years later, relations between mother and daughter were severely strained, and if Sophie actually attended the brief register-office ceremony she did not sign as one of the two witnesses. That was done on the family's behalf by Sheila, the second witness being one H.H. Olley. 'A number of friends' attended, or so the press said.

And Christabel seemed to have dressed for going away as swiftly as possible, rather than adapting her ivory satin Callot Soeurs number as a substitute for pure bridal white. She wore a velvet costume with fur collar and cuffs and a small round hat, and carried a daintily worked wrist-bag. The newly-weds posed for photographs which showed the groom to be a big, moustachioed man in a light-coloured three-piece suit and soft hat, as though he might have been going to the races. According to one family member, he was 'most unpleasant [and] smelled strongly of drink'.

They left for a honeymoon in Paris — and one report said Sophie went with them, perhaps having refused to let her daughter leave the country solely in the company of this raffish fellow, even if he was now her husband. She was right to keep a close eye, as it turned out, because much more embarrassment was on the horizon.

The trouble was, not everyone thought Charles Olivier Maurice Gervais was a major — or at least, certainly not 'Major 12th Lancers', which was how he had signed his name in the marriage register. Lieutenant-Colonel O.W. Brinton, commanding officer of the 12th Lancers, swiftly announced that 'Major Gervais does not hold and has never held a commission in the regiment.'

Gervais laughed when asked about this confusion:

It has been said that my name is not Major Gervais. I am not a major in the 12th Lancers but I was once. Why does not the colonel of the regiment consult the army list? I was born at St John's, New Brunswick. In 1898 I was a sub-lieutenant in the Royal Canadian Infantry. In 1914 I was in Paris, having finished my service. I wired to Lord Kitchener offering my services. A few days later I was posted to the 12th Lancers. In 1915 I joined the Royal Canadian Dragoons and afterwards the 87th Battalion Canadian Grenadier Guards. I was demobilized in 1918 as a major.

The dates incidentally, suggest that he was in his forties at the time of the wedding, although another newspaper report gave his age as 38. He also faced insinuations that the marriage had been contracted in suspicious haste; it did not help that the engagement announcement had been published only the day before the ceremony, which was presumably when Sophie had realised it was pointless to go on arguing with Christabel against the match.

'I made the acquaintance of Miss Bevan after the charge had been brought against her father,' was Gervais's response on this point. 'Some people want to know why I did not wait until after the decision in his case. What does that matter to me? I was marrying his daughter. I do not know and don't care whether he's guilty or not.'

But there were more oddities to come out about Gervais. Although he had been living at the Grosvenor Hotel above Victoria Station, he was also discovered to have been renting for the past twelve months — though rarely visiting — a small room behind a barber's shop in Churton Street, Pimlico, furnished only with a writing table, an armchair and a camp bed.

A reporter found a sword, spurs and a uniform there (of which regiment it was not revealed) and also tracked down the information that Gervais had once been a Mountie — a trooper in the Royal Canadian Mounted Police — but had been discharged in 1901.

Sophie not only had a husband who was about to go to prison. She had acquired a wrong'un for a son-in-law. And her fears were to be confirmed in full when the son-in-law went to prison too.

In 1924 Gervais was given a nine-month sentence at the London Sessions for obtaining a cheque from a Dr Shaw of Bedford Place by false pretences. A detective told the court that for the whole duration of his marriage to Christabel, 'Gervais has been living on his wits by means of fraud.'

Though there were no previous convictions against him, it had been definitively established that he never held the rank of major, in the 12th Lancers or any other regiment. He had come to England in 1918 after an incident in which he had claimed to be an officer and behaved in an objectionable manner at the Fort Orange Club, a prominent social club in Albany, New York.

Police in Paris were now investigating a complaint against Gervais by a Mr Talbot, involving money obtained under false pretences. A warrant was also out against him for a paternity order at Westminster police court. And that was the end of his marriage to Christabel.[5]

Sheila's Wedding

Sheila fared better. On 16 July 1927, aged 22, she married Leslie Boore, whose parents lived in Croydon and of whom nothing is known except that a Bevan aunt once described him as 'a little working upholsterer — dreadful', and that he served as an RAF officer during the second world war. When Hugh and Pleasance Bevan met him they formed the view that he was not dreadful at all, but in fact one of the nicer members of the extended family.

---

5 See Endnotes on page 329

And unlike Christabel's hurried register-office ceremony, Sheila's marriage took place in good style at the fashionable church of St George's Hanover Square in Mayfair. It was conducted by the long-serving rector there, Prebendary Thicknesse, assisted by Prebendary Gough, vicar of the equally fashionable Holy Trinity, Brompton — and best known as a founder of the anti-socialist British Workers League during the first world war, so perhaps someone Sophie had come across in her political campaigning days.

The ceremony marked a brief comeback in polite society for Sophie. Sheila was announced as 'younger daughter of Mrs S.K. Bevan of Wickhurst Manor, Sevenoaks' without mention of Mr G.L. Bevan of a different address in Kent but with the addition of a nice touch of respectability: '…and grand-daughter of the late F.A. Bevan, Trent Park, chairman of Barclays Bank'.

Perhaps that wedding day was also the last time Sophie, Sheila and Christabel were all together. Estranged from her mother, Christabel fell on hard times and took a small room in Paris where she supported herself by teaching English. She had her father's gift for gardening and kept a beautiful balcony of flowers in pots, but became increasingly eccentric, wearing long, flowing purple dresses, announcing that she could not sleep in a bed if its head was not to the north, and dabbling in exotic religions. The Bevan family thought she was touched in the head like her mother.

On one occasion, Christabel conceived an urge to visit the holy city of Lhasa in Tibet. She had no idea how to get there but set off anyway, equipped only with an umbrella and a belief that she would be spiritually guided. She eventually reached the gates of Lhasa by donkey, and got back to England again, but little more was heard of her.

As for Sophie, after Sheila's wedding she disappeared from public view. She put Wickhurst Manor up for sale in 1929 — perhaps out of financial necessity, if the investments that provided her income suffered in the crash of that year.[6]

Though the reference to Frank Bevan in Sheila's wedding announcement suggests that Sophie was keen to maintain

6 See Endnotes on page 329

a connection with her respectable Bevan in-laws, the feeling was not mutual. When Cosmo Bevan died in October 1935, Sophie caused a stir by turning up unexpectedly at the funeral at Christ Church, Cockfosters, the Bevan church near Trent Park. Cosmo's widow Marion hissed that she would on no account have Sophie in her house (in nearby Barnet) for tea afterwards. Owen Bevan was delegated to break this news to Sophie, and to escort her back to Cockfosters tube station.

It was the last time any of the Bevans set eyes on her. She died aged 74, on 11 January 1941, at a nursing home at Borth, a long, windswept coastal village north of Aberystwyth in Wales, bleak in winter but much favoured in summer by holidaymakers (in modern times, many of them caravan enthusiasts) from the West Midlands.

Perhaps that included one of her sisters — Mabel, Dorothy or Rosa — who helped her when she became infirm or mentally unstable. Her death notice implies that she had returned to the bosom of the family from which she came, describing her simply as 'daughter of the late J.A. Kenrick of Edgbaston'.

Christabel and Sheila, poignantly un-mentioned in that notice, died respectively at Plymouth in 1971 and at Watford in 1988. Neither had children, and Gerard fathered no offspring with Jeanne nor, so far as is recorded, with any of his other mistresses. So he has no known descendants.

CHAPTER TWELVE

Last Years

'*A duke who has served a prison sentence is still a duke, whereas a mere "man about town", if once disgraced, ceases to be "about town" for ever more.*'

George Orwell, in *Raffles and Miss Blandish* (*Horizon* magazine, 1944), an essay on E.W. Hornung's tales of A.J. Raffles, the Mayfair socialite and 'amateur cracksman'

What Happened to Hatry?

Bevan left prison on 7 February 1928. Unlike Horatio Bottomley, whose release a few months earlier had attracted a frenzy of attention and who later published a series of articles about his jail experience entitled 'Five Years of Hell!', Bevan just slipped quietly away.

Five and a half years in custody had taken a heavy toll on his health. His rheumatism was much worse, and his sister Evie described him as looking like 'a broken man'. But he rallied to marry Jeanne — whose name was entered in the register as Maria Letitia Pertuisot — on 10 April.

They were reported to have made a new home in the elegant and very Anglophile French resort of Biarritz on the Atlantic coast, where they could visit the English tearoom on the Avenue Edouard VII, though they probably steered clear of the casino on the beachfront below.

Thereafter, their trail becomes much harder to follow — but there was at least some tidying up of financial loose ends. In August 1930 a third and final dividend in bankruptcy of two pence in the pound was declared in respect of the Ellis & Co partnership, and a little over three pence in the pound in respect of Bevan's personal debts, following a seven pence dividend in 1927. It was very small recompense for those who had put their trust in him.

And there were echoes of Bevan's story in the fate of Clarence Hatry — who some influential voices in the City, including Lord Revelstoke of Barings, thought should have been in the dock alongside Bevan back in 1922, but who had climbed back to City prominence if not quite to respectability.

The Commercial Corporation (formerly Commercial Bank) of London had gone into receivership in 1923 with a deficiency of some £3 million, the value of most of its strategic investments having been wiped out. But Hatry promised to safeguard the interests of his shareholders, and liquidated many of his personal assets in order to do so.

He made great efforts to pay off his remaining creditors, first through a vehicle called Aylesbury Trust and then through Austin Friars Trust, the vehicle for his last and ultimately disastrous forays into the field of company reorganisation. It became a 'central sun', in the attorney general's description during the subsequent prosecution, 'with the other companies circling around it like its satellites'.

These satellites included the Drapery Trust, an amalgamation of numerous London and provincial department stores which Hatry sold on to Debenhams at a large profit. Then there was Corporation and General Securities, which managed some £35 million of loan issues for local authorities, including a £5 million loan for the city of Birmingham.

This typical Hatry venture grabbed market share by using a variant of the mechanism he had often used for company flotations, whereby his companies bought the whole issue (thus guaranteeing the local authority its money) at a discount, then made a turn by selling the paper into the market at a smaller discount or at face value.

And a third string to his corporate bow was Photomaton, which commercialised a patent photographic process for use in public booths.

Hatry was feverishly active in the market for speculative new share issues of 1928, and went on in 1929 to bring a number of smaller English and Scottish metalworking businesses together to form Allied Ironfounders. From there he attempted to restructure the entire British steel industry by taking over the United Steel Company and building a new group around it.

But as Photomaton and some of his other businesses fell into difficulties, Hatry could no longer muster the cash resources needed to carry his steel plan through. And he had made too many enemies.

Brokers who had been cut out of local authority loan stock issuance by Corporation and General were keen to see him fail. And he found himself implacably opposed by Montagu Norman, the Bank of England's autocratic governor, who persuaded several finance houses to withdraw support for the steel project.

Under extreme pressure to fill the funding gap, he resorted to fraud via Corporation and General by diverting the proceeds of genuine loan issues for the local authorities of Swindon, Wakefield and Gloucester and by issuing unauthorized additional paper in their names and using it as collateral to raise short-term loans. Likewise, spurious share certificates were printed for various Hatry companies and used as fake collateral for borrowings.

But to no avail. By mid-1929 rumours were rife in the City that Hatry was in trouble, and by September the game was up. Dramatic falls in the share prices of companies associated with him were later seen by some commentators on both sides of the Atlantic as harbingers of the Great Crash.

Hatry made a partial and inaccurate confession to Sir Archibald Bodkin, the Director of Public Prosecutions, as his group collapsed with debts of some £14 million. When he came to trial at the end of the year, according to one account, the financier 'conducted himself with great dignity and took all the responsibility upon himself', but that cut little ice with Mr Justice Avory, who handed down a sentence of 14 years' penal servitude and told Hatry that he stood convicted of 'the most appalling fraud that has ever disfigured the commercial reputation of this country'.

The sentence was upheld on appeal, and Hatry in due course occupied a cell at Bevan's *alma mater*, Maidstone, where he was even a successor to Bevan as prison librarian. With the help of influential friends, he gained early release in 1939 and soon made another business career for himself. Librarianship had evidently encouraged his interest in the written word, and in 1940 he became the owner of Hatchards, the famous Piccadilly bookshop.

The manner in which he bought Hatchards was a fine illustration of Hatry's financial ingenuity at a time when his own resources, after a decade in jail, were very limited indeed. The business was for sale partly because its regular customers, many of them members of the upper classes, were habitual bad payers. Hatry agreed a bargain price for the acquisition — only £6,000, of which half was payable immediately and half later.

He borrowed the first tranche from his wife, who had made money from dealing in shares (ironically including steel shares) on the strength of her husband's advice from his prison cell. Having gained control of Hatchards, he then wrote to all its delinquent customers saying that he proposed to place a list of their names in the shop window — provoking enough of them to pay up to enable him to pay off the balance of the purchase consideration.

He went on to create a publishing business attached to Hatchards, and later to invest in West End coffee bars. Despite continuing ups and downs of financial fortune, he retained an impish sense of humour, and employed as his office doorman a former warder from Maidstone — on the grounds that 'anyone who was good at keeping people in should be good at keeping unwanted visitors out'.

Hatry died in 1965. The parallels between him and Bevan hardly need to be laboured. The Marquess of Winchester, who was chairman of Corporation and General Securities, described Hatry in terms that could very well have been applied to Bevan: '[He had] the supreme quality of dangerous optimism coupled with inordinate conceit ... his brain was honeycombed with crevasses into which unpleasant facts were allowed to slip and there he permitted them to remain in the hope that the glacier would never reveal its secrets.'

But perhaps what is most interesting to ask, in both cases, is to what extent their actions revealed an inherently criminal nature, or to what extent they were both merely acting out of desperation and panic as their legitimate business schemes and aspirations foundered.

Hatry's deceits — involving borrowing against bogus securities — were more blatant than Bevan's, which were to do with disguising mismanagement and inappropriate risk-taking by presenting false accounts. And Hatry in the end served a longer sentence.

But there were still plenty of people willing to defend Hatry on the grounds that he had a genuine grand plan for the steel industry, whereas Bevan despite his patriotic rhetoric at City Equitable meetings was really never more than an opportunistic money-man.

And, so his sympathisers said, everything Hatry did might have come right in the end if market circumstances had allowed — as indeed they might have done for Bevan. Here is part of the foreword, signed by six MPs and a dozen other public figures, to *The Hatry Case: Eight Common Misconceptions*, a book by Hatry's son Cecil which helped to secure his release in 1939:

> We know that Mr Hatry… erred, and in seeking to retrieve his error did much that should not have been done. But he was never a reckless adventurer of the vulgar legend. He was a man of high quality and notable achievement who was caught in a world of depression and hoped, by taking certain risks, to win through, not for himself but for his enterprises. By the narrowest of margins he failed. He has taken harsh punishment.

Put plainly, neither Hatry nor Bevan was a wholly bad person from beginning to end. Neither was an incorrigible swindler of small savers as Horatio Bottomley had been. But both had an inclination to sharp practice and imprudent dealing which mutated into blatant dishonesty when their backs were against the wall.

And the defence offered for Hatry by his barrister, Norman Birkett, that he did what he did merely 'to avert a disaster which would bring many innocent people a loss they could not bear', was far from convincing. Sir Horace Avory certainly had no truck with it: 'What does the plea amount to, when stripped of its rhetorical language? It is nothing more than the threadbare plea of every clerk or servant who robs his master and says he hoped to repay the money before the crime was discovered by backing a winner.'

Finally, there is the issue of trust in financial systems: the damage done by fraudsters is limited in its direct impact and the number of its actual victims, but it invariably has wider and more insidious consequences. As R.A. Haldane concluded in his account of the Hatry case in *With Intent to Deceive* (1970):

> It has been said of Hatry that he was unlucky in that, but for the unexpected and unparalleled collapse of money markets late in 1929, the scheme might have worked. That may be. But crime is crime, concealed or exposed. The convicted men were guilty of frauds on a gigantic scale and... the credit of the City of London was the chief victim.

Russet and Asp

Sitting in a French café reading the London papers, Bevan must have felt a wry sense of *déjà vu* as he watched not only what was happening to Hatry's empire but the increasingly febrile state of the stockmarket as the Great Crash of 1929 impended. But his most immediate preoccupation in the year after his release and new marriage had nothing to do with finance. It was a literary endeavour.

One of the most intriguing glimpses of Bevan at any stage of his life is to be found in the memoirs of the novelist Anthony Powell, who as a young man worked for the publishing firm of Gerald Duckworth & Co in Henrietta Street, Covent Garden.

In *To Keep the Ball Rolling* (1983) he wrote:

When I was at Duckworth's the firm published 'on commission' (i.e. paid for by the writer) a volume of verse in the manner of Swinburne put out after release from prison by a financier called Gerard Lee Bevan, who had in some manner transgressed in City dealings. Bevan's poems appeared at least once if not more in the Bestseller Lists, when in fact Duckworth's had disposed of only three copies.

This not-so-slim volume — 236 pages, containing 83 poems — was evocatively titled *Russet and Asp*, which is of course a reference to what happened to Eve in the Garden of Eden. It appeared in June 1929, and contained this curious dedication:

We can assume that 'C' is Christabel, 'J' is Jeanne and 'S' is Sheila rather than Sophie. That aside, the mystery of *Russet and Asp* is how the reputable and somewhat stuffy firm of Duckworth, publisher of Anton Chekhov, Hillaire Belloc and John Galsworthy among other literary lions of the era, came to accept a fraudster and jailbird onto its list of authors.

The answer seems to be — apart from a matter of money changing hands — old school connections, once again. Gerald Duckworth, the founder-proprietor, was a contemporary of Bevan at Eton and Cambridge, where he was at Clare College. It seems they were friends — and Duckworth must also have known the most literary member of the Bevan family, Edwyn, a fellow member of the Savile Club where Duckworth was for many years honorary secretary.

Edwyn, it will be remembered, acknowledged the advice of Gerard Bevan in his translation of Aeschylus many years earlier, and had gone on to become a published author on subjects ranging from

Indian nationalism to ancient Mesopotamia. We may guess he had a hand in persuading Duckworth to bring Gerard's verses into print.

If Powell's biographer Michael Barber is to be believed, publisher and financier would have been comfortable in each other's company anyway — Duckworth was a shrewd man of business; and if anything, Bevan was the more intellectual of the two.

According to Barber, Duckworth 'seems to have entered the [publishing] trade for want of anything better to do during daylight hours (after dark he found plenty to occupy him)... a typical Edwardian clubman, portly, pompous and self-indulgent... he had, by the time Powell joined Duckworth, relinquished whatever pleasure he ever took in books and reading.'

Virginia Woolf, Duckworth's half-sister, had a particularly low opinion of him even though he published her novels, likening him to 'a pampered overfed pug dog with white hair, hardly a gleam of life, let alone intelligence in his eye'.

Whatever the proprietor's shortcomings, Powell must have been exaggerating when he claimed that only three copies were ever disposed of by Duckworth. The book was something of a collector's item. It was announced, at eight shillings and sixpence, in prominent newspaper advertisements which carried a quote from the *Daily Express*: 'Mr Bevan stands revealed as a poet of vivid imagination and genuine feeling.' Indeed, John Galsworthy — a close observer of Gerard Bevan's fall, as we shall see in a moment, as well as the chronicler of the wider milieu in which he lived — must have been miffed to find his own latest published work, *Exiled*, a play then running at the Wyndham Theatre, listed two places below Bevan's in the Duckworth ads.

Most likely, Bevan wanted to send the book as a gift to City friends who had not shunned him after his disgrace. It must have been an expensive project, so perhaps Edwyn also helped to pay for it. The author's copy, discovered in 2009 in a secondhand bookshop in Ramsgate, contains the *Ex Libris* label of Sir George Alexander Touche, a highly reputable accountant who was a City contemporary of Bevan's and chairman of numerous public companies. The copy does not look as though it has passed through many other hands, so it is pleasing to think that the neat pencil marks beside striking poetic phrases are Sir George's own.

We can only wonder what he and other readers who knew Bevan's story made of the archaic style and unworldly sentiment of most of the poems. Powell was right to compare them to Swinburne. *Russet and Asp* is an unequivocal echo of the aesthetic movement of the last third of the 19th century, with its rejection of Victorian materialism in favour of an idealised chivalric and pastoral world.

It is possible that some poems in the collection were written in Bevan's undergraduate days in the early 1890s. But they must have felt extraordinarily dated to the reader in 1929 who was familiar with T.S. Eliot's *The Waste Land* (1922), or the modernist oeuvre of Ezra Pound, or had chanced across a copy of W.H. Auden's first little book of poems, hand-printed by Stephen Spender for limited circulation in 1928.

Even in poems that were clearly written after his City fall, Bevan remains in the realm of the long-dead Dante Gabriel Rossetti and the quintessential 1890s poet Ernest Dowson, author of the phrase 'the days of wine and roses'. Bevan steers clear of their unrestrained eroticism and inclination to decadence — but who knows, perhaps the buttoned-up, church-going undergraduate Bevan had inwardly yearned in that direction.

Was he a talented poet, even if he was a self-consciously old-fashioned one? He was certainly a careful craftsman, working in a variety of metres and rhyme schemes, and perhaps at his best with the sonnet form, a couple of examples of which we have already encountered. Here is another, *Toledo*, which shows considerable skill:

> *Thou lonely citadel of shrunken creeds,*
> *Is this the end of all thy majesty?*
> *The foster-mother once of high-born deeds,*
> *Of faith the fortress, sword the armoury,*
> *Deep in thy crypts lie cardinals and kings*
> *Who once to Lima's beaches pushed their sway;*

Above, the skies are dark with raptors' wings,
Augurs of evil, omens of decay.
Well may the dusky waves of Tagus weep
Along thy bases held impregnable;
Well may the snows hang wreaths about thy steep
And the far Sierras answer to each knell:
For thy dead greatness clothes thee like a sleep
Wherein still hover ghosts of Heaven and Hell!

Yet elsewhere he makes clunking errors of rhythm, and resorts to tongue-twisting vocabulary which can have been no more familiar in 1929 than it is today, and only serves to make the reader stall. In one nine-line stanza of *Pilgrims*, for example, we stumble over *tortuousest, eclogue, shalm, jesserant* and *heaume*, (the last two being items of medieval armour) and the deeply unpoetic *paludal*, which refers to swamp or marsh. In *Sonnet II*, the poem that is reproduced as this book's prologue and the source of its title *Fortune's Spear*, we puzzle over *oboli*, a small ancient Greek coin, and *accompt*, a Frenchified archaism for 'account'.

We can picture Bevan cloistered in the Dutch parlour at Littlecote or the billiard room in Upper Grosvenor Street, surrounded by leather-bound, gold-tooled translations, travelogues and dictionaries, jotting curious new words into a notebook, imagining himself transported to exotic places. But this does not always make for good poetry.

On the other hand, he reveals a charming, boyish fascination with birds: bitterns, plovers, flycatchers, cuckoos and owls populate his poetic landscape, sometimes far removed from their natural habitat. And just occasionally, he offers a glimpse of his real life.

At Auction, for example, muses on the provenance of an ancient Persian painting about to go under the hammer. This poem was, according to the *Daily Mirror* (which in those days interested itself in contemporary poetry) 'seemingly written in his prosperous days'. In it, Bevan — the great collector of Chinese porcelain, most of which must have been looted by foreigners from its original owners to be sold and re-sold before it finally came into his hands — expresses contempt for the very trade of which he was himself such an active beneficiary:

> *E'en now they're holding up their impious prize*
> *Above the rostrum, and begin to bray*
> *And brag as though possession made them wise.*
> *By what themselves allege*
> *They stand attaint in grossest sacrilege.*
> *"A clever dealer brought it from the east."*
> *"He heard of it at feast*
> *And bribed the keepers of the Holy Place."*
> *"'Twas wasted where it was; 'twas hard to trace."*

> *And in a moment when the bidding's done,*
> *This jewel, where five centuries have prayed*
> *And worshipped, this pure-flowered paragon*
> *Of constancy where not a seed has strayed*
> *On wings of the night air,*
> *This, the epitome of all that's fair,*
> *Ousting revenges, like wild animals,*
> *To its remotest walls,*
> *Will be a thing to boast of, a pretence*
> *Of culture at the beck of insolence.*

But only a few of the poems make reference, obliquely, to the last phase his life. One such is *Sonnet II* and another is *Exile*, which he might well have written in Vienna before his arrest — perhaps, as a neighbour there reported, 'gesticulating wildly' as he composed it.

It expressed his sadness at the thought that he would never 'look on the green fields again' — English fields, obviously — having been separated from them by 'misunderstandings madder than typhoons'. And it tells us that 'one red apple on a wrinkled tree / Means more than a whole Amazon to me', confirming that the exile he imagined for himself could well have been in Brazil. In order to give Bevan the last word from afar, in every sense, in his own story, *Exile* is our epitaph on page 321.

Russet and Asp confirms what a complex person Gerard Lee Bevan was: a 'Napoleon of finance' capable of large-scale deceit, yet also a genuine lover of beauty, an amateur scholar capable of withdrawing into a distant realm of fantasy. Many fraudsters are fantasists, but their dreamworlds are projections of the material wealth and power they imagine their financial alchemy will conjure up — not vistas of knights and pilgrims and arcadian peasants.

It is disappointing, in a way, that Anthony Powell did not use Bevan as raw material for one of the characters in his great 12-novel sequence *A Dance to the Music of Time*. But the truth is that Powell was not terribly interested in business. His rather sketchy references to financial machinations in the lives of characters such as Kenneth Widmerpool and Sir Magnus Donners — displaying varying degrees of ruthlessness, but never straying towards outright fraud — were informed by conversations with one particular source, the banker, soldier and MP Sir Harry d'Avidgor Goldsmid, an establishment figure a generation younger than Bevan.

The only possible sighting of Bevan in the *Dance* is a very oblique one: it must have been a broker very like him who in *A Buyer's Market*, the second volume of the series, set in 1928, offers a South American share tip to Uncle Giles, the former army officer and mildly disreputable uncle of the narrator Nick Jenkins.

Uncle Giles turns up from time to time (until his death in *The Kindly Ones*, the sixth volume of the series) worrying about the affairs of the family trust on which he relies for income. After a long and eventful night out, Nick Jenkins returns at dawn to his bachelor rooms in Shepherd Market, the red-light area of Mayfair, to find his bowler-hatted uncle lurking in front of a nearby pub.

> "Tell your father to try and get some San Pedro Warehouse Deferred," he said, shortly. "I have had reliable advice about them."
>
> "I'll say you said so."
>
> "Do you always stay up as late as this?"
>
> "No, it was an especially good party."

Whereupon Major Jenkins, who might so easily have been a former client of Ellis & Co alongside Colonel Grove and Colonel Richmond-Brown, shoulders his umbrella and marches off as if departing a surrendered town at the head of his troops.

The PPRS

To claim to have glimpsed Bevan in Powell's fiction clearly verges on the tenuous. There is, however, one character in 20th-century English literature who was very obviously modelled on Bevan (or at least on an amalgam of Bevan and Mansell) in a way that suggests the author concerned had done painstaking research to capture the detail and ambience of a real-life boardroom drama. The character's name is Elderson, and he appears in *The White Monkey*, the first volume of John Galsworthy's second Forsyte trilogy *A Modern Comedy* — later repackaged as Volume II of *The Forsyte Saga*.

The White Monkey was not Galsworthy's best work, according to his critics, but was much enjoyed by the elderly Thomas Hardy, whose wife wrote to Galsworthy's that it was 'the first time I have ever known him to have a novel by his bed'. It was published in 1924, and Galsworthy had begun writing it in London in November 1922, when Bevan's trial was the talk of the town. He finished it while staying in Italy, Madeira and Portugal in the course of 1923.

It is a curious thought that Bevan might have had the opportunity of reading *The White Monkey* in the library at Maidstone. We can only wonder what impact it made on him. He must have been startled to find that Galsworthy had, in effect, adopted the entire story of the City Equitable and given it the thinnest fictional varnish.

In doing so — even Bevan might have acknowledged — he had captured better than any newspaper reporter the patterns of corporate life which so often repeat themselves: the placing of excessive trust in a powerful chief executive, the failure of non-executives to challenge the executive until it is too late, the collective unwillingness to face the truth when conditions turn bad; the recriminations and excuses afterwards.

Galsworthy was the son of a City solicitor, and had practiced as a barrister in the 1890s before his writing career took off. Some of his ripe, whiskery boardroom characters might have seemed a touch Victorian — Dickensian even — in 1924, but his fictionalisation of Bevan is well worth re-telling, because in an entertaining way it draws many of the morals of the real story.

Soames Forsyte, the prickly, self-centred solicitor and 'man of property' who is the central figure of the *Saga*, has been appointed a non-executive director of the Providential Premium Reassurance Society, at a fee of a thousand a year. This nice little earner has come to him through the influence of another of the Society's directors, Sir Lawrence Mont, a baronet whose son Michael has recently married Soames's daughter Fleur. But Soames is immediately troubled by the nature of some of the business accumulating on the Society's books, and has his beady eye on its general manager, Robert Elderson.

Never a man to offer his trust freely, Soames is a good deal more suspicious than any of the City Equitable board members had been when business conditions turned against Bevan and Mansell. But he realises that the law of averages, as applied to underwriting risks, is 'perhaps the most reliable thing in the world', and worries that it might seem presumptuous to raise the alarm in such an 'imposing concern' as the PPRS, especially when he has been connected with it for such a short time.

As for Elderson, with his 'sweetish face' and bald pate, there is nothing about him to suggest 'irregularity or excessive optimism'. Even so, the Society's circumstances cause Soames 'disquietude', not least because his sister Winifred, encouraged by Soames's presence on the board, has recently bought some of its shares.

'I'm not easy,' he tells Sir Lawrence (known to the Forsytes as 'Old Mont') over Sunday lunch at Fleur and Michael's house. 'If I'd realised how that chap Elderson ruled the roost, I doubt if I should have come on to that Board... I don't believe in trusting a man's judgement as far as we trust Elderson's; I don't like this foreign insurance.'

'You're quite wrong about Elderson', replies an affronted Old Mont, as he tucks into Fleur's risotto of chicken livers: 'His grandfather was my grandfather's parliamentary agent at the time of the Reform Bill... first-rate head, Elderson; I've known him all my life, we were at Winchester together.'

But that's the nub, Soames thinks to himself: 'On the Board they had all, as it were, been at Winchester together! ... They were all so honourable that they dared not scrutinize each other, or even their own collective policy. Worse than their dread of mistake or fraud was their dread of seeming to distrust each other.'

And who were his fellow directors? The PPRS's chairman, Sir Luke Sharman, 'seemed always to be occupied in not being taken for a Jew' but his clothes 'had a suspicious tendency towards gloss'. Anti-semitism in the world to which Soames (and Bevan) belonged was a theme Galsworthy had recently explored in a much-acclaimed stage play, *Loyalties*.

As to the rest, they sound like a pretty good replica of the City Equitable board. In Lord Ribblesdale's seat is 'old Lord Fontenoy [who] was there for his name, of course; seldom attended, and was what they called a 'dud'.' Mont, who prefers talking about shooting and is fond of a nap during board meetings, is a fair facsimile for those other ineffective toffs at the City Equitable, Lord March and Sir Douglas Dawson: 'What was the good of a ninth baronet on a Board?'

Then there is a King's Counsel, Guy Meyricke, 'a good man in court, no doubt, but with no time for business and no real sense of it'; he is the fictional equivalent of the solicitor Henry Grenside. Finally, there is 'that converted Quaker, old Cuthbert Mothergill', in whom Galsworthy encapsulates the reputation of the Bevans (except Gerard of course) and their ilk, 'whose family name had been a by-word for successful integrity throughout the last century, so that people still put Mothergills on to boards almost mechanically'. But this Mothergill, unfortunately, was 'rather deaf, nice clean old chap, and quite bland, but nothing more'.

'A perfectly honest lot, no doubt', but all in the pocket of Elderson:

Clever chap, bit of an artist... with everything at his fingertips! Yes! That was the mischief! Prestige of superior knowledge, and years of success — they all kowtowed to him, and no wonder! Trouble with a man like that was that if he once admitted to having made a mistake he destroyed the legend of his infallibility. Soames had enough infallibility of his own to realise how powerful was its impetus towards admitting nothing.

Conditions have been deteriorating in the twelve months since Soames had joined the board, in part due to currency fluctuations affecting the company's foreign reinsurance portfolio, much of it German. And he suspects that not even Elderson himself knows how badly matters really stood, 'or, if he did, he was keeping knowledge that ought to belong to the whole directorate severely to himself'.

What follows is a masterclass by Soames — more instructive, in its way, than any corporate governance code — in how an independent director should behave if he thinks he has spotted a serious problem that the management is trying to cover up. At a board meeting called to approve the Society's accounts ahead of its annual general meeting, he speaks up:

> I'm not satisfied that these accounts disclose our true position. I want the Board adjourned to this day week, Mr Chairman, and during that week I want every member of the Board furnished with exact details of the foreign contract commitments... Unless there's a material change for the better on the Continent, which I don't anticipate (quite the contrary), I fully expect those commitments will put us in Queer Street... For all I can tell, instead of paying a dividend, we ought to be setting this year's profits against a certain loss next year.

This intervention is met with 'the scraping of feet, shifting of legs, clearing of throats which accompany a slight sense of outrage', as well as expressions of confidence in Elderson and objections to the inconvenience of another meeting. Soames holds back from demanding an independent scrutiny of the accounts (*'Mustn't overdo it!'*) but insists that he will resign if he does not get the information he has asked for — and in the end the chairman coldly assents. 'First time I remember anything of the sort on that Board,' comments Old Mont as they leave.

When they come back a week later, the figures he has asked for are on the table — and they don't look too bad, certainly not bad enough to justify foregoing the dividend. 'But suppose there were another Continental crash and they became liable on the great bulk of their foreign business, it might swamp all profits on home business next year, and more besides.'

So Soames sticks to his guns, agreeing to the dividend but demanding that 'we drop this foreign business in future, lock, stock and barrel'. If not, he will resign and raise the matter from the floor at the forthcoming general meeting.

The other directors demur. But to Soames's surprise, Elderson gives way graciously, declaring that he will not press the board to maintain the foreign business if one member is so vehemently opposed to it. The matter is decided Soames's way.

'That's very handsome of our manager,' says Mothergill, to Soames's irritation. For Soames sees Elderson's volte-face in a different light:

> What's he ratting for? ... He recalled the shift and blink of the fellow's steely eyes at the idea of the question being raised at the general meeting. That had done it! But why? Were the figures faked? Surely not! That would be too difficult in the face of the accountants. If Soames had faith, it was in chartered accountants... It couldn't be that!

Despite Soames's continuing misgivings, the general meeting of the PPRS passes without incident, on the strength of 'a watertight rigmarole' from the chairman and 'butter' from a couple of reliable shareholders. But the German mark is falling fast, endangering the company's foreign business. Soames is convinced there will be no dividend next year, and has already persuaded his sister to sell her shares at a loss, lest she should lose more later.

So far, so very like the City Equitable story: a supine board placing too much trust in one charismatic executive and too slow-witted to spot the looming impact of a downturn. The fictional Elderson turns out to be plain corrupt, rather than merely deceitful and unwilling to face the truth like Bevan, but the two stories end in a very similar way.

Out of the blue, Soames receives a visit at his office from a PPRS employee called Butterfield, who is, in modern parlance, a whistle-blower. This young man has overheard a conversation between Elderson and 'a man called Smith — I fancy by his accent his name's a bit more foreign — who's done most of the agenting for the German business'. He feels duty bound to reveal to Soames what he heard Smith say, namely, '...Quite so, Mr Elderson, but we haven't paid you a commission on all this business for nothing; if the mark goes absolutely phut, you will have to see that your Society makes it good for us.'

So the truth appears to be that Elderson had been taking back-handers to pile on German business, and with no 'limit of liability'. With the mark indeed going phut, Soames is now worrying about the prospect of an action for gross negligence against the whole board, including himself:

> ... at his age and with his reputation! Why! The thing was plain as a pikestaff; for omitting a limit of liability, this chap had got his commission! Ten per cent probably, on all that business — he must have netted thousands! A man must be in Queer Street indeed to take a risk like that!

With no evidence other than hearsay, he attempts to cross-question Elderson in front of the chairman: 'What on earth were you about, Mr Manager, when you allowed these contracts to go through without limit of liability? A man of your experience! What was your motive?' But Elderson smoothly deflects him, replying that the latest plunge of the mark 'must be considered just bad luck'.

Soames is now tortured by worry about his reputation if a scandal breaks, and by self-criticism. Why had he allowed himself to be seduced by 'the names, the prestige and not looking a gift horse in the mouth' into accepting a directorship of such a can of worms? The German business has lost the Society a quarter of a million, and the interim dividend will have to be abandoned. He resolves to share Butterfield's revelation with Old Mont — but gets the conventional answer: 'Hallucination, my dear Forsyte! I've known Elderson all my life. We were at Winchester together.'

'You can't tell from that,' replies Soames.

A man who was at Marlborough with me ran away with his mess fund and his colonel's wife and made a fortune in Chile out of canned tomatoes. The point is this: if that young man's story's true, we're in the hands of a bad hat.

Mont grudgingly concedes the point, and they set off to confront Elderson. 'He'll deny it, of course,' says Soames, as they wait in the boardroom. 'I should hope so,' says Mont. 'Elderson's a gentleman.' 'No liar like a gentleman,' mutters Soames, under his breath.

And sure enough, having heard the accusation, Elderson summons poor Butterfield, accuses him of making his story up, and sacks him on the spot — telling Soames and Mont that he has had his eye on him as a troublemaker for some time. But why on earth would he make up such a damaging tale? 'Foresaw dismissal and thought he would get in first.'

Soames is not done with the matter, however, not by any means. He asks his son-in-law Michael Mont, who works in a publishing house no doubt rather like Duckworth & Co, to find a job for Butterfield, who has a wife and two children and no reference from the PPRS. Michael, who has had the opportunity to observe Elderson at close quarters playing cards in his club and thinks he has the look of a womaniser, is sympathetic. So Butterfield is taken on as a book salesman — and promptly makes a point of calling on Elderson to sell him some books.

'He didn't like it a little bit,' Butterfield reports back to Michael,

> My being in this firm. He knows you're a partner here and
> Mr Forsyte's son-in-law, doesn't he? Well, sir, you see the con-
> nection — two directors believing in me, not him. That's why
> I didn't miss him out... I happened to see his face in the side-
> board glass as I went out. He's got the wind up all right.

But curiously, that is not how Soames finds Elderson when he next
drops in at the PPRS: the man looks positively jaunty, in 'a suit of
dittoes' — a frock-coated three-piece suit, less formal than the City's
traditional dark coat, silk lapels and striped trousers — and a buttonhole carnation. He thanks Soames for taking such a close interest in
the Society's business, and is apparently unperturbed when Soames
remarks that it is time to call a meeting of the shareholders. The rest
of the board and even the shareholders themselves may not like it,
Soames acknowledges, but such a response would be 'all a part of
the vice of not facing up to things'.

'I don't think, Mr Forsyte, that you will accuse me of not facing
things, in the time to come... Goodbye, Mr Forsyte. I'm so grateful to you.' The fellow 'was actually squeezing Soames's hand', a
rare sensation for Soames, and seems to be 'armoured like a crab,
varnished like a Spanish table'. What on earth does he mean, 'in the
time to come'?

A few days later all is explained, however, by a letter:

Dear Mr Forsyte,

> Perhaps you will be good enough to tell the board at the meet-
> ing on Tuesday that I am on my way to immunity from the con-
> sequences of any peccadillo I may have been guilty of. By the
> time you receive this, I shall be there. I have always held that
> the secret of life, no less than that of business, is to know when
> not to stop. It will be no use to proceed against me, for my per-
> son will not be attachable, as I believe you call it in the law, and

I have left no property behind. If your object was to corner me, I cannot congratulate you on your tactics. If on the other hand you inspired that young man's visit as a warning that you were still pursuing the matter, I should like to add new thanks to those which I expressed when I saw you a few days ago.

Believe me, dear Mr Forsyte,
Faithfully yours, Robert Elderson.

And so the tale reaches its denouement at a meeting of PPRS shareholders, a comic gallery of characters who exhibit varying degrees of disgruntlement or anger at the board's failure to stop Elderson departing and leaving such an unholy mess behind, even after two of the directors suspected him of wrongdoing. For a moment it looks as though a vote of no confidence in the whole board may be proposed.

'Unless you've got something up your sleeve, Mr Forsyte, we're dished,' says Lord Fontenoy. 'Damn it, sir, you put the chestnuts in the fire, it's up to you to pull them out. I can't afford to lose these fees!' To which Soames retorts, 'You may lose more than your fees!'

Soames himself is quite prepared to lose his director's fee, but not his dignity. He watches Old Mont tender his resignation: a gallant gesture, but Soames 'distrusted gallantry — there was always a dash of the peacock about it'. He rises to his feet, feeling 'curiously savage', and delivers his own magisterial farewell to the Society:

I, apparently, am the other incriminated director. Very good! I am not conscious of having done anything but my duty from beginning to end of this affair. I am confident that I made no mistake of judgement. And I consider it entirely unjust that I should be penalised. I have had worry and anxiety enough, without being made a scapegoat by shareholders who accepted [the policy of piling on high-risk Continental business] without a murmur, before I ever I came on the Board, and are now angry because they have lost by it.

You owe it to me that the policy has been dropped: you owe it to me that you no longer have a fraudulent person for a manager. And you owe it to me that you were called together today to pass judgment on the matter.

I have no intention whatever of singing small. But there is another aspect to this affair. I am not prepared to go on giving my services to people who don't value them. I have no patience with the attitude displayed this afternoon. If anyone here thinks he has a grievance against me, let him bring an action. I shall be happy to carry it to the House of Lords, if necessary. I have been familiar with the City all my life, and I have not been in the habit of meeting with suspicions and ingratitude. If this is an instance of present manners, I have been familiar with the City long enough. I do not tender my resignation to the meeting; I resign.

With that, Soames stalks out of the meeting — which proceeds to reaffirm its confidence in the remaining members of the board. 'It was the speech of your life, Forsyte!' Old Mont congratulates him, but Soames, still stung by the aspersions cast against him, limits himself to 'a bitter little smile' and decides to have no more to do with the boardroom world. 'It was all of a piece with the modern state of things,' he thinks to himself as he walks past the Bank of England.

Hand to mouth and the steady men pushed to the wall. The men to whom the pound was a pound, and not a mess of chance and paper... One by one, they would get the go-by — as he had got it — in favour of Jack-o'-lanterns, revolutionaries, restless chaps, or clever, unscrupulous fellows, like Elderson. It was in the air. No amount of eating your cake and wanting to have it could take the place of common honesty.

And with that fine aphorism, Galsworthy concludes this sub-plot of his saga. We never find out what happened to Elderson — whether he was apprehended like Bevan, or made good his escape. All we know is that every generation has its Eldersons and Bevans, and that many of them are beyond the reach of the law before their misdeeds are uncovered.

A Pauper's Grave

Gerard and Jeanne took ship to Havana some time in 1931. There they lodged in a small hotel in the city, and Gerard found work as a manager for the Mill Creek Distillery Company, whose principal function was almost certainly as an offshore source of liquor for the bootleggers who thrived during the Prohibition era in the United States, which lasted until 1933.

No trace of the company survives — hardly surprising after half a century of Fidel Castro's communist rule. But references to it crop up in accounts of the career of Leon M. Gleckman, a Jewish ex-convict who earned the nickname of 'the Al Capone of St Paul, Minnesota', the Midwestern city where he once ran his own illicit distillery making a million dollars a year profit, and where he effectively controlled the police department and the mayor's office in the early 1930s.

When Gleckman was investigated for tax evasion, it was found that he had been laundering money through (among other channels) the Mill Creek Distillery in Havana, in which he had a large shareholding. *United States vs Gleckman* (1935) became a much-quoted case in US tax law.

Bevan must have been looking after the finance and administration of the distillery at the time of Gleckman's involvement — paying the wages and the local suppliers of cane sugar, organising and invoicing shipments of liquor, keeping the books of account in good order. We can but wonder how good a job he did, given his old City habits of signing cheques without enquiring what they were for and striking deals without proper contract paperwork.

But he could hardly have been taken on to manage the actual distilling process, of which he knew nothing. Either way, his name does not appear in any account of the Gleckman case, so it would be fanciful to suggest that he was in league with the American gangster even if he could not have failed to be aware of the connection.

Reports of Bevan in these last years say he was well regarded in Havana society. He and Jeanne, accompanied by Christabel when she joined them to live there for a while, even played regularly at a bridge club — a sure sign of respectability.

But working in the racket-driven booze business meant Bevan would have had to rub shoulders with some pretty dangerous people. Havana was not an easy place to lead a quietly respectable life. The biggest and most sophisticated city in the Caribbean, it was by no means the safest, despite its growing reputation as a playground for tourists to rival Miami.

Cuba had been ruled since 1925 by Gerardo Machado, an elected president who outstayed his term of office to become a dictator. His regime was notoriously brutal and his political opponents were frequently murdered. Machado was overthrown in 1933 by the 'revolt of the sergeants', which led to a period of chaos from which one of those sergeants, Fulgencia Batista (himself eventually to be overthrown by Castro) emerged as the dominant political figure. Batista was also an important offshore ally of American mobsters such as Lucky Luciano and Meyer Lansky, who followed after Gleckman.

So the streets of Havana were far from calm for long periods during the Bevans' sojourn. And the climate cannot have been good for Gerard's health either. The great Cuban novelist Alejo Carpentier (who had himself been imprisoned by Machado, and spent much of the 1930s as an exile in Paris) wrote in *Explosion in a Cathedral* (1962):

> Strangers praised the town's colour and gaiety after spending three days visiting its dance halls, saloons, taverns and gambling dens… But those who had to put up with the place all the year round knew about the mud and the dust, and how the saltpetre turned the door-knockers green, ate away the ironwork…

Outside the drier winter months, Havana was perpetually hot and sticky and its air was foul. In the early autumn it was prone to hurricanes. It was a place of shuttered windows, slow fans, bad drains, crowded streets, raging infections, opulent hotels, inadequate hospitals, corrupt policemen, languid prostitutes, and hypnotic dance music everywhere.

In this edgy and exotic milieu, as far removed from Mayfair or Maidstone as it was possible to be, Bevan lived out his last years. And so we leave him as we found him, the former titan of the stockmarket, magnate of the City Equitable and squire of Littlecote, reduced to a crumpled, regretful, nervous shadow hiding behind his newspaper at a café table as he waits for his loyal wife to take him home. 'Character is fate', indeed: and the interaction of character, fate and money can be particularly cruel.

Bevan died in Havana on 24 April 1936. The cause of his death was announced in the London press as 'sleeping sickness' — which would normally be read as a reference to African trypanosomiasis, the debilitating parasitic illness transmitted by tsetse flies. But that makes no sense in Cuba. Bevan must have been suffering from Chagas disease or American trypanosomiasis, sometimes referred to as 'American sleeping sickness' and endemic throughout Central and South America.

Transmitted by a bloodsucking insect known as the 'kissing bug', Chagas begins with relatively mild symptoms of fever, fatigue, muscle aches, diarrhea, vomiting, headaches, and localised swelling — often around the face, where the insects prefer to feed. Swollen eyelids can be a particular sign of Chagas infection.

A small number of sufferers — more usually the very young — develop fatal infections of the heart or brain during the early, acute stage of the illness. Otherwise, the symptoms simply drag on, and if untreated, the infection can persist for years.

In Bevan's case we do not know whether he had suffered previous bouts, but we do know that he died after 12 days of illness complicated by pyelonephritis, a urinary tract infection leading to kidney failure, which was recorded as the official cause on his burial certificate. The announcement placed by his daughters in *The Times* described him as 'dearly-loved father of Christabel Bevan and Sheila Boore (née Bevan)', with no mention of Jeanne.

Gerard Lee Bevan's ghost may pace the Long Gallery at Littecote to this day — and he certainly haunted the London auction rooms for some years after his death, as paintings and *objets* which had passed through his collection continued to come up for sale. But his mortal remains were interred in the Colon cemetery (named after Christopher Columbus) in the Vedado district of Havana, a necropolis of some 800,000 graves, many of them very ornate.

He was preceded there by a roll-call of Cuban heroes such as former president José Miguel Gomez and the (female) nationalist revolutionary Candelaria Figueredo. He would be followed by the likes of José Raúl Capablanca, considered by some to have been the greatest chess player of all time.

But there was to be no fancy memorial for Bevan. His remains were placed in what his great-nephew Sir Timothy Bevan describes as 'a pauper's grave':

> One evening during the [second world] war, my father [Gerard's nephew Hugh] told us that he had received a letter from Christabel in Cuba asking him for money so that Gerard could be moved from a pauper's grave to a rather classier one. My father initially declined, saying that with two sons to educate on a Lieutenant RNVR's pay, he had better things to spend his money on.

None of the surviving brothers — Bertie, Owen, Ivor — were prepared to cough up, so Hugh eventually did so and Gerard was indeed moved to a more dignified spot in the cemetery. But in order to track down his true final resting place, a little deceit had to be exercised — which does not, in the end, seem wholly inappropriate to the Bevan story.

The journalist Elliot Wilson, visiting Havana in October 2008, sent the following email to the author, together with two photographs (see plate section):

Hi Martin. Exciting Bevan update forthwith: I found him. I went along [to the cemetery] this morning and tipped the clerks a few coins. They went into the archives for a while and found, I hope, your man. He was registered as Gerard Lee Bevan, father Frank (Is that right? The writing was a bit smudged.) The records show that he died in 1936 aged 67 and was buried in the cemetery in what was, as you say, a pauper's, or temporary, grave.

The actual date of death was not clear, but the records, written in beautiful copperplate hand, state that he was exhumed on 21 May 1941 and laid back to rest in a grave or catacomb owned by two families, the Fernandez (Juan Bautista) and Brendes (Juan Federico).

I found the unmarked catacomb — at least, the one that the authorities say is his. They say the names on the catacombs change regularly as ownership changes, but that the remains inside stay untouched. I then went back and checked with the bookkeepers a second time and there is no record of his remains having been moved again, so Mr Bevan must still be there.

I couldn't find any records at the cemetery, which is an enormous place, of anyone called Maria Letitia Pertuisot or Bevan, by the way. The only mass French grave there, a pantheon near the British and American one, has no one who died around that period with either of her surnames.

But there you have it: your man in Havana and — or so the authorities there now think — my grandfather. That was the only way they would let me see the records, if I declared I was a blood relative. All in all, quite an adventure.

Exile

I'll never look on the green fields again!
Springs turn to summer, June to autumn's rain,
The autumns dissipate their majesty
In tumbling tumulus along the lea,
But I shall never watch their falling showers,
Or grudge the passage of the golden hours.

I'll never see the gateway of the mist,
The great white gates a million waves have kissed
Since dawn, and died in kissing — Oh! the joy; —
There's glory here; the Paschal buds deploy
Purples imperial, but the flowers I know
Are far away, where I shall never go.

I plunge into the forest; all around
Are tiers of topless ancients, many-crowned
With fruitage out of some Aladdin tale,
Bosses of fire and silvered chevesaile;
But one red apple on a wrinkled tree
Means more than a whole Amazon to me.

Is that the toucan's cry? 'Tis no relief.
Or dropping palm-fruit? Fuel to my grief.
These are all strangers to me, and they play
Strange instruments; as of a far mêlée.

I knew a heaven once — the thrush's song —
And now I've lost it, none can do me wrong.

I plunge into the thoroughfare; but as,
Through the sonata's ever-swelling phrase,
From bar to bar some simple burden breaks,
— A nuthatch knocks perhaps, a cuckoo wakes, —
So through the labyrinth of the loud street
I hear the plain-song that once fell so sweet.

I'll never laugh with the green fields again.
Walls are between us of unappeasable pain,
Misunderstandings madder than typhoons,
Resentment rolling on like tired simoons.
I go down to the beaches, watch the sea;
A thousand leagues flow 'twixt my fields and me.

Last night I heard spring calling: 'Follow me
Beyond the meadows to the alder-tree;
The daffodils are dead, but there's a spot
Where you shall gather bright forget-me-not."
I woke, and lo! The whispers of the stream
Were my heart's sobbing, and the rest — a dream.

Gerard Lee Bevan
1869–1936

Acknowledgments

Gerard Lee Bevan was a footnote both in *Falling Eagle*, my account of the modern history of Barclays Bank published in 2000, and in *To Keep the Ball Rolling*, the abridged version of the memoirs of the great novelist Anthony Powell. As a long-time devotee of Powell's work, I was intrigued by that conjunction. I wanted to know more about Bevan.

I began gathering material — but a decade passed before I had time to complete the research and turn it into this book. During that time the internet has expanded exponentially as a research resource, but it is still no substitute for personal guidance and well-stocked libraries.

David Kynaston, author of a magisterial four-volume history of the City, was the first person to set me on the right track. Professor Richard Roberts of King's College London and Dr Terry Gourvish of the LSE Business History Unit were very helpful, as was Roy Church, the historian of Kenricks.

I am grateful to Rev. Peter Kettle of Holy Trinity, Prince Consort Road, for information on All Saints, Ennismore Gardens; to Michael Churchill at Cheam School; Penny Hatfield, Christine Vickers and Charlotte Villiers at Eton College; and Adam Green at Trinity College, Cambridge, where my godson Joshua Hardie delved into the archives on my behalf.

Chris Swinson OBE, whose day job is as Comptroller and Auditor General of Jersey, shared with me his expert studies of Clarence Hatry and his companies. Richard Ellis shared his research into his ancestors' stockbroking firm, Ellis & Co, and Willie Dickson unearthed additional material on the stock market boom of 1919–20.

Josceline Grove volunteered correspondence from the files of his grandfather, Colonel Reginald Grove, a disgruntled Ellis & Co customer. Michael Bloch introduced me to Hugo Haig-Thomas, and Hugo and his cousins Peter and Tony provided rich details of their grandfather's life. Emma Hicks explored Claridge's in Paris on my behalf. James Nye helped me track down a rare copy of Bevan's book of poems, *Russet and Asp*, and Andrew Carter, Director of Arts at Ampleforth College, offered a critical assessment of it. Elliot Wilson tracked down and photographed Bevan's grave in Havana.

Mark Amory, St John Brown, Louise Hallam, Joshua Hardie, Richard Lesmoir-Gordon and Chris Swinson read and commented on sections of my text in draft, but I should of course add that despite these many contributions by others, the errors and the inevitable exercises in guesswork are all my own.

And I am especially grateful to Sir Timothy Bevan, the former chairman of Barclays Bank and Gerard Lee Bevan's great-nephew, who answered many intrusive questions and allowed me to see his mother Pleasance Bevan's unpublished memoir, *Various Reminiscences*. Given that I have not always written kindly about Barclays during Sir Tim's era, this was a particularly gracious gesture — and it revealed aspects of Bevan family life which I could never have uncovered elsewhere.

Finally, at a time when all our treasured libraries are under threat, it would be remiss of me not to thank the staff of Westminster Reference Library, Guildhall Library and British Library Newspapers at Colindale.

The publishing team of Lorne Forsyth and Olivia Bays at Elliott & Thompson could not have been more amiable or more professional. On a more personal level, I was encouraged to persevere by Katie Walsh, Andrew Rosenheim, John Marshall and Andrew Hewson. And on the home front, I would not have been able to complete this or any of my projects, literary and otherwise, without the assistance of Erica Zarb.

MVW

Helmsley, July 2011

Bibliography

Bevan Family

Bevan, Gerard Lee: *Russet and Asp*, Duckworth, 1929

Bevan, Pleasance: *Various Reminiscences*, unpublished, 1972

Bevan, Sophie K.: *Letters from a Veiled Politician*, Everett, 1910

————: *The Parting of the Ways: or Conquest by Purchase*, J Murray, 1911

————: *The Path to Peace: A Short Handbook on National Training*, Everett, 1913

————: *The Home and the War*, J Murray, 1918

Business History

Ackrill, Margaret and Hannah, Leslie: *Barclays The Business of Banking 1690–1996*, Cambridge University Press, 2001

Church, R.A.: *Kenricks in Hardware – A Family Business 1791–1966*, David & Charles, 1969

Elliott, Geoffrey: *The Mystery of Overend & Gurney – A Financial Scandal in Victorian London*, Methuen, 2006

Ellis, Charles D.: *The Partnership – A History of Goldman Sachs*, The Penguin Allen Lane, 2008

Endlich, Lisa: *Goldman Sachs – The Culture of Success*, Little, Brown & Co, 1999

Haldane, R.A.: *With Intent to Deceive*, Blackwood, 1970

Hennessey, Elizabeth: *Coffee House to Cyber Market*, Ebury Press, 2001

Holmes, A.R. & Green, Edwin: *Midland – 150 years of Banking Business*, Batsford, 1986

Jenkins, Alan: *The Stock Exchange Story*, Heinemann, 1973

Kynaston, David: *Cazenove & Co: A History*, Batsford, 1991

———: *The City of London – Vol II Golden Years 1890–1914*, Chatto & Windus, 1995

———: *The City of London – Vol III Illusions of Gold 1914–1945* Chatto & Windus, 1999

———: *The Financial Times – A Centenary History*, Viking, 1988

Matthews, R.W. & Tuke, A.W.: *History of Barclays Bank Ltd*, Blades, East & Blades Ltd, 1926

Meredith, Hubert A.: *The Drama of Money Making* Sampson Low, Marston, 1931

Michie, Ranald C.: *The London Stock Exchange*, Oxford University Press, 1999

Robb, George: *White Collar Crime in Modern England: Financial Fraud and Business Morality 1845–1929*, Cambridge University Press, 1992

Vander Weyer, Martin: *Falling Eagle – The Decline of Barclays Bank*, Weidenfeld & Nicholson, 2000

Vallance, Aylmer: *Very Private Enterprise*, Thames & Hudson, 1955

Wake, Jehanne: *Kleinwort Benson – The History of two Families in Banking*, Oxford University Press, 1997

Biography

Barber, Michael: *Anthony Powell – A Life*, Duckworth Overlook, 2004

Dawson, Sir Douglas: *A Soldier Diplomat*, J Murray, 1927

Dupré, Catherine: *John Galsworthy – A Biography*, Collins, 1976

Dutton, David: *Austen Chamberlain – Gentleman in Politics*, Ross Anderson, 1985

Hart-Davis, Duff (ed): *End of An Era – Letters and Journals of Sir Alan Lascelles from 1887–1920*, Hamish Hamilton, 1986

Masters, Anthony: *Rosa Lewis – The Life Story of the Duchess of Duke Street*, Weidenfeld & Nicholson Ltd, 1977

McKie, David: *Jabez – The Rise and Fall of a Victorian Rogue*, Atlantic Books, 2004

Powell, Enoch: *Joseph Chamberlain*, Thames & Hudson, 1977

Social History and Miscellaneous

Ferguson, C.L.: *A History of The Magpie and Stump Debating Society 1866–1926*, Heffer, 1931

Haig-Thomas, P., and Nicholson, M.A.: *The English Style of Rowing*, Faber, 1958

Hunter, Eileen: *Christabel – The Russell Case and After*, André Deutsch, 1973

Norwich, John Julius: *The Architecture of Southern England*, Macmillan, 1985

Parker, Eric: *Eton in the Eighties*, Smith Elder, 1914

Phillips, Gregory D.: *The Diehards — Aristocratic Society & Politics in Edwardian England*, Harvard University Press, 1979

Priestley, J.B.: *The Edwardians*, Heinemann London, 1970

Taylor, A.J.P.: *English History 1914–1945*, Oxford University Press, 1965

Thomas, Hugh: *Cuba – A History*, Penguin, 2010

Thompson, F.M.L.: *The Rise of Respectable Society – A Social History of Victorian Britain 1830–1900*, Fontana, 1988

Wilson, A.N.: *The Victorians*, Arrow, 2003

Selected Fiction

Barker, Harley Granville: *The Voysey Inheritance* (play), Sidgwick & Jackson, 1909

Galsworthy, John: *The White Monkey* (*The Forsyte Saga, Volume 2*), Heinemann, 1924

———: *Loyalties* (play), Duckworth, 1922

———: *The Skin Game* (play), Duckworth, 1924

Gissing, George: *The Crown of Life*, 1899

Grossmith, George & Weedon: *The Diary of a Nobody* 1892 (Penguin, 1945)

Hornung, E.W.: *The Complete Short Stories of Raffles*, Heinemann, 1924

Marsh, Ngaio: *Death at the Bar*, Collins, 1939 (Fontana, 1954)

Powell, Anthony: *A Question of Upbringing*, Heinemann, 1951

————: *A Buyer's Market*, Heinemann, 1952

Simenon, Georges: *Les Caves du Majestic*, Editions Gallimard, 1942

Trollope, Anthony: *The Way We Live Now*, Chapman & Hall, 1875

————: *The Prime Minister*, Chapman & Hall, 1876

Waugh, Evelyn: *Decline and Fall*, Chapman & Hall, 1928

————: *A Handful of Dust*, Chapman & Hall, 1934

Wells, H.G.: *Tono-Bungay*, Macmillan, 1909

Endnotes

Chapter Eleven

Page 290: One confusing piece of evidence suggests either that Gervais had been offered the commission he claimed to have held but had never taken it up, or that he was not quite as mendacious as the press painted him to be: The London Gazette of August 25, 1914, listed one 'Charles Oliver Gervais (late Canadian Militia)' under Special Reserve of Officers, 'to be Second Lieutenant, 12th Lancers'.

Page 291: When her brother John Archibald Kenrick died in July 1933, a Letter of Intent was found with his will to the effect that Sophie was not to be pressed by his executors for repayment of loans that he had made to her.

Index

3/3/2016